NOTES

ON THE

VOLCANOES OF THE HAWAIIAN ISLANDS.

WITH A HISTORY OF THEIR VARIOUS ERUPTIONS.

BY

WILLIAM T. BRIGHAM, A. M.

[FROM THE MEMOIRS OF THE BOSTON SOCIETY OF NATURAL HISTORY, VOL. I, PART III.]

BOSTON:
PRINTED AT THE RIVERSIDE PRESS, CAMBRIDGE.
1868.

X. *Notes on the Volcanic Phenomena of the Hawaiian Islands, with a description of the modern Eruptions.* By WILLIAM T. BRIGHAM, A. M.

Read June 20th, 1866.

AS the study of the volcanic phenomena of the Hawaiian Islands requires a survey of the whole group, a physiographic sketch of all the Islands, even of those on which volcanoes have been long extinct, forms a part of the plan of this essay.

The Hawaiians reckon twelve islands: four large and four small ones inhabited, and four which are little more than barren rocks. They are named as follows: —

Nihòá,[1]	Barren Rock.		
Niihau,	20 miles long,	5 miles wide,	elevation of highest point 1800 feet.
Kaùla,	Barren Rock.	Tufa cone.	
Lehùa,	" "	" "	
Kauaì,	30 miles long,	28 miles wide,	" " " " 8000 "
Oáhu,	35 " "	21 " "	" " " " 4000 "
Molokaì,	35 " "	7 " "	" " " " 3000 "
Lanai,	20 " "	9 " "	" " " " 2000 "
Máui,	54 " "	25 " "	" " " " 10,200 "
Kahooláwe,	12 " "	5 " "	" " " " 600 "
Molokìni,	Barren Rock.	Tufa cone.	" " " " 200 "
Hawaii,	100 miles long,	90 miles wide,	" " " " 13,950 "

The smallest, Kahooláwe, has an area of about fifty square miles, and the largest, Hawaii, of about three thousand eight hundred. The group extends in a north-north-west direction from this last island, and has nearly the average trend of the Pacific groups.[2] The Islands are all high, increasing in height and size, towards the south-east, where they culminate in the lofty domes of Hawaii. The rock of the whole group is volcanic, with the exception of the ancient elevated coral-reef and the resulting sandstone. No true fossiliferous rocks are found; although the tufa cones often contain fossilized shells, and corals of recent species. It has been the general impression that the lavas were wholly basaltic, but on the tops and in the interior of the mountains a variety of trachyte is found, and the bulk of the mountains seems to be composed of phonolites and graystones, forming a complete series from basalt to trachyte. These lavas contain few mineral species, but assume forms of great variety, and while tolerably uniform in composition, present structural differences in great number.

Occupying a central position in the Pacific these Islands have been visited, since their discovery by the Spaniards, by many government exploring expeditions, whose published accounts have intimated the interesting nature of the volcanic developments constantly taking place; but, except by the United States Exploring Expedition, no attempt has been made to examine carefully the geology. The Rev. Titus Coan, who has been for thirty years a missionary at Hìlo on Hawaii, has constantly observed every outburst of the volcanic fires during this period, and to his accounts we are principally indebted for what is known of their history on these Islands. Professor James D. Dana, also in his "Geology

[1] For the pronunciation and signification of the native names see Appendix.

[2] The principal groups in the Eastern Pacific have the following trends: —

Hawaiian Range,	N. 64° W.
Marquesas Islands,	N. 60° W.
Hervey Group,	N. 65° W.
Samoan Islands,	N. 64° W.

of the United States Exploring Expedition," and in subsequent memoirs, has done much to explain and extend our knowledge of the Hawaiian volcanoes. The information from these two sources is scattered through many volumes, and it has seemed desirable to collect and compare with the writer's own observations made during a residence of eighteen months, all hitherto published on the Geology of the Hawaiian Group.

KAUAÌ.[1]

[See Map, Plate XI.]

General Features. — Kauaì is from twenty-eight to thirty miles in diameter, nearly circular in form, and has an area of six hundred and forty square miles. As will be seen, it forms with Niihau, Lehùa, and Kaúla, a group closely connected in structure, as well as position. As on the other Hawaiian Islands, two centres of formation may be noticed, and the mountain summits are said to be thickly dotted with craters. Waíaleale, the highest peak, is situated a little east of the centre of the Island, and is supposed to be eight thousand feet high. West of this is a high table-land more than four thousand feet above the sea, which, extending over forty square miles, terminates in a precipice two thousand feet high. Waíaleale is much furrowed by deep valleys, the intervening ridges being sharp and irregular; the lava of which the whole Island is composed is much decomposed on the surface, and where not covered by the profuse vegetation of the tropics exhibits strata with a gradual dip of from 5°–10° towards the sea on every side.

On the coast of the north-eastern to the south-eastern part of the Island is a ridge, interrupted in many places, and of no great height, but seemingly detached from the great central mountain, being placed tangentially to the main ridges. The shore on the western side is precipitous, but elsewhere it is a sand beach interrupted by basaltic cliffs from ten to a hundred and fifty feet in height. The valleys are long, widening towards the sea and very fertile, the soil being sometimes ten feet deep. The rivers on the windward side of the Island are numerous, although not large, and as most of the low land lies on that side, Kauaì possesses a larger proportion of arable land than any of the other Islands. The south-west, or leeward district, is dry and barren, although several rivers descend from the mountains above.

It is more difficult to trace the original plan of Kauaì than of any of the other Islands, as its mountain summits are difficult of access, its valleys and ridges larger and more irregular, the lavas more decomposed, and the natural sections more concealed beneath the vegetation than on any other Island of the Hawaiian group. From the degradation of its ridges, and the absence of any very recent volcanic products, it has been supposed to be the oldest member of the group, and it cannot be disputed that volcanic action ceased here before it became extinct on Oáhu or the other Islands. Many years must have elapsed, — how many it is useless to conjecture, — to convert the hard basaltic lava into the rich soil which nourishes trees of immense size; and which is so abundant as to give Kauaì the name of The Garden.

[1] The most northerly island of the group, Nihòa or Bird Island, has never been visited by scientific men, but from the description of natives and others who have landed to collect the eggs which the birds deposit there in large quantities, it would seem to be the remains of an ancient crater, as it exhibits tufaceous and basaltic formations.

The rock of which the mountain is built, is a heavy compact ferruginous basalt, tolerably uniform throughout; while the shore ridges contain less iron, are more cellular, and vary in their structure from a compact phonolite to a heavy basalt. Crystals of quartz and iron pyrites are found in various parts of the Island, and in some places the silica of the lava has been converted into an opal-like irregular mass.

The valley of Hanaleì opens on the northern coast, and at its mouth is one of the best harbors in Kauaì. At the shore the valley is two or three miles wide, but its bounding ridges gradually approach each other, and five miles from the sea a narrow gorge alone remains, the bed of the largest river on the Island, of the same name as the valley. This river takes its rise in the swampy summit of Waíaleale and descends gradually without high falls. The last four miles of its course it has but little current, is from fifty to two hundred feet wide, and from two to fifteen feet deep. The bottom is gravelly or sandy, and free from stones. The plain bordering its banks is very fertile, and has been occupied in succession by plantations of mulberries, coffee, and sugar-cane.

Westward of the valley of Hanaleì there is a region about twelve square miles in extent, quite mountainous and much cut up by deep ravines. The valley of Waiòli is remarkable for its circular form and precipitous walls formed by the ridges Namalahóa and Namalokáma, between two thousand five hundred and three thousand feet high. Extending to the westward Namalahóa ends abruptly at the sea in a *pali* (precipice) about two hundred feet high. The cañons of Lumahaì and Wainìha are narrow and picturesque, with nearly perpendicular sides and frequent cascades. Every ravine is a watercourse, and after the frequent rains the white threads of the waterfalls are seen breaking out all over the palis among the bright green of the Kukùi (*Aleurites moluccana*) and the darker ferns.

The soil of the ridges near the shore is reddened by the oxidation of the iron which forms an important part of the Hawaiian lava,[1] and contains small boulders formed of concentric layers of a loose friable stone around a hard, amorphous, argillaceous core. These coats are loose and may be easily separated like the skins of an onion. The strata nearer the mountains where the rivers have exposed sections, are deep, (thirty to eighty feet,) and have a regular dip of 5°–10° towards the north. The exposed edges are much decomposed, the lava being generally cellular but not scoriaceous, and the soil formed is of a very dark color from the combination of the oxide of iron with organic acids, while the entire wall is often covered with the luxuriant foliage of the ferns, leguminous creepers, and Lobeliaceæ.

In the valley of Wainìha, some five miles from the coast, is the precipitous ascent to the high table-land of the western district of Napàli. This valley is exceedingly fertile, and is filled with the kukùi-tree, bread-fruit, orange, banana, the fragrant pandanus, and kalo (*Colocasia antiquorum, var. esculenta*). The ford of the Wainìha River is difficult at high tide owing to the large and small loose, smooth stones on the bottom; the beds of the other rivers here are usually smooth and sandy.

Two miles beyond on the coast are the remarkable caves of Haéna formed in the abrupt broken end of the ridges of Mauna Hina. The largest cave is more than a hundred feet wide at the mouth and twenty feet high, extending into the mountain several hundred feet, gradually becoming narrower and lower, until the explorer is obliged to creep on hands and knees to an artificial wall which is said to block up a sepulchral cave. The roof is very

[1] See Analyses below.

rough, and water drips through in many places. The floor is tolerably even and level and covered thinly with a black mould. This seems to have been one of those gigantic bubbles common in all lava streams; but half a mile beyond are two caves of less simple form, both occurring in the solid compact lava a few rods apart and half a mile west of the first cave. The more westerly one contains a pool of fine cool water, perfectly fresh, although on a level with the sea and but a few hundred feet from the shore. As the water extends the whole width of the cave, about one hundred feet, it is not easily accessible, but at a short distance from the entrance, which is fifty feet perhaps in height, the walls contract until only a low arch is left, hardly high enough to admit the passage of a canoe. The water is said to be forty feet deep, natives diving and bringing up stones from that depth. The other cave between the two former is much more remarkable; the water which fills it is of a most remarkable clearness. A scum of some insoluble white substance, of such tenuity as to render futile all attempts to collect it for analysis, usually covers the surface when the wind does not blow into the mouth of the cave. A few yards from the shore, where the water was thirty feet deep, the smallest pebbles could be seen with great distinctness. The shore-line of this reservoir was one hundred and eighty feet long. The entrance was formed by a low arch traversed by a narrow dyke, and seemed to have been opened by the falling away of a mass of rock which now forms an embankment of the pool which is above the sea-level. At Haéna the shore road ends in rock wall, and the only passage along the western coast is by water.

The district of Haleléa which extends from Haéna to Mauna Puéo, a distance of fifteen miles, is the most fertile and best watered on the Hawaiian Islands; and eastward of Waiòli the valleys are wider and the ridges lower, more rounded and covered with a deeper soil, rendering this a region admirably adapted for agricultural purposes, although the frequent rains, extending over nine months of the year, are said to injure certain crops. Hanaleì is reputed the place on all the group where the rain falls oftenest and most abundantly. The upper ridges are heavily timbered, and four or five miles above Hanaleì the soil becomes black and marshy, and the Ohia trees (*Metrosideros polymorpha*) attain a circumference of twenty-five feet three feet from the ground. Further than this the natives consider the way to the summit impracticable, owing to the closeness of the vegetation and the swampy nature of the ground.

Kalihikaì and Kalihiwaì are valleys of little depth, well adapted to the cultivation of rice and kalo from the deep fertile soil, and abundant supply of water. Here, as elsewhere when not occupied by trees, the soil of the ridges is red, and when wet is very clayey and slippery; it supports a coarse grass, not very nourishing to the cattle.[1] At Kilauéa, six miles east of Hanaleì in the district of Koolaù, the coast is an abrupt pali of inconsiderable height, and of an intense red color; a small island near the shore has been considered the remains of an ancient coast crater, but is probably only a portion of the cliff which has been cut off by the waves, an agent which the natives say is constantly reducing its size. In many

1 In the *Journal of the Boston Soc. of Nat. Hist.*, vol. iv. p. 147, Mr. J. P. Couthouy has described the stratification in this neighborhood near the shore, and expresses the opinion that "These laminæ were evidently formed by successive horizontal depositions, but have since been tilted up so as to dip about 5° north to the sea." From a careful examination of the place I am convinced that no tilting has taken place, but that the reef has been elevated, and the inclined strata of coral refuse, sand, and soil are the combined result of wash from the valleys and sand and coral fragments driven in from the sea by storms of unusual violence. It must be remembered that this is on the windward shore, and peculiarly liable to incursions of the sea as well as rain torrents.

places in this district the elevated coral-reef forms the roadway, and the coral-sand has often blocked up the mouths of the small streams which are compelled to seek another outlet through the porous reef beneath the surface, and the traveller may pass over the breach after a storm unconscious of the existence of a watercourse until his horse commences to sink in a quicksand.

Very curious masses of black basalt occur imbedded in ochreous earth in the hills near the shore. They often exhibit a columnar structure, are always smooth on the surface, as if long exposed to the action of water, and are seldom found in masses of more than two tons weight.

The southern boundary of Koolaŭ is formed by Mauna Kaléa, a curved ridge meeting Mauna Puéo nearly at right angles. Its peaks are sharp, thin, and needle-like, about a thousand feet in height, often columnar. Near Anahòla, the ridge ends rather abruptly, and is so thin that a round hole has been formed through the wall high up the slope, through which the sky may be seen, from a base line of more than a mile at an average distance of half a mile. The dip of this ridge is quite regular seaward. From Anahòla southward the mountain slopes are more gentle, not so much broken by ravines, and the streams of water are small. Seven miles beyond is the Wailŭa River, the second in size on Kauaĭ, and navigable for canoes two miles and a half from its mouth, which is sometimes nearly closed by a changeable sand-bar which reduces its breadth from one hundred and fifty to twenty-five feet. Its depth does not exceed fifteen feet.

Two miles and a half from the sea on the western branch is a fall one hundred and sixty feet high, which, after a rain, presents a most beautiful spectacle as the river dashes over the rocks, finally leaping in a broad sheet of foam into a dark basin walled on either side by cliffs so steep and rocky that even the ferns and mosses which revel in the spray cannot cover the naked rock. These walls continue nearly to the sea, and often present a columnar structure. One of the layers of basalt on this river is convex in the manner of a lava bubble, leaving a cave underneath. The fractures in this rock seem to follow nearly the course of radii drawn from the centre of the sphere of curvature.[1] The cave underneath the fall seems to be of similar structure, but can only be examined during very low water.

Several dykes intersect the high walls of the gorge about a mile from the sea, where the river changes its course. They are from three to six feet wide, and seem to have the direction of radii from the centre of the Island. On the eastern branch of the Wailŭa is a fall of exceeding beauty.

Both above and below this the river passes through a deep cañon with nearly inaccessible walls. The whole region about these falls abounds in small cones, some of which have crateriform cavities at the top, several are broken down, and many of them are wooded to the summit. Probably this region was once a *malpays*, quite like that described by Humboldt as surrounding Jorullo in Mexico.[2]

The Wailŭa intersects a mountain ridge about half a mile from the sea, which presents many curious features. The northern part is about six hundred feet high, extending two miles, and is called Mauna Nóunou, while the southern ridge, Mauna Kápu, is about two thirds this height and extends double the distance. Both of these ridges are nearly parallel with the coast line, are uneven, much degraded, and face the interior of the island with an abrupt wall. The stratification is not very apparent from the decomposed state of the lava,

[1] *Geology of the U. S. Expl. Exped.*, p. 269.

[2] *Vues des Cordillères*, pl. xliii. p. 239.

but the dip is towards the sea in every part examined, and sometimes exceeds 10°. Dana noticed, in a height of one hundred and fifty feet, ten layers each from ten to thirty feet thick.[1]

South of Nawiliwíli, and separating the district of Púna from that of Kóna, is a ridge of similar appearance, but much greater height (2290 feet by triangulation). The side towards the north is steep and generally inaccessible, except where two breaks occur, the western one affording an excellent roadway. So far as examined the dip was towards the south, about 10°–12°, and the seeming dip on the northern side was due to the successive deposits of wash from the mountains.

The region between Mauna Kaléa on the north, Mauna Nóunou and Kápu on the east, and the Kolòa Ridge on the south, forms a semicircle of about seven miles radius, elevated about two hundred feet above the sea, and is mostly rolling land covered with grass and occasional groves of pandanus or koa (*Acacia koa*). Near Kolòa at the south-eastern end of the island, is a very interesting region where the volcanic fires have left their latest traces. Over nearly ten square miles the lavas are fresh and but little decomposed, although the cluster of craters from which it probably came occupies but a tenth of that space. From the Kolòa ridge to the sea the *pahoehoe*, or smooth lava, extends, in some places covered with large blocks lying loosely together, or with a red earth which nourishes a few argemone, sida, and indigo bushes. This barren surface is uneven, being in many places bulged up in immense bubbles some of which have fallen in, leaving caverns, one of which near the shore is paved with the ancient coral reef.

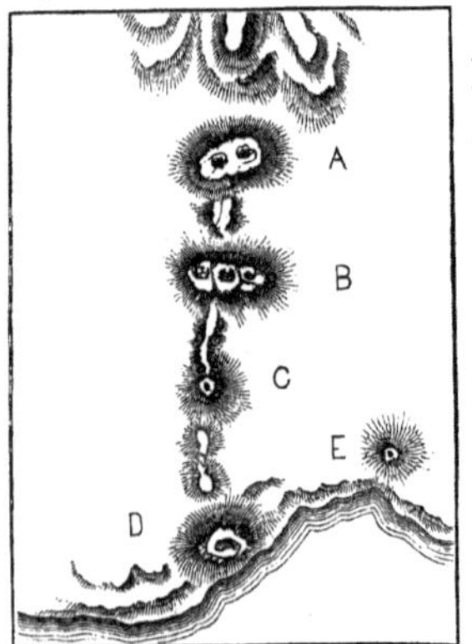

Fig. 1, Plan of the Kolòa Craters.

Dana's description of these craters is very complete, and leaves little to be added. He says:[2] "The old crater (C) has a steep and ragged summit, consisting of dark-brown lavas and scoriæ The cone stands about one hundred and fifty feet above the plain. The bare sides are smooth until near the summit, where the lava breaks out in columns, so rude and jagged as scarcely to justify the term, yet appearing columnar from below. It forms a narrow wall, or crest, broken by numerous rents, and is mostly wanting on the east-south-east and west-north-west sides. The crater is about one hundred and fifty yards wide at top, and has a depth of thirty or forty yards. The surface within is smooth, and consists of red earth like the lower slopes of the interior. The lava of the crest owes its roughness, in part, to a thin laminated structure and numerous vertical fractures. The laminæ are from half an inch to two inches thick, and although not easily separated, they stand out prominent over the worn or decomposed surface. The rock has been rendered very irregular from disintegration, and, at top, the columns are sometimes unevenly tapering. Besides these sources of its rough features, the walls within are covered with lava in twisted shapes, forming patches plastered on the surface, or hanging in stalactites. The rock of the crest is very cellular, and much of it is scoriaceous.

To seaward from the old crater, the observer looks down upon a low, broad elevation (D), with a shallow crater at top. Its smooth surface, covered with scanty vegetation, at first suggested that the lava had not flowed from it. But the crater proved to be half filled

[1] *Loc. cit.* p. 270. [2] *Loc. cit.* p. 273.

with black basaltic rock, lying in huge blocks, averaging more than a cubic foot in size. There were no scoriæ about the crater. The lavas were ejected, and subsequently cinders were thrown out, the decomposition of which covered the exterior with earth. The rock resembles that about Kolôa.

"A little to the east of north from the old crater, there are two hills, of oblong form, and about one hundred and eighty feet high. The near one (B) contains three craters, and the other (A) two. These are alike in their red, earth-covered declivities, unfurrowed by a single ravine or depression. The central crater in B, has a diameter of a hundred yards. On one side the lava is piled up in columns, somewhat as in the old crater; the bottom of the cavity is very evenly concave, and covered with red earth, like the exterior. The western crater is about half the diameter of the central, and has an earthy margin around the shallow cup-shaped cavity. The rock crops out in one place, and shows the same features as above described. Ejected cinders probably covered the lavas, as in other instances; the red color is the result of decomposition setting free the iron in a state of red oxide.

"In A, the larger crater of the summit is nearly two hundred feet across. The same red earth characterizes it inside and out. The smaller crater lies adjoining, and is forty feet across, and twelve deep. The walls around consist of cellular lava in layers which appear to have flowed from the larger crater; the rock is the same as that of the plains below. On one side of this small crater there is an entrance to a cavern which appeared to run down the hill; it could not be traced beyond thirty feet, on account of the rocks that had fallen in from above. The entrance is eight feet high and fifteen wide, and the walls are, in part, incrusted with lava stalactites. The cavity appears to indicate that a stream of lava had flowed from the small crater. There is still another depression on the western slope of this volcanic hill, that may have been a third crater." At present the large sand-hills on the shore have reached D, and partly filled it.

Near these craters the sand-drift has formed large deposits more or less consolidated, which have been worn into the most grotesque forms, sometimes resembling branching coral both in color and hardness.

The blowholes on the shore cliffs have attracted the attention of all travellers. At half-tide, during a heavy sea, the largest one throws up a column of water to a height of over sixty feet, from an orifice five feet in diameter; and the effect of the air rushing through the small crevices is very startling to the bystander, who feels the rock tremble beneath him, with groans and shrill shrieks, as the surf comes thundering into its midst. These caves are sometimes bubbles in the lava stream, and sometimes seem to have been formed by the washing away of loose scoriæ underlying the solid lava.

All the lava of this neighborhood is dark-red or brownish-black ferruginous basalt of solid appearance, and contains very little chrysolite. Near a small brook in the village of Kolôa, the lava assumes a prismatic structure, the prisms being from ten to eighteen inches in diameter, having from five to seven sides, and are more regular than any others seen on Kauaì.[1] Horizontal fractures are flat instead of convex, and the part adjoining these transverse fissures, is harder than the interior, and forms projections on the sides of the exposed columns; but where the ends are exposed to the weather they are convex from the abrasion of the edges.

[1] My friend Mr. Sanford B. Dole, a resident, informs me, since the above was written, that the columnar structure is much more perfect near Hulèia north of the Kolôa Ridge.

West of this lava region are many round smooth grassy hills of no considerable elevation, composed of red earth, and destitute of any depression on the top. The intervals between these hills are generally swampy, or the beds of winding sluggish streams. Beyond these the land becomes dry and barren near the shore, owing to the slight amount of rainfall on the lee side of the mountains. A few streams find their way down from the heights above, and the Wahiawà runs over a stony bed several miles in extent, from a very beautiful cascade in the mountains.

On the southern side of Kauaì opposite to Hanaleì is the valley of the Hanapépé, — a type of a certain class of cañons common on the Hawaiian Islands.

For two or three miles from the sea the river is several hundred feet wide, ten feet deep in some places, with an even bottom, and winds through a nearly level valley bounded on either side by cliffs two hundred feet high. These cliffs are nearly perpendicular, much grooved vertically, and present fine layers of basaltic conglomerate and gray basalt. This plain produces the kalo and bananas which supply the neighboring country, and is thickly dotted with the grass houses of the natives. It is a mile wide and four miles long. Beyond this the bed of the river becomes steeper, and the mountain walls close in upon the stream, forming a cañon a thousand feet deep. The walls are by no means even and unbroken, but here and there steep ravines and arched recesses, Gothic clustered columns and broken buttresses, astonish and delight the explorer, while the solemn stillness, broken only by the ripple of the stream over its rocky bed, completes the illusion of some vast aisle of an ancient temple.

The stream of cold clear water winds from side to side, constantly cutting off the pathway, and receiving from the heights above a tributary waterfall. The walls rise generally clear from the bottom of the valley; the agent that formed the gorge has removed all debris; even the little ravines that open on either side do not accumulate any wash in the main bed. This is doubtless owing to the force of the Hanapépé which, during the rains, often fills its channel from wall to wall, moving stones of considerable weight with its impetuous current.

After a ride of four miles through this cañon, the fall is reached, and horses can go no further. The pali on the right curves round and closes the chasm with an abrupt wall over which the stream pours from a height of three hundred and twenty-six feet. Two high, sharp, and somewhat inclining peaks stand on the left, forming a colossal gateway for a small stream which enters from a broader valley beyond. All around the circus of the falls small white cascades dart out among the dense foliage, sometimes spreading like fingers over the black rock they in vain endeavor to conceal, or side by side in a large company, like the burnished pipes of some vast organ, warble forth an accompaniment to the diapason of the fall. The effect of the light, sunny-green foliage of the kukui, contrasted with the dark green of the orange and coffee overhanging the stream, is very pleasant in a place where only the noonday sun penetrates.

A curved fracture is quite evident behind the fall, although the columnar structure is no longer so evident as when Dana visited the place. Several large dykes occur two miles below the fall, extending through the whole height of the cliff on the right bank of the stream, although their existence is concealed by dense foliage on the left. They seem to proceed, like those in the Wailùa valley, from the mountain towards the sea. Where the gorge opens upon the plain a beautiful example of prismatic structure was observed.

A small spur of the wall exhibited the appearance represented in the margin. Three layers of gray cellular basalt were capped by the soil formed by the decomposed scoriæ of the bed above, and formed terraces which were covered with grass and convolvulus vines forming a curtain over the dark rock beneath. The prisms were very irregular, none having parallel sides. Near this terrace, one of the streams of prismatic lava had passed over a rounded mass of lava resembling blue clay, fissured as in the figure.

Fig. 2. Cliff in Hanapépé Valley.

The Waiméa River is similar to the Hanapépé, but larger, and its valley is neither so deep nor so picturesque, but it is nevertheless an oasis in the barren red plain of this part of Kauaì, and its green kalo-ponds and banana plantations furnish the principal food of the inhabitants of the village of Waiméa, which is situated on the dry plain at the river mouth. Canoes pass up the river several miles, and at its mouth it is too deep for fording. It rises on the uplands of Napàli, but receives some tributaries from Waíaleale.

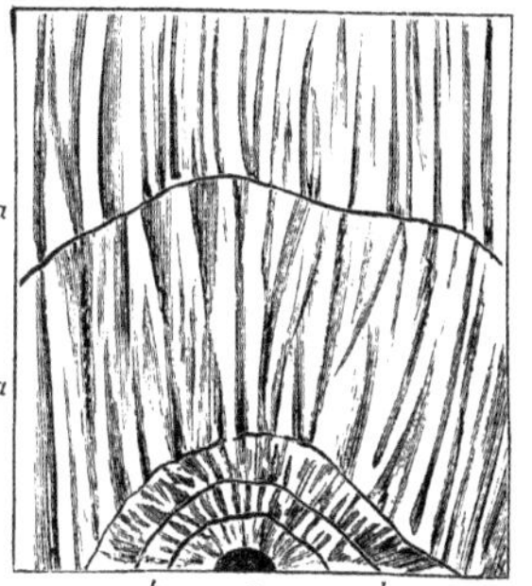

Fig. 3. Natural Section in Hanapépé Valley.

a, a, prismatic basalt; b, b, blue stone with concentric coating much fractured; c, solid amorphous nucleus.

Beyond Waiméa the mountain region of Napàli approaches the shore, leaving a narrow strip of land usually less than a mile wide, without permanent surface stream, but abounding in springs along the shore near the sea level, which supply large kalo-ponds, and water fields of sugar-cane, cocoanuts and bananas, forming a green belt between the ocean and the dry and rocky slopes of the mountains. Anywhere over this land water may be obtained by sinking wells eight to fifteen feet deep, and large tanks are dug to water the herds pastured on the scanty beach grass.

Waiméa is the usual place to ascend the mountain. The table-land to the west is wet, and during the rainy season dangerous without guides. Since the introduction of horses, the path across Napàli has been quite forsaken, and few old natives know the way. Several caves occur near the centre of the plain a little west of the pathway. Dr. Charles Pickering, in crossing the island in October 1840, passed along the course of the Waiméa River some miles through an exceedingly interesting botanical region, but on reaching the table-land found it very difficult to pass, owing to the marshes and quagmires which abound over a tract twenty miles square. This was in a favorable season. Waíaleale has been seldom ascended, although the ascent is possible from Hanaleì and Lihùe as well as from Waiméa. The summit is an extensive bog like Napàli, abounding in deep mud-holes, and several natives having lost their lives there, it is difficult to obtain guides or even bearers to ascend except during very dry seasons, as in September.[1]

Ten or twelve miles west of Waiméa in the district of Mána, the coral reef has been elevated in a long wide ridge transversely to the present shore line. It is much fissured, as if a stream of lava had forced its way beneath it. Near Lápa, in this same district at the south-western end of the Pali, is a very curious sand-bank formed by the wind and currents which strike the island here with great force. This bank is nearly sixty feet high,

[1] The author found it impossible, even with the offer of five times the usual wages, to obtain guides in July 1865, although the streams were low and the weather favorable.

and is constantly advancing on the land, the front wall being of as steep an angle as the sand will permit; the same angle is preserved from top to bottom, without the slightest debris at the base. The sand is white, coarse and composed of coral, shells and lava. When two handfulls are slapped together a noise resembling the bark of a dog is heard, the place being known as the "Barking Sands." This phenomenon also occurs near Kolòa and at other places, but requires that the sand be very dry. It is a common amusement for visitors to slide their horses down the steep incline, when a noise as of subterranean thunder is heard, which greatly terrifies animals not used to the experiment. The mirage is often seen on this dry hot soil so perfectly, that strangers endeavor to ride round the extensive lake they see before them.

No scientific observers have examined the western pali thoroughly. The water is very deep close to the shore, and the walls so perpendicular that canoes often pass between the rock and the waterfalls, which are common after a rain, and sometimes strike the sea twenty or thirty feet from shore.

NIIHAU.

Fifteen miles from Kauaì is the Island of Niihau, which is different in many respects from other islands of the group. It is twenty miles long by five wide, and consists of two portions, the mountain region, and the plain which meets this on three sides, the latter so low as to be almost invisible from Kauaì. The mountain is not much channelled by the rains,

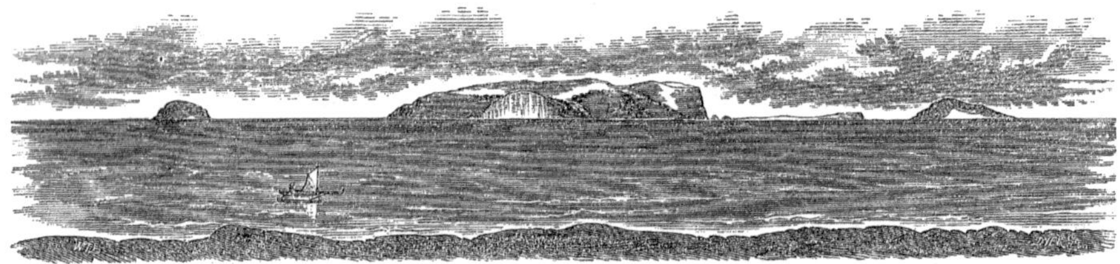

Fig. 4. View of Niihau from Waiméa, Kauaì. On the left is Kaúla, on the opposite side Lehùa.

which, however, are infrequent from the leeward position of the island, nor are the lower slopes covered with vegetation; small shrubs, (*Compositæ, Euphorbiaceæ, etc.,*) and succulent plants, constitute nearly the whole flora, indicating a dryness of the soil. The summit is remarkably flat in a distant view, but on closer inspection appears undulating and irregular, but wholly destitute of sharp peaks and narrow ridges. There is said to be no evident crater. On the windward side the mountain meets the sea in a pali of nearly eighteen hundred feet, exhibiting evident stratification. The rock is quite identical with that of the western part of Kauaì.

The craters of Kaúla and Lehùa belong to this island, and the latter is separated from Niihau by a channel only half a mile wide, and one and a half fathoms deep, in which the connecting bed of lava is plainly visible through the clear water. This lava is dark, in layers of about a foot in thickness, and seems to dip toward the north-west. Lehùa is mostly composed of tufa, has a crater much broken down towards the south-west, and a spring of good water. A colony of rabbits has for some years held undisputed possession, and is said to have increased rapidly.

Kaúla (*The Red*) is further from the opposite end of Niihau, and except in very smooth seas is difficult of access. It has no water, and is wholly barren. On the shore of Niihau, opposite these islands, are shore craters, especially near Kaúla. They are composed of red tufa, and although much broken down, exhibit clearly the anticlinal axis of true tufa cones. In the tufa, chrysolite and small clusters of calcareous crystals occur, and also fragments of coral reef.

The plain land of Niihau comprises two thirds of its surface, and all the habitable part. It is composed of coral reef, sand, and the wash from the mountain in successive layers. Although destitute of running streams, the soil is fertile, producing under cultivation the best pine-apples and bananas found on the group, as well as indian-corn, beans, cabbages, onions, squashes, and most of the vegetables of temperate climates.

The coral reef has been elevated from fifty to one hundred feet, and at the south-east end of the island is quite level, indicating that the rise was not gradual. This level portion is bare and very hard; the coral structure is not evident, its fracture is conchoidal, and it has a metallic ring. The surface is very uneven; the large caves and channels, always found in such formations, are here filled with breadfruit-trees and sugar-cane, which grow well in these pits, which are sometimes twelve feet deep and a hundred in diameter. They seem to be rooted on a base of lava or scoriæ, and only the topmost branches of the breadfruit-trees appear above the coral bed, the cane being usually wholly below. The rich deposit of vegetable mould in these pits would indicate great age, and it is worthy of note that the cane which grows here on little else than silica is harder, and leaves more ash than that on the richer plains of the other islands.[1]

Opposite Kaúla the reef is covered with sand in round hills which have a thin crust of earth in which grass grows well. Wherever the wash from the mountains has accumulated, sweet potatoes and yams grow abundantly. In a well sunk in this region, the earth was three feet deep, the sand five, and the coral reef beneath this contains water which is slightly brackish. In all places where exposed, the stratification of the sand indicates a wind rather than a sea deposit, probably filled up subsequently to the elevation of the reef. On the leeward side of the island, near the centre, are fresh-water ponds covering several acres very little above the sea-level. Salt-ponds occur at the southern end of the plain, where formerly the natives gathered much salt.

In some places the hard lava crops out, although no flow has been traced to the mountain, and is sufficiently hard to hold water. The natives in ancient times, further back than tradition extends, built reservoirs to hold water, some of which have been recently discovered, and are in good repair.

The absence of craters on the mountains of Niihau seems to have been settled by several natives who frequently make the ascent, and assure us that there are no valleys nor breaks of any size. None can be seen from below, and as there are no forests to conceal the irregularities of the slope, it would not be difficult to discover from the shore any true craters or large rents. On the other hand the dip is quite regular so far as examined, from the high wall fronting Kauaì to the opposite shore. As the cliff is on the windward side of the island comparatively little rain falls on the lee slopes, and in consequence there is but little soil and a scanty vegetation.

1 The crushed cane called *trash* or *bagasse*, is used as supplementary fuel under the train of sugar-pans, and the silica is melted into spongy masses of glass.

The channels between the different islands are deep and quite irregular, so far as soundings have been made. These have been limited to the principal harbors and shores where shoals were suspected. Generally where rock cliffs meet the sea, the water is deep and the shore destitute of coral reefs. Where a sand-beach or low lava streams are found, the fringing reef extends some distance from the shore, but it is generally quite level to its outer edge where it meets deep water at once. The limits of these reefs may be readily seen by the marked change in the color of the water. In none of the channels are there known to be detached coral reefs; there seem to be no sunken rocks at any considerable distance from the shore which might indicate the existence of some submerged or abortive volcanic peak. It is well known, however, that to the north-west of the Hawaiian Group, a long range of shoals extends many hundred miles, but beyond the mere fact of its existence, we know nothing. It would be most interesting to institute a series of soundings to the south-east of Hawaii, and it is hoped that the Hawaiian Government will undertake a complete hydrographic survey of the "Seven Seas."

OÁHU.

(See Map Plate XII.)

General Description.—Oáhu is ninety miles distant from Kauaì, in a S. E. direction, the channel between being called Ieiewàho. Its shape is somewhat irregular, the greatest length being thirty-five miles, the breadth twenty-one, and the area six hundred square miles. Unlike Kauaì, Oáhu has no central mountain, but on the N. E. and S. W. coasts, two high ridges extend in a nearly parallel direction for many miles, the plain between being the base of the N. E. or Konahuanùi range.

The windward side of the island is well watered and fertile, and even the leeward side possesses several streams besides many subterranean springs. As on all the other islands of the group, except perhaps Kauaì, the larger portion of the surplus rainfall passes to the sea by subterranean channels, often appearing as springs near the line of low tide. The lava of the mountains is more porous and less decomposed than on Kauaì. Dykes are not so common, nor so large, nor have the valleys such high and closely approaching walls, with the single exception of the valley of Kaliiwàa.

The shores of Oáhu are mostly fringed with coral reef which is often half a mile or more in breadth, and is composed of the cemented coral fragments, shells, sand and growing species of zoöphytes. The ancient reefs are elevated thirty, forty, or even a hundred feet in various places, and several of the valleys have by this barrier been changed from lagoons to solid ground. Volcanic action is perhaps more evident than on Kauaì, although many ages must have elapsed since any outbreak. Vegetation extends to the summits of the mountains, and during the rainy season even the dry plains and tufa cones support a crop of grass.

South-west Range.—The mountains on the S. W. were perhaps the earliest formed, and from the overlying strata of the eastern range, it is evident that they first ceased to give out lava streams. They are much broken into peaks and ravines, the slopes are steep and difficult to ascend, the summits are often marshy, and on one of them a lake of some size is said to exist. This range is usually called the Kaàla from its highest peak, which Dr. Gairdner ascertained to be three thousand eight hundred and fifty feet high (3850). There are two breaks or passes, one to the south of Kaàla, only fourteen hundred feet high, while the other near the southern end is sixteen hundred.

Between the mountains and the shore is a narrow, desolate, stony region called Waianaè, above which Kaàla towers with abrupt precipices strengthened by narrow buttresses, and generally inaccessible. In various parts of Waianaè are detached hills composed of a hard lava of various colors, some of it quite similar to the clinkstone found on Hawaii, while most of it is peculiar to this place, becoming white on decomposition, and so soft as to serve for chalk. This white formation is quite distinct from the decomposed coral reef which is sometimes found near by. The whole appearance of this barren, desolate district, without streams, and almost without vegetation, hedged in towards the land with dark red cliffs two thousand feet high, bending on either hand towards the shore, is that of a vast crater broken down towards the sea.

The pass near Kaàla exhibits several fine dykes, in one place eleven occurring within fifty yards, some projecting from the softer wall of the precipice, while others have broken out leaving narrow slits in the rock. A conglomerate is very common near by, as are also the small boulders with concentric coatings mentioned in the description of Kauaì.

Towards the centre of the island the slopes of the Kaàla mountains are less abrupt although still quite steep, the valleys are deep, although of small extent, and the ridges so sharp in many places as to render walking decidedly dangerous in wet weather. The rocks are mostly of gray basalt alternating with a red cellular lava. They are often porphyritic, containing small tabular crystals of feldspar.

These mountains completely cut off the trade wind, and are much dreaded on this account by mariners on their voyages to and from Kauaì. At Barber's Point (Laelóa) the sand extends some distance from shore, forming a rather dangerous shoal.

Fig. 5. Eastern end of Oáhu. From the north, distant fifteen miles.

North-east Range.—The mountains of the Konahuanùi range are higher and much more extensive than those of Waianaè. Commencing at the northern end of the island near Kahúku, the mountains rise gradually with a slope of less than eight degrees for nearly ten miles; then the summit becomes broken and jagged, valleys of increasing size cut the mountain to its core on either side, until it culminates in the two peaks of Waiolàni and Konahuanùi, four thousand feet above the sea, and which seem rent asunder to form the valley of Nuuánu. Beyond this towards the east the valleys decrease in size on the leeward side, while on the N. E. an almost perpendicular wall extends for thirty miles unbroken by any valley, ending at last abruptly at Makapùu Point. The range is simply a midrib some thirty miles long with a complete series of lateral ridges or pinnæ on the S. W., but without these for two thirds its length on the N. E.

The valleys are of exceeding beauty, and many travellers have pronounced the scenery unsurpassed by any in the world. Nuuánu opens on the coast not far from the centre of the range, directly behind Honolulu, and was once a bay or lagoon, protected towards the sea by a reef of coral a mile wide, through which the fresh-water streams from the valley made their way. This bay was nearly two miles deep and of the full width of the valley. The elevation of the reef some twenty-five feet has furnished a site for Honolulu which covers its whole width, and has converted the bay into a low but pleasantly situated plain. Near what was formerly the head of the bay, the stumps of large tree ferns have been dug up from a depth of five to ten feet, in such quantities as to serve for fencing material on a small cane-field. No such ferns are found at present north of Hawaii.

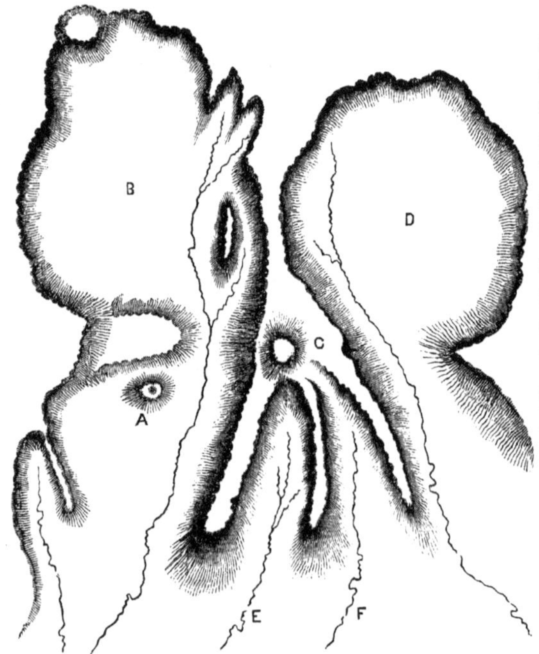

Fig. 6. Map of the Valleys near Honolulu.
A, small cone in Nuuánu; B, circus of Nuuánu Valley; C, smooth conical peak; D, Manóa Valley; E, stream from Pauóa Valley; F, stream from Makiki Valley.

Ascending the valley by a gentle slope among the gardens of the foreign residents, and the equally beautiful kalo-ponds of the natives, one sees the ridges on either side, at first broad and smooth, covered with grass; but soon these ridges become steeper, their walls rise nearly perpendicularly, fluted with the pathways of the rain torrents, mantled with every shade of green, and fringed at their base by dark densely wooded dells. The origin of Gothic architecture is referred to the study of the form of trees, but here the Divine Architect has reared a structure far more suggestive than the forests; and the green archways of covered rock extend in long colonnades up the aisle leading to a nave crowned by the spires of Waiolàni, the "waters of Heaven."

The valley becomes narrower, although never a gorge; and about four miles from Honolulu, a low ridge crosses the road, beyond which the walls are higher, more precipitous, and seem to form an amphitheatre around a small cone crater which occupies nearly the middle of the valley. Two miles beyond, the valley terminates on the brink of a precipice twelve hundred feet in height, above which on either hand Konahuanùi and Waiolàni tower three thousand feet higher. This is the famous Pali of Nuuánu, down whose steep although not difficult descent, lies the road to the district of Koolaù. The cliffs near the Pali are much worn by the rain and wind which sweep through the narrow pass with terrific violence during a storm, and several hills of red ochreous earth are ground and channelled by the same agency into forms resembling those described in Colorado by Dr. J. S. Newberry.[1] Two dykes occur in the hard graystone of the cliff, and several rents at right angles to these have formed small ravines. There are some indications of volcanic action in the neighborhood, as scoriæ and cinder deposits, but they are probably much older than the shore craters. No distinct crater is visible, although the sides of the valley much resemble the encircling

[1] Report on the Colorado, by Lieut. J. C. Ives. Part iii., p. 82, *et passim*.

walls of some vast pit. On opposite sides of the valley there is very little to indicate that they were ever nearer to each other than at present; they are not always of the same height, their spurs and side ravines are different, but the arrangement of lava beds and their dip is essentially the same.

In Nuuânu Valley at the head of the ancient bay, and along the base of all the ridges towards the east, a coarse black gravel is found at various depths, owing to the irregular surface of the ground, but apparently nearly on the same level, in layers of one or two feet in thickness. This gravel seems to be comminuted pitchstone, and contains a very large amount of iron. It is often used to cover road-beds, and when crushed by the unshod hoofs of the horses, forms a coarse powder, and an electro-magnet drawn through it for ten inches becomes charged with particles of iron. The wash of the hills and the tufa of the coast craters is often directly superimposed upon this bed. Near the lower end of Nuuánu a stream of dark compact basalt crops out in the bed of a river, exhibiting rude columnar forms.

Next to Nuuánu on the east is Paućá, a small but very beautiful valley filled with rice-fields, kalo-ponds, banana plantations, and the grass houses of the natives, and remarkable as affording a pathway for horses to the summit of the mountain at its head, the valleys of the Hawaiian Islands usually ending in an abrupt wall often inaccessible to man. East of this, Manóa Valley forms a broad circular plain inclosed by high and steep walls. The soil is deep and rich. The rock is usually a gray or red cellular basalt, which becomes quite soft on decomposition, so that when wet it may be easily cut with a knife, though when dry it is as hard as an ordinary unpressed brick. It retains the shape of its nearly spherical cells through these changes which must take place several times each week, as the showers and sunshine alternate with wonderful rapidity in these mountain recesses. In many places large bubbles have been formed in ancient lava streams which now form caverns, sometimes of considerable extent with rough sides and roof. These are often exposed by the breaking off of the outer wall, and have for ages formed convenient receptacles for the dead.

The spurs of the side ridges project towards the mouth of the valley usually, but in several remarkable instances the direction is reversed. During the rains, the circus at the head of Manóa presents a hundred cascades whose white threads may be seen several miles at sea. The ascent to Konahuanùi by the western ridge of Manóa is not difficult, although beyond the first few miles the pathway becomes narrow in places, and the ridge almost knife-edged. Swamps and pools are met with on the way, and the whole soil is wet, even to the summit, where moss covers the trees, and is usually saturated with water from the clouds that settle upon the mountain. Two cracks or rents occur, neither of them of any great size, but remarkable for their position. They are both about twenty feet wide, and nearly the same depth, the bottom being filled with loose earth and stones. The rock exposed by these sections is the red-brown cellular lava which crops out below, and the strata are much confused as if different streams

Fig. 7. Side Ridge in Manóa Valley.

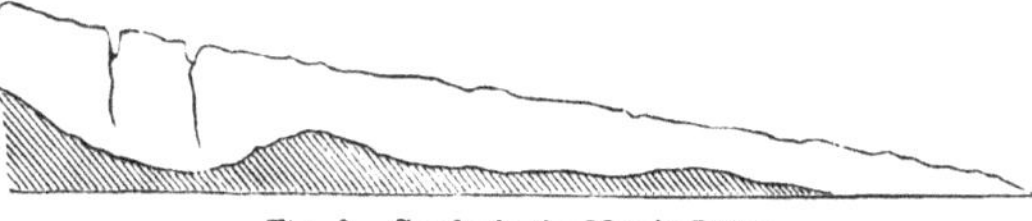

Fig. 8. Cracks in the Manóa Ridge.

had met here. The soil is in many places quite red from the oxide of iron, and the water in the pools is often coated with the iridescent film of the hydrated peroxide.

In the valley of Palòlo the decomposed lava has formed a stiff, tenacious, light-colored clay which constitutes so large a proportion of the soil as to give the valley its name. Towards the east the valleys are small, destitute of running streams, and the ridges point inward as in the figure. Caves are more frequent near this end of the island, and some are of considerable extent. The soil is red, dry and covered with loose stones. In ancient times this barren land was cultivated, and the small piles of loose stones show where the sweet-potatoes were planted, the stones retaining moisture, and serving as supports. At present, wild cotton (*Gossypium tomentosum*), a few *Convolvulaceæ*, sidas, and argemones constitute the vegetation during the summer. There are no trees, save a few Nawiliwili (*Erythrina monosperma*).

Fig. 9. Plan of the Makapúu Ridges.

The mountain ends abruptly at Makapùu, and the only pathway leads over an almost perpendicular precipice nearly eight hundred feet high. From this the whole aspect of the island changes. The deep valleys like Nuuánu and Manóa, and the sterile rock-paved region of Kóko, have alike disappeared, and a narrow strip of bright green land extends for eight or ten miles, bounded on one hand by the green ocean, and on the other by an almost unbroken wall nearly two thousand feet high. A section through the island here at right angles to the main ridge would be approximately represented by the annexed diagram. The summit is a very sharp edge through which many holes are visible from beneath, and the base is covered with fallen rocks and earth so as to furnish a pathway for the goats to the top.

Fig. 10. Section of Konahuanùi from North to South.
a, *a*, compact basalt; *b*, debris from the cliffs; *c*, dunes of coral sand.

The reef has been raised nearly twenty feet at this point, and the whole coast is fringed with a reef now growing and extending out in some places four thousand feet. From this reef the sand is washed in, forming dunes thirty feet high in some places, of a dazzling whiteness. There are several small islands off the shore, evidently the remains of tufa cones; the largest is represented in the accompanying figure.

Fig. 11. Island Crater off the northern coast of Oáhu.

The pali of Koolaù is one of the most remarkable formations on Oáhu, and the interest with which it is regarded by geologists is much increased by the explanation Prof. Dana gives of its origin.[1] It must not be inferred from that explanation that this wall is a clear unbroken perpendicular precipice of regular curve. Whatever may have been its condition a quarter of a century since, at present there is a considerable talus at the base, composed of fragments of rock intermingled with the earth washed from above. It is quite difficult to ascertain the dip of the exposed strata, as the cliffs are quite inaccessible. From below they certainly seem to dip towards the

[1] *Loc. cit.* p. 258.

interior of the mountain, and this is particularly the case in the projecting buttresses. Low ridges run out like projecting arms, often encircling crater-like valleys. This is especially common through the region from Waimanálo to Kaneóhe. Two ridges, one of them nearly two thousand feet high, extend completely to the sea enclosing the district of Kailùa, and between these occur many circular depressions with smooth rounded walls, and hills of red ochre. The many brooks in this neighborhood have confused the original outline of these hills and valleys by cutting through them and sometimes nearly filling the hollows with alluvial deposits. The coast ridge is very sharp and needle-like, and must have occupied nearly the centre of Prof. Dana's supposed crater.

From Kaneóhe to Kahúku is the most fertile region of Oáhu. The soil is deep, well watered, and is covered in many places by fields of sugar-cane. Tobacco, cotton, and ground-nuts also do well here. Kaneóhe is directly opposite to Nuuánu Valley, and is remarkable for its series of coast craters. The main ridge changes its character beyond towards the west, and valleys and ravines cut their way into the interior of the mountain. A curious circular valley is directly opposite the village of Kaneóhe, and is a fair type of many valleys on the islands.

The strata evidently dip towards the N. E. as well as to the S. W., and in the valley of Ahumánu a fine spring gushes forth from the mountain wall in the direction of the strata. Farther to the west, the scenery grows wilder and more grand. The lateral ridges approach the sea; retaining, however, the identical appearance of the Koolaù Pali, their black, almost perpendicular rock-walls often being destitute of vegetation for eight hundred feet in height, and above and below this bare space clothed with dense foliage. At the head of Punalúu Valley is a large cone crater, from which radiate several valleys, as the Kahàna, Kaliiwàa, Punalúu, and others. This crater is densely wooded, and occupies nearly the centre of the range. No one seems to have ascended it, and it is impossible to say how deep the cavity may be, but the internal slopes as seen from below seem to be quite steep, and probably the outer wall is broken down. Around the base is a large swamp in which several streams take their rise, the Kahàna being one of the largest in Oáhu.

The adjoining valley of Kaliiwàa or Kaliuàa, much resembles that of Hanapépé on Kauaì. Entering the lofty portals which rise in pinnacles a thousand feet, the explorer finds himself in a dark and narrow aisle, less than sixty feet wide, and enclosed with inaccessible walls at least eight hundred feet high. A clear cold stream runs over the stony bed shaded by the dark green foliage of the ohia ai (*Eugenia malaccensis*, Linn.). In ancient times this was a place sacred to the native divinities, and even now, so impressive is the solemn grandeur of the scene, that the natives make an offering of a few leaves placed beneath a stone, that the wrathful gods may not hurl rocks from above upon the sacrilegious intruder.

A quarter of a mile from the entrance is one of the curiosities which gives the valley its name (Ka-lii-wàa, the chief's canoe). On the right, at the head of a small ravine, some fifty yards from the stream, is a perpendicular wall over which a former stream fell nearly three hundred feet; and the water has worn a perfectly regular, smooth groove, much resembling a cast of a native canoe. About a mile beyond this is a similar but more perfect channel. For nearly a thousand feet the vertical wall is cut into by a conical groove twenty-five feet wide and fourteen deep at the bottom, but regularly diminishing as it approaches the top of the cliffs. That this was formerly the bed of a stream, and that water was the sole formative agent, is very evident, although the perfection of the work, the smoothness of the sides, seem beyond the power of a rude waterfall. A few rods beyond this is the present waterfall, which has worn its way down from above until its waters gush out of a narrow cleft, clear of the wall, into a dark pool below, which only the mid-day sun ever shines upon, so close are the walls above it. There is no possibility of scaling the walls of the valley; and to examine the gorge above, one must retrace his way to the shore and ascend the ridges. There are two falls above this, one of them invisible but audible; the other, some three or four hundred feet high, may be seen from the shore some four miles distant. It may be a matter of interest to some future traveller to trace the ancient conduits, and see what has twice diverted the stream.

At Laié the drift-sand has formed hills of sand-stone hard enough for building purposes. These hills are thirty or forty feet high, much broken by earthquakes apparently, and worn by the action of wind and rain, into grotesque honey-combed masses and ragged pinnacles. From the white color of this stone it has often been mistaken for elevated coral reef. Near Kahúku the sand-hills are of greater size and height, and much resemble an elevated beach. The tracks of a plover, identical with the existing species, were discovered imbedded in the sand-stone nearly a hundred feet above the sea. The stone splits readily into slabs, and is white, hard, and of a coarse texture. The elevated reef near Kahúku, and all along the north-west end of Oáhu, is quite distinct and full of large caves. A light-colored rock in rounded masses is sometimes met with at this end of the island. It is a light, porous gray-stone, and always occurs beneath beds of red cellular lava.

The Shore Craters of Oáhu. — Although the main mountains of Oáhu exhibit few craters or cones in perfect condition, there are along the shores fine examples of tufa cones. These occur in six groups: at Kaneóhe, Kóko, Leáhi, Puawaìna, Aliapaakaì, and Laelóa.

Kaneóhe Group.

On the peninsula that forms the eastern side of Kaneóhe Bay are four hills, three of which exhibit craters. Excepting these volcanic hills the surface is flat and formed of coral limestone elevated but a few feet above high-water level. The largest crater (A) is much broken down by the sea; no lava stream has been discovered. The next cone towards the land (B) is almost wholly composed of a compact, black, heavy lava, which has flowed out towards the sea, although now wholly hidden by accumulating sand. The other two hills (C, D) are small, and made up of lava similar to the last. A crater (F) some rods from shore has not been examined; it much resembles the island off Makapùu. At E is a low ridge nearly covered by sand, which appears to be the remains of a crater nearly as large as A. Both C and D have been much worn by the waves on the sea front, while they have been covered by sand towards the shore, a fact that would render their identification difficult were it not for the description of Dana written some twenty-five years ago. This erosion has taken place in spite of the protecting coral-reef which fringes this coast. Along the shore to the west are one or two small islands of like origin, but much worn away by the sea which has obliterated all traces of craters.

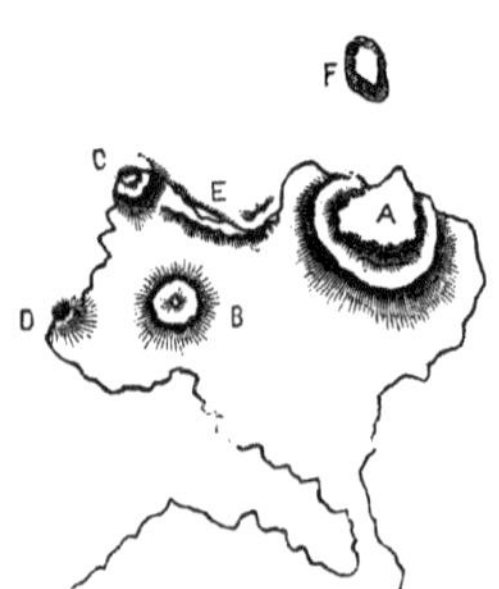

Fig. 12. Plan of Kaneóhe Craters.

Fig. 13. View of Kaneóhe from the East.

Kóko Head Group.

The south-east promontory of Oáhu is composed of the remains of cones so closely crowded that the strata and slopes are very perplexing. Kóko is a smooth rounded eminence with no traces of a crater on the top. The ascent is remarkably gradual, and there is a good horse-path to the summit (A), where the grass grows well. Blocks of lava are scattered over the level top, probably brought there by the natives for burial purposes. At B is a small crater, now covered with grass; the walls are low, rounded, and smooth. D is open to the sea, and the blue color of the water indicates great depth; at its head is a house belonging to the king, and a spring (C) of fresh water issuing at the base of the cliff supplies several kalo-ponds. The walls are steep but not high. Near the signal station between D and E, there is a large amount of augite imbedded in the tufa, also incrustations and thin layers of calcareous matter. E is the largest crater, and its walls are broken towards the sea, leaving the bottom dry and level a few feet above high water. All through the tufa of this crater fragments of coral rock are thickly scattered. The tufa is hard, brown, and coarse, much resembling sand-stone; where the sea has undermined the cliffs, projecting striæ parallel to the dip seem to indicate varying hardness in the layers. Inland of this is a very high and steep cone quite different in its outline from the other craters in the neighborhood. The internal cavity descends nearly to the sea level, and is open towards the north-east. The cone is obliquely truncated, owing to the trade-winds, which, besides modifying the form in this way, render the plan oval with the acute end towards the wind, as during

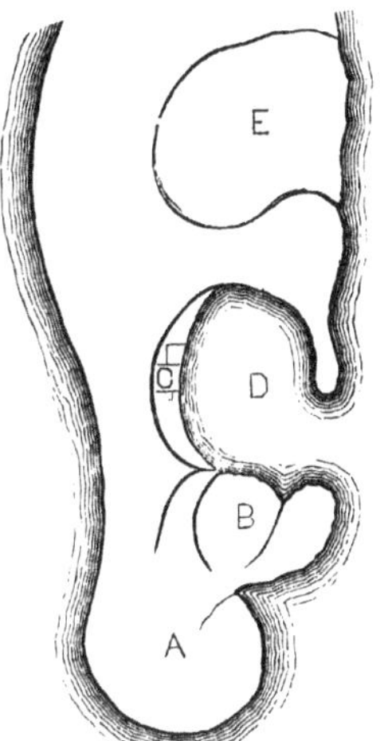

Fig. 14. Plan of the Kóko Craters. A, smooth grassy summit; B, small crater; C, spring of fresh water; D, deep crater open to the sea; E, large dry crater broken down towards the sea.

Fig. 15. View of Kóko Craters from the outer Signal-Station.
The bay in the foreground is represented by D on the plan (Fig. 14), and the small house on the right marks the position of the spring.

the eruption the ashes are blown to leeward. The windward side would, therefore, be the weakest, and is most easily breached. Lava streams are common about Kóko, although it is often difficult to trace them to their source, and both the graystone and red vesicular varieties are found, the former often imbedded in large fragments in the tufa, the edges being as sharp and uneven as if recently fractured.

Leáhi Group. The most remarkable object on approaching Oáhu, is the high cone of Leáhi or Diamond Hill. It is situated on the shore nearly between Kóko and Honolulu, and about eight miles west of the former. Its height at present is from four to seven hundred feet,[1] and its longest diameter at the top, about half a mile. The crater is deep, reaching nearly to the sea level, and contains no lava rock. At the bottom, during a third of the year, a pool of water collects which covers nearly half of the tolerably level bottom; on the remainder, which is deeply furrowed by rains, wild cotton, a few sidas and argemones flourish, and enough grass to tempt horses to make the difficult ascent and descent.

Fig. 16. View of Leáhi from Punahoù (⟶East).

This cone is rapidly diminishing. In the winter of 1864, during a severe rain, when thirty-six inches of water fell in a week, a deposit of mud two feet in depth was formed over the inner basin, and the degradation of the exterior was still more extensive. The south-west end, which is the highest point, was formerly quite accessible, but now can only be scaled with ladders or ropes. Most of the exterior has been washed down upon the elevated coral bed which surrounds the cone, forming a deep layer of soil, frequently cut through by rain-channels. The strata exposed by the removal of the exterior, have a dip towards the centre, showing that the whole outside has been removed towards the south and west. The rim of the crater is narrow, and where the exterior slope remains, exhibits an anticlinal axis, the dip being about 35°.

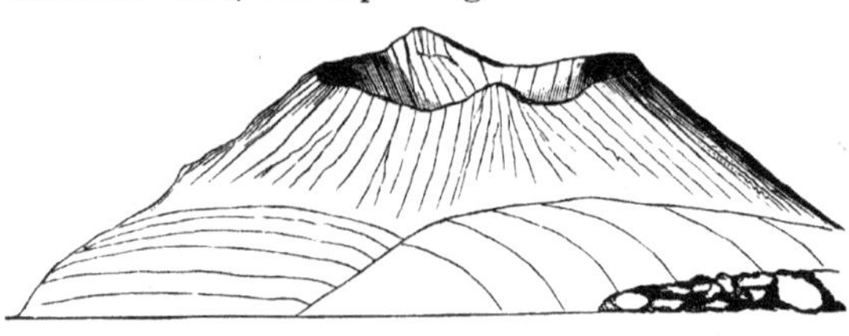

Fig. 17. View of Leáhi from Kóko (N. N. E. ⟶.)

The tufa of which the hill is composed, is light brownish, inclining in some places to red, and is very friable, breaking easily in the fingers. It consists of thin laminæ usually separated by a calcareous deposit. Coral of recent species occurs imbedded in considerable quantity, often undecomposed, and in masses of two to twenty cubic inches. The whole region about Leáhi is an elevated reef.

No lavas have issued from this cone, but two large streams surround it, and have poured into the sea at its base over a deposit of sand. The sand has been washed away leaving the lava in broken slabs. In one place this lava, in passing over a stratum of tufa, has

[1] Since the above was in print (1867), President Alexander, of Oáhu College, has found the highest point to be 760 feet.

baked it hard and given it a deep red color; at the same time its structure has been rendered beautifully prismatic, the penta-hexagonal prisms being about an inch in diameter and two or three long. The lava above is in a thin sheet, and probably cooled rapidly, as no effects of heat are visible half a foot from the surface.

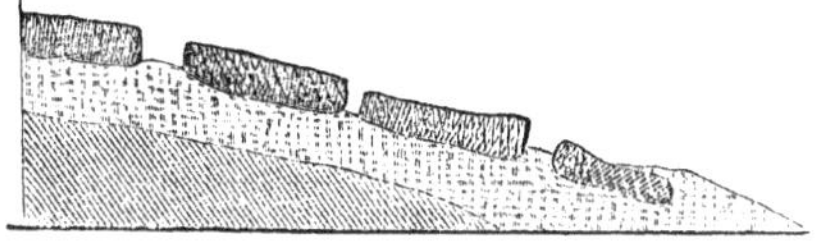

Fig. 18. Section of a lava stream at Leáhi.

There are two other craters nearly in a line with Leáhi, but low, and mostly composed of lava; probably they were the vents which supplied the lava covering this region. All the country in the neighborhood is dry and barren. Smooth beds of lava are covered with blocks of similar rock of all sizes from one to one hundred cubic feet, indicating that a lava flow had underrun and burst up a previous stream. Where a river from Palòlo Valley has broken through the deposit, three or four strata are visible near the base of the Konahuanùi range — their probable source. The coral reef is much cracked and tilted, and is of great thickness, some of the natural pits or caves being twenty or thirty feet deep with a coral bottom. The upper surface is rough, and so colored by the ochre of the earth in the neighborhood, as to lose all appearance of organic origin, and to closely resemble lava.

Puawaìna Group. Punch-bowl, or Fort Hill, is directly behind Honolulu, adjoining the west ridge of Manóa Valley, and blocking the entrance to Pauóa. It much resembles Leáhi, but is much smaller. Its brown tufa sides have an arid aspect, except during April

Fig. 19. Puawaìna from Punahou (← East).

and May, when the rains water the scanty crop of grass which covers the whole hill with an evanescent mantle of green. The summit is about five hundred feet above the sea,[1] and as its substance is harder and more closely bound by the roots of the grass and shrubs on its surface, it has suffered less than Leáhi, still an examination of its southern edge shows that less than one half of its pristine size remains. In Dixon's "Voyage Around the World," a view of the cone is given, presenting high peaks; this was in 1786, and the natives declare that "many ages since, it had such a form."

The crater at the top is very shallow and covered with green sward. Its diameter is about six hundred yards, and it is of the usual oval form. The tufa is beautifully laminated, and well exhibits the double dip of about thirty degrees on each side of the rim. Lime encrusts the tufa on the south side, and seams of the same white substance occur in such abundance as to give the outer slope in many places a whitewashed appearance.

Near the little battery on the summit, is a rough pile of cellular lava and scoriæ which

[1] Found by President Alexander to be 460 feet.

seems to have risen to its present height, and, prevented by the superincumbent tufa, remains in the branched and ragged form in which it cooled. At the eastern side is a deep break, and another mass of dark basalt of slightly columnar structure. From the appearance of this side it is by no means evident that this break is coeval with the eruption which marked the formation of the cone; during the rains water collects in the crater, and a stream of some size rushes over the cliff, carrying with it a large quantity of earth and stones, and this agent has enlarged if not originated the ravine whose former contents are spread in a thick layer over the plain east of Honolulu. Two dykes are seen on this side, the one two, and the other ten feet wide. The basalt of these, as of all the masses visible in this cone, contains some chrysolite and minute grains of augite. On the northern side a conglomerate occurs, seemingly due to the ejection of scoriæ from the crater. In several places near the base, masses of rock occur imbedded in the tufa, the latter being raised around them precisely as a thick mud would rise around a heavy body dropped into it.

Near Punahoù at the entrance of Manóa Valley, are marks of another crater, and beyond this is much fresh looking basalt. Some disturbance seems to have caused the appearance of the spring which gives the name to the land of Punahoù (*New Spring*), and which evidently flows over extensive lime deposits, probably coral beds, the water being very hard.

Aliapaakaì Group.

Six miles west of Honolulu, and three quarters of a mile from the sea, is a region of tufa craters of considerable interest, extending over ten square miles, and bearing marks of greater antiquity than any other similar formation on Oáhu. Several vents have coalesced, or rather the ejections of several have commingled as in the Kóko region, forming confluent arcs enclosing a plain almost a mile and three quarters in diameter and nearly level. The bounding walls are low, being on the northern side two hundred, and on the south not more than fifty feet high. They are formed of layers of tufa of a red color, more granular than that of Leáhi, but arranged in the same way. The *inner* slope and a portion of the outer have disappeared from the Aliapaakaì craters, while at Leáhi the *outer* has suffered most. In the tufa large masses of agglomerated chrysolite (*olivine*) are found, often four or five inches in diameter, also augite in dark green crystals, black mica, and garnets. Salt impregnates the whole mass of the inner walls, and is found in places on the cliffs where it could hardly have been brought by human hands. A large portion of the plain is occupied by the salt lake which gives the place its name (*Aliapaakaì*). In the rainy season large quantities of water rush in from the mountains through a hole near the centre of the basin, often bubbling above the surface, and extending the lake to the borders of the plain. At such times the water is about three feet deep, clear and dense, and intensely salt. The bottom is covered with a blue clay-like mud several inches deep, and is smooth and nearly level. During the dry season when the supply of fresh water is cut off, and the evaporation is very great, the lake is contracted to a third of its former extent, the water becomes oily and burning to the skin, the whole bottom is encrusted with large cubical crystals of salt, and along the shore the cakes of salt are sufficiently solid to bear the weight of a horse

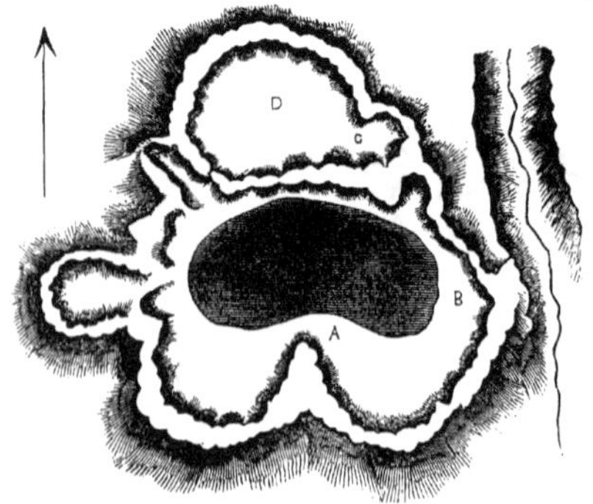

Fig. 20. Plan of Aliapaakaì.
A, raised coral reef; B, spring of fresh water; C, small crater; D, large crater, generally dry.

and his rider without cracking. The salt covering the bottom is much fissured, and it is on the edge of these cracks that the finest crystals occur. Large nodules, composed of brilliant cubes more than a third of an inch in diameter, are quite common in the water, and usually contain no nucleus. The salt is quite pure, and large quantities have been taken away for sale.

On the shore towards the mountains (B) fresh water oozes in through the remains of abandoned kalo patches, but the cattle have so trodden the miry soil that it is difficult to trace any stream. It is not possible that this lake has any communication with the ocean, as the tides rise and fall nearly two feet on the adjacent shore, a change of level sufficient to alternately drain and fill the shallow basin; and a rise of an inch would cause an advance in the shore line of at least a foot, while the most careful observations have failed to perceive any change which could not be attributed to the varying winds.

On the southern ridge near its base is a raised coral reef (A) much cracked and displaced, and fragments of coral are imbedded in the tufa of the walls on every side. Towards Éwa on the west is a hollow (D) which during the severe rains of the winter, contains a muddy pool of brackish water; this is separated from the salt lake by a narrow ridge, and is of similar formation.

Laelóa Group. At Laelóa, the south-western point of Oáhu, is a cluster of small cones, distinctly visible from Honolulu, which bear marks of comparatively recent origin. All these have craters, and in two of them the rock projects in rude columns. They are mostly composed of a tolerably compact black lava, and are surrounded by lava of a red color broken into large loose blocks from two to twenty cubic feet in size, precisely resembling the masses so common near Leáhi. The highest of these cones is but three hundred feet above the sea, and, although from a distance conspicuous from its regular conical form, is hardly larger than some of the lava bubbles on Hawaii.

MÁUI GROUP.

(See Map, Plate XIII.)

The third division of the Hawaiian Islands consists of a group of islands of considerable extent. Máui, the largest, is next to Hawaii in size as well as in height, and contains the largest known crater. Molokaì, Lanai, Kahooláwe, and Molokíni are small, seldom visited by travellers, and have never been thoroughly explored.

Although closely clustered, and forming, as it were, the fragments of a former island of semicircular form, the members of this group exhibit some remarkable differences, both in form and constitution. Máui contains a lava which has never been found on Kauaì or Oáhu, while Molokaì abounds in a light gray stone, which is not known to occur anywhere else. Máui and Molokaì are islands of double summits like Oáhu, while Lanai and Kahooláwe are single, and resemble Niihau. The distribution of land-shells and of plants is also various, each island having several peculiar species. Whether they ever composed one island, or what their true relation to each other may be, will be examined further on; at present it remains to examine their physical and geological characteristics as separate islands.

Fig. 21. View of the Southern Islands from Molokaì.
Máui. Molokìni. Hawaii. Kahooláwe. Lanai.

MAUI.

Máui is a double island consisting of two peaks connected by a low isthmus, and its plan somewhat resembles the human bust, the head being towards the north-west. Its greatest length is fifty-four miles, breadth, twenty-five, and its area is six hundred and fifty square miles. East Máui is the larger, and is a mountain dome rising more than ten thousand feet above the sea. Háleakala (*the house that the sun built*) is quite regular in its slopes, which vary from eight to ten degrees, being somewhat steeper on the windward side. The lava beds of which it is composed vary much from those of Kauaì or Oáhu, being of a lighter color, less cellular, and more impervious to water. This is particularly the case with the lower beds where exposed by the ravines; and the beds of the streams are much worn into pot-holes, which serve as reservoirs during the part of the year when the stream ceases to run. On the surface the rock is more red and broken, closely resembling that near Leáhi on Oáhu. Lateral cones abound, some near the base, although on the northern side they seem very ancient, and no streams of lava have been traced from them. On the western side, near Ulupalakúa, several distinct streams of very fresh looking lava are found near the coast. All the windward side of Háleakala is much cut up by ravines, rendering travelling in the district of Hána laborious, and when the streams are high, even dangerous. The road winds up and down precipices over which the wind rushes with such violence as to sometimes oblige the traveller to dismount and seek shelter against the cliff on one side to avoid being dashed over the precipice on the other. Travellers among the Alps see less wildness of mountain scenery than the Hawaiian who rides from Hána to Lahaìna. On no part of the islands are the roads so dangerous, yet such is the skill of the riders, or the sure-footedness of the horses, that accidents seldom occur. Water is abundant in all the gorges, especially after a rain on the mountain, and the ridges are generally well wooded.

On the north-west side the path to the summit passes over a bare tract of land, destitute of trees save a few straggling koa or sandal-wood bushes, but covered with wild sage (*Sphacele hastata*), ohelos (*Vaccinium reticulatum*) and grass. In September 1864, the grass was thin and dry but extended to the highest point, as did a common *Sonchus*. The ascent was gradual and far more even than that of Mauna Lòa; indeed, a carriage-road might be built to the top with very little difficulty, the slope being much more regular than that of Mt. Washington in New Hampshire.

The immense size of the terminal crater does not at first strike one; but a brief examination of the cliffs which stretch their black precipices for a circuit of thirty miles, enclosing

Fig. 22. The Crater of Háleakala, from a Photograph by Weed Bros.

several hills which seem from the top like mole-hills, but in reality are five or six hundred feet high, springing from a base eighteen hundred feet below the upper wall,— a glance at the small white specks which move along the cliffs at the beholder's feet,— and the full wonder of the place is recognized. It is not like the solemn grandeur of Mokuawéowéo on Mauna Lòa, nor like the black terrors of Kilauéa, but it is still a scene of desolation, and a mighty monument of the forces with which God builds the world.

Although the walls are steep, it is possible to descend almost anywhere, the sand or cinders having accumulated about the base of the rock cliffs. On the north and east are two vast breaks from one to three miles wide, as deep as the crater, and extending to the sea. Through these gateways two streams of lava found their way out, when, no one can say, although native tradition would leave us to infer that it took place since the Hawaiians came to these islands two thousand (?) years ago. Their appearance is in many places as fresh as the streams of 1801 on Hualalaì.

The eastern or Hána break is completely floored with the hard lava stream and occasional clinker beds, and for more than three miles from the crater a line of small cones extends along the centre. About half way down the mountain, this flow emerges from its gorge and spreads over the slopes to the southward in the form of a huge delta. It has blocked up several ravines, showing its comparatively recent origin. The northern or Koolaù break is quite similar in its formation, and extends directly to the sea. Both streams doubtless belonged to the same eruption. The bottom of the crater is dotted with sixteen large cones of regular shape, the acute end of their oval base being towards the north-east.

They are composed of cinders and scoriæ, generally of light specific gravity and reddish tinge, sometimes black, and again colored with the hydrated oxide of iron, as if steam had acted upon them while highly heated.

On these cones we find the first appearance of sulphur. Kauaì and Oáhu were free from it, and it is here in small quantities, much weathered, and quite impure; with this exception Hawaii is the only island where this common volcanic product is found. There is no steam or vapor, and not even a hot spring to mark the forces once so active in this mountain. A pool of cool and sweet water on the floor of the crater is carefully protected with stones.

This crater has never been surveyed, and the size is estimated by Mr. Drayton, of the United States Exploring Expedition, to be from one to two thousand feet deep, and fifteen miles in circuit. This is, however, much below the true circumference, which is nearer thirty miles. The highest point of Háleakala was determined by barometer to be ten thousand two hundred and seventeen (10,217) feet above the sea.

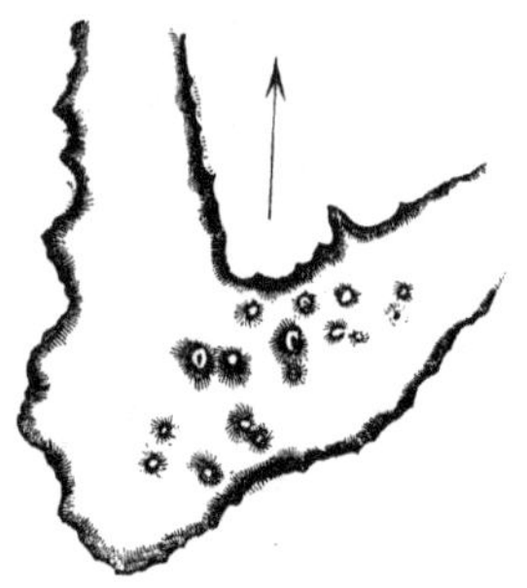
Fig. 23. Plan of Háleakala.

Caves are of frequent occurrence near the top, and have every appearance of lava bubbles. The rock of the crater is a hard gray clinkstone, much fissured, and in many places resembling artificial walls of cubical stone blocks; lower down the mountain the rock is softer and of a bluish tinge. A variety of feldspar, which Prof. Dana named Mauilite, occurs in the loose sand of the cones.

Háleakala has been long extinct. No warm springs or steam-jets, no mineral springs nor solfataras exist on Máui. Earthquakes are not more frequent, nor are there indeed any signs to indicate that it will ever shake off its slumber of two thousand years, and again pour forth lava. The slopes of Hána are as old to all appearance as those of Kauaì, and the soil is as deep and as productive.

Old as is East Máui, West Máui is older still, as is shown by its more broken surface, deeper soil, and extensive degradation. Its summit, Eéka, is six thousand one hundred and thirty (6130) feet high. No single terminal crater exists, although there seem to be the remains of several: the valley behind Lahaìna being one, and Wailùku Valley perhaps another. On a clear day, when the trade-wind clouds that usually hang over Eéka pass away, the clustered peaks as seen from Ulupalakúa more closely resemble the walls of a central terminal crater than when examined from a nearer point. Indeed, no one who had only seen this distant view would hesitate to declare that a crater of considerable size and distinct outline crowned the mountain.

Several of the valleys of Eéka have much the appearance of rents like the vast breaks in Háleakala. The valley of Io, near Wailùku on the south-eastern slope, is deep and wild; several curious pinnacles or needles have been formed by the degradation of the very sharp, thin ridges. The head of the valley forms an amphitheatre half a mile in diameter, and is raised above the level of the valley-slope by a terrace nearly a hundred feet high. It is not impossible that this was once a crater, and the lower part of the valley where the high and nearly perpendicular walls closely approach each other, was a rent which the waters and decomposition of the lava have enlarged. In no valley on the islands are the ridges so sharp as here; they often seem mere laminæ set up on edge, — almost the leaves of this vast volume of Nature.

Near Haikù on East Máui the soil is deep and productive. Many acres are covered with kukui-trees of large size, and on the cultivated ground sugar-cane yields good crops. Several of the broken-down tufa-cones produce good crops of cane, and as the rain-fall is frequent, the absence of all permanent streams is to some degree compensated. The shore is a cliff nearly perpendicular, washed by the surf. Where the rain-streams have broken through at Maliko, the section is as represented in the margin. There are three distinct layers, each twenty or thirty feet thick, of tufaceous lava, the top of each layer being burned red by the stream above it, and rendered prismatic for nearly a foot in depth, indicating great and uniform heat, as each stream is similar to the preceding one both in size and composition. The lower portion of each stratum is composed of loose rounded masses that are gradually forming a conglomerate. To the west of Haikù is a large tract of land of many hundred acres, formed by the wash of Háleakala, and capable of producing a large amount of cane, but wholly destitute of water. Should enterprise and capital ever unite in building an aqueduct from the streams of Hána to this dry plain, few places on the Hawaiian Islands would produce larger crops. Further up the mountain at Haliimaìla the rain-fall is sufficient to water large fields of cane.

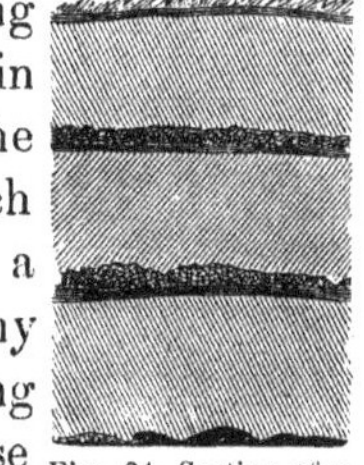
Fig. 24. Section of a cliff at Maliko.

On the western slope the soil is light, and at Ulupalakúa the dust in dry seasons is often a foot deep. Cane grows well here, although from the great elevation of the arable land, four years are sometimes required to ripen it. Below Ulupalakúa is the most recent lava-flow on Máui. Large fields of a-a, as fresh as if ejected but yesterday, line the coast for nearly a mile, while tufa-cones, some of considerable size, abound, indicating this as a line of extensive eruption; and it seems highly probable that Molokìni belongs to this series.

The low plain which connects East and West Máui is but a few feet above the sea, and several vessels have sailed upon the land not doubting the existence of a passage. On the windward shore the coral-sand is piled up in ridges nearly a hundred feet above the sea; shifting with the wind which sometimes drives columns of sand miles along the beach. As on Kauaì the large proportion of lime contained in this coral-sand, has a tendency to form a concrete; and perpendicular rods, often a foot in length and several inches in diameter, are found on the slopes of the more permanent hills near Wailùku.

KAHOOLÁWE.

Kahoolâwe is twelve miles long and about four broad, with an area of about forty square miles, and its elevation is nearly six hundred feet above the sea. The surface is comparatively level, not broken by ravines, owing to its slight elevation and its situation on the lee of East Máui. It possesses no streams nor fresh water, except in several pools of small extent. Grass and a few euphorbiaceous plants constitute the entire vegetation, and afford pasturage for a large flock of sheep. It is said that a crater exists on the summit, and that the strata have a slight dip from the centre of the island; but an examination from a vessel at a distance of a mile seemed to show a dip from the cliffs on the leeward side of the island, which are two hundred feet high, towards the centre. These high, and nearly perpendicular cliffs are highest on the south-west side, but extend nearly around the island, leaving few landing-places.

LANAI.

Lanai is eighteen miles north of west of Kahooláwe and but eight miles from the south-west shores of Máui. Its length is twenty miles, breadth eight, and its area about one hundred and fifty square miles. It is much higher at the south-eastern end where a mountain rises to a height of nearly two thousand feet, sloping gradually to the north-west, where its dry, almost barren declivities, terminate in a cliff a hundred feet high. On the leeward side the shore is a steep rock-wall three or four hundred feet high, exhibiting thick strata dipping from the centre of the island, while on the opposite side the mountain slopes nearly to the sea.

Fig. 25. Lanai from Molokaì.

Many valleys intersect the south-eastern end, and one of them is doubtless the remains of an ancient crater. There are no streams on the island, and it is difficult to account for the formation of the valleys on the supposition that they are wholly the result of wearing waters. While these valleys radiate from the highest point, which is near the south-eastern end of Lanai, the opposite end has hardly a gully, and presents an unbroken surface of gentle inclination towards the sea. The soil is red and the vegetation appears stunted.

Kahooláwe and Lanai are the only two islands that present high cliffs to the lee shore, and gentle slopes to the windward. On all the other islands the reverse is the case, and the rocky barriers are placed as it were to oppose the surf driven in by the prevailing winds.

MOLOKAÌ.

Molokaì is about nine miles distant both from Máui and Lanai. It is a long and narrow island, and closely resembles the eastern mountain-range of Oáhu. Its length is thirty-five miles, its breadth averages seven, and its area two hundred and twenty square miles. It presents from the north the appearance of a wall with ragged edge and varying height, rising nearly perpendicularly from a narrow level plain, and cut towards the western end,

Fig. 26. Molokaì from the North, distant fifteen miles.

where its height is least, by a low isthmus like that of Máui. The eastern end is far the higher, and Mauna Olokùi attains an elevation of nearly three thousand feet, while the western portion is a mere hill of about a fifth of that height.

Kaluaáha is the principal landing on the southern coast, and the mountain rises directly back of this, leaving but a narrow strip of cultivable land, except in the mountain valleys. The slopes are generally steeper than those of Eastern Oáhu, and are covered with grass and small shrubs to the top, while in the valleys and ravines trees of large size are found. From Kaunakakaì, seven miles west of Kaluaáha, the ascent is quite easy on horseback, although the surface is much broken by ravines. The soil is stony and of little depth, owing to the comparative infrequency of rain on the leeward side; but on the summit, where the trade-wind clouds settle, there is abundant moisture, and the trees and shrubs form a thick jungle in the numerous depressions. Olokùi is not flat like Mauna Lòa nor so narrow as Konahuanùi, but is exceedingly uneven on the top, and abounds in large irregular depressions between the summit peaks. Whether these are the remains of craters it is difficult to determine, they are so completely overgrown with a dense jungle. It is said that near the eastern end there is a large crater, but none of the inhabitants seem to possess any definite information regarding it.

The rock of the mountain summit much resembles hardened blue clay, and is of light specific gravity compared to the lavas of the side, and base. It is porous and splits to pieces with loud detonations when exposed to fire.[1] On the north the mountain ends in a high wall extending nearly its whole length, with a rough barren plain at its base containing many craters and lava bubbles: one of the craters is filled with sea-water and is quite deep. The appearance of this plain of Koolaupápa from the sea, is of a region flooded with lava-streams of a more recent date than any others on Molokaì, and these streams have issued from the small craters on the plain or from the very base of the precipice. There are but few places on the northern side where valleys afford the natives an opportunity of raising kalo and potatoes, and much of their food is brought from the eastern end. The low western point is white and sandy, and quite barren. Eastward of Kaluaáha the scenery is beautiful and romantic. Deep, narrow valleys open towards the coast, and often contain plantations of oranges and bread-fruit. The head of these valleys is frequently a perpendicular precipice, before which the gorge divides and smaller ravines open to the right and left. Mapuléhu is the largest, and is subject to torrents of water after severe southerly storms. The sides are very steep, and the stones at the bottom are much worn. Moanùi Valley contains several large caves in the side ridges, in one of which, now quite concealed, the ancient kings of Molokaì were buried. The eastern end of the island is a high bluff of smooth grass-land, and at the extremity the fine valley of Halàwa cuts through the strata for five hundred feet in depth, exposing a series of thin, almost horizontal layers of ochreous earth. The slope to the mountain from this place is less than ten degrees, while on the south it is nearly fifteen.

HAWAII.

The last and largest of the Hawaiian group is Hawaii itself. All the other islands exhibit only the effects of the volcanoes of ancient times, long since extinct; even sulphur-beds, solfataras, or hot-springs, which so often mark the expiring efforts of internal heat, are not found, nor does tradition notice their existence. The other members of the group are interesting, from the traces of former volcanic action, and for the effects of time on the igneous

[1] The author was obliged to remove a camp-fire which had been built on this rock, as the fragments were thrown several feet by the explosion.

products which they exhibit in such variety, but the geologist must look to Hawaii for the explanation of much that he sees on Kauaì, Oáhu, or Máui; and here better than at any other known place on the globe may the phenomena of an active volcano be studied. On Hawaii is the largest active crater in the world, and the whole island presents, in an accessible form. models and specimens of the work which has constructed the whole group. At all times the explorer may see the melted lava boiling and surging in its ragged caldron; he may approach it with an impunity which is marvellous in view of the mighty forces at work; and during the occasional eruption, may stand by the side, nay, even on the surface of a resistless torrent of melted rock often several miles in breadth, and flowing on for months in undiminished volume. Probably in no other place can the volcanic work be better examined than here, where for thousands of years — how many thousand who shall say? — fiery floods have poured forth, and still pour forth, until they have builded mountains of vast extent. All conditions of the lava-rock are seen here: basaltic and trachytic, solid and cellular, from the rich black soil, deep and fertile as on Kauaì, to the smooth hard rock of this year's flow.

To obtain the best idea of Hawaii it may be well to make the circuit of the island near the coast, to ascend the mountains, and finally examine the great volcano Kilauéa.

The form of Hawaii, as will be seen on the map, is roughly triangular, the western coast being eighty-five geographical miles in length, the south-eastern sixty-five, and the north-eastern seventy-five miles; the area is three thousand eight hundred square miles. Its whole surface pertains to the slopes of its four mountain summits,—Mauna Kéa on the north, which rises 13,950 feet above half-tide; Mauna Lòa on the south, 13,760 feet high; Mauna Hualalaì on the west, 8,500 feet high; and Mauna Koháła on the north-west, about 5000 feet: — and so distinct are these summits, that a subsidence of six thousand feet would leave three islands, two of which would be eight thousand feet high, and the third would still equal the heights of Molokaì. From the sea on the east side the two mountains, Kéa and Lòa, are alone visible, and so slight is their elevation compared with their great horizontal extent that the voyager is wholly deceived in estimating their height. Their surface seems smooth and unbroken, their slope so gentle as hardly to be perceptible, and their rounded summits seem easy of access.

Starting from the western coast at Keálakeakùa Bay — the memorable scene of Cook's punishment — the island may be described as the traveller journeys along the coast towards the south and east. Keálakeakùa presents several points of interest. At the head of the bay is a nearly perpendicular rock-wall eight hundred feet high, on either side of which recent lava-streams have descended. The face of the cliff is broken in several places by large caves, and seems to be the section of a lava flow of great size, of which the extremity has been engulfed in the sea by some violent shock. The northern point on which Cook was killed is a lava-stream, and the bare black rocks on which he landed are part of a flow which may be traced up the steep ascent, and over the precipice in a black rock-fall, where every wave and curve and twist of the once molten torrent has been transformed into an iron-like mass, as if instantaneously. It is a remarkable fact that this cliff is the only similar one on this coast, while further south they are of frequent occurrence. Although they have not been tracked to the vent from which they issued, it is probable that the Keálakeakùa streams originate from Mauna Lòa, not from the nearer Hualalaì.

From the top of the cliff, the slope towards the interior is more gentle, and is covered with a deep and productive soil. Thick forests extend more than six miles up the sides of the mountain, and although no streams are found on the surface, the soil is moist and in many places even swampy from the frequent rains. Where the forests have been cleared away, oranges grow well, and the Kóna coffee is quite equal to the Mocha or Wynaad. The soil is full of small fragments of the spongy lava called *a-a*, which keeps it loose, and at the same time retains moisture in its pores. The red clayey earth, so common on northern Oàhu, is rare here, as the vegetation has converted the red and brown iron oxides into organic salts. The climate of Kóna is one of the finest in the world; the thermometer ranges annually from 60°–80° Fahr.; the nights are always cool with the mountain breezes, while the fresh sea-breeze during the day tempers the heat of a tropical sun, and while cooling the atmosphere for man, yet permits the luxuriant growth of bread-fruit and pines side by side with Indian-corn and apples.

Descending to the coast on the southern side of the bay, the steep, winding path leads under bread-fruit and kukùi trees, while the pandanus, and caricas (*Papaya vulgaris*), covered with yams and a beautiful convolvulus, clothe the slopes. On the shore, all is changed. A bare sand-beach, and black lava-rocks take the place of the luxuriant vegetation of the cliffs above, and only the cocoa-nut trees seem to flourish. Two miles to the south is a recent lava-stream a mile broad, which has passed through a grove of these palms, and the impressions of the fallen stems are stamped in the smooth lavas with wonderful clearness, the depth of the cast being often more than a third of the diameter of the stem; and it was easy to distinguish the casts of several fan-palms among the cocoa-nuts. The trees generally fell towards the advancing stream, sometimes in the opposite direction, and always left a deep round hole to mark their former position. By measuring the depth of these holes, the depth of the stream at this place was found to be between three and four feet, which would make its approximate bulk, from its source some thirty miles distant, nearly four hundred million cubic yards of rock! The surface of this, as of all other Hawaiian streams, presents three aspects: the *pahoehoe* or velvety lava, which is folded and twisted, in the manner of a viscid fluid, and may be compared to the homely illustration of a thick coat of cream drawn towards one edge of the milk-pan; the *clinkers*, or scoriaceous lava, rough and covered with fragments; and the *a-a* or spongy lava, a form of which no description can convey an idea of the horrible roughness and hardness. The pahoehoe is the most common form, and occurs when the flow passes over rocks or dry earth at a gentle slope, although the inclination may be more than 50° without the formation of scoriæ if the ground be tolerably even and the current unimpeded. The scoriaceous lava or clinker fields are found wherever the stream passes through woods, wherever its course is impeded by obstacles or inequalities in the ground, or where the heat of the melted rock causes the explosion of caverns in the former flows over which it passes. The a-a is the most puzzling to one who has never seen the actual process of formation, but it seems to occur when the lava meets with an impediment, which gives way just as the lava is granulated, rolling the spongy mass over, and building up huge piles from which the still liquid lava drains away.

The shore where this flow reached the sea exhibits no signs of a violent encounter of fire with water, but the lava has run into the sea with scarcely a break and may be seen beneath the water for several rods where it projects above the white coral sands which cover the larger portion.

Beyond this the shore is wholly black lava-rock, which often rises in cliffs from fifty to a hundred feet high, rough and jagged, full of rents and caverns, through which the sea rushes with great violence during a storm, leaping in vast white columns upon the shore above. Islets of every form have been broken off from the cliff, and form with their black rugged sides towering above the white surf a beautifully picturesque scene, which claims the admiration of the passer-by. Vast bubbles have broken down, opening large caves, and the whole surface of the rock is very uneven and broken.

At Kaulanamàuna the road leaves the coast and ascends a rather steep hill to the wooded region. Near Manukà a region of a-a commences, extending for many miles. No soil is found here, yet the traveller passes through forests of ohia-ha (*Metrosideros polymorpha*) where the trees average twelve inches in diameter, and sometimes exceed twenty, growing in the loose a-a, which forms a layer of unknown depth. It would seem unreasonable to select a pile of the slag from a blast furnace as a spot for potato raising, yet the Hawaiian makes a hole in the a-a, which looks quite like furnace refuse, plants a banana shoot, filling the hole with stones around the tender plant, and in ten months he gathers the fruit. Or he buries a sweet-potato cutting in the stones, covering the place with fern-leaves as a mulching, and in due time digs, it may be, a bushel of large fine potatoes. Awa (*Macro-piper methysticum*) grows well, and since the removal of all prohibitions against its culture, has been extensively planted. Beyond this ancient a-a, a more recent flow of the same material covers an extent of six miles, and its ridges, although scantily covered with vegetation, present a horrible scene of roughness and desolation. Piles of a-a fifty feet high, rents in the more solid pahoehoe beneath it, make the path uneven and tedious. The road is built with care, and where worn is good, but the fresh a-a, with which the bed is repaired, is as hard as glass, and although the iron shoes of the horses grind it down, the bare feet of the natives, or even the leathern soles of the foreigner, suffer exceedingly. Next this rough region which extends over nearly sixty square miles, a tract of pahoehoe stretches from the mountain to the shore, so hard that no tracks are worn by the horses, and it would be difficult to mark the road were it not for piles of stones erected for the purpose. This extends a mile, and is succeeded by a green grassy ridge of totally different character from any yet met with on Hawaii, and much resembling the rocky uplands of New England. This ridge of Kahúku seems to proceed from the upper mountain regions, with a slope of less than eight degrees, to the sea, where it terminates in a steep bluff surrounded by cone-craters of red earth. None of these cones are very large, and their sides are steeper than those of Oáhu, resembling in outline cinder-cones rather than tufa, not being much furrowed or broken down. The grass-land extends five miles, and is then interrupted by the large valley of Waiohínu, where is the only running stream on this side of the island for a hundred miles. This brook rises from several springs not many miles up the mountain, and is clear, cold and never-failing, although small in volume. The Waiohínu Valley contains the principal settlement and the mission-station of the district of Ka-ù; it is very fertile, and many fruit-trees of temperate regions grow here with wonderful rapidity.[1] No valleys have been met before, but beyond for fifteen miles the country is broken with ridges and valleys, the former broader and rounder, and the latter smaller and shallower than those of Oáhu or Máui. The soil is seldom more than a foot deep, but is productive, and the district seems to have been long exempt from the lava-streams from the mountain above. The explanation of this seems to be, that this part of the island was in ancient time by some great convulsion broken

1 The writer has seen in the garden of Mr. Spencer a peach-tree which had attained a height of ten feet, and was wide spreading, six months from the time it sprung from the stone.

from the mountain-side precisely as the portion between the breaks of Háleakala on Máui, the lava flowing on either side of the wedge-shaped fragment. In support of this view a valley running transversely to the Ka-ù ridges may be cited, which bears evidence of disruption, and which has received and turned many streams of lava from the mountain above.

Near Punalúu, along the shore for four miles, the lava is hard pahoehoe intersected by a ridge of clinkers twenty feet high, three quarters of a mile wide, and at right angles to the shore, bearing marks of comparatively recent formation. From its relation to the smooth grassy hills above it, it would seem to have issued from the plain and not from the ridges. More than thirty lava-streams have been counted on this side of the island from Keálakeakùa to Punalúu, marked by slight differences of shade or decomposition.

Fifteen miles from Punalúu the fertile soil ceases, and pahoehoe takes its place. Trees still border the pathway, and in several places deposits of volcanic sand are found which are said to have been thrown out of Kilauéa in 1790. Here the road branches to Kilauéa, whose smoke is clearly seen. In this neighborhood in 1823, the Rev. William Ellis found what he considered a nascent volcano; deep rents and chasms, from which steam and smoke were issuing, and masses of fresh black lava, scattered on the scorched trees and bushes near by, gave evidence of recent if not continuing action, and the natives told him that the ground had fallen in and the lava was ejected in September 1822. The place is called Ponahohòa, and at present there are no signs of steam or smoke, although the lava looks fresh. It was probably in the track of a subterranean eruption from Mauna L`a or Kilauéa.

Passing again to the shore down a steep declivity two thousand feet high, near a row of cones extending from Kilauéa to the coast, the road crosses what the natives call *pahoehoe lapalapa* — lava that looks like boiling water. It was formed by passing over caves in the older rock, exploding them and raising in this way bubbles and cones, as well as small tracts of a-a. It is very easy to see, even at a distance, where the a-a occurs, as there trees spring up, while the solid pahoehoe forbids the entrance of a root except along the cracks. The former is often covered with vegetation a few months after its ejection in regions where rain falls, but the pahoehoe may remain bare and fresh-looking for centuries.

Fig. 27. Plan of the Sunken Plain at Kalapànu.

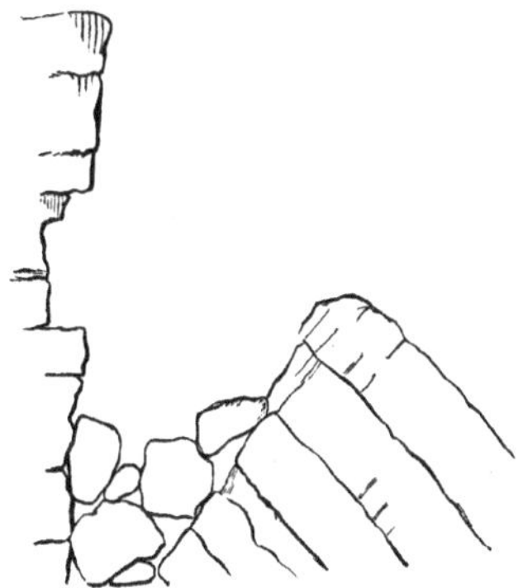
Fig. 28. Section of Cliff at Kalapànu.

At Kalapànu a very considerable subsidence has taken place. A plain a mile wide and two miles long has sunk nearly fifty feet, leaving the surface not more than two feet above high water. A precipice fifty feet high bounds this sunken area on the south, having a fosse at its base partly filled with blocks of lava.[1] A raised coral reef extends along the shore half a mile, forming an embankment against the sea, and would seem to indicate another change of level in more ancient times. The mountain meets the sea in a long, high ridge- and there is no marked break between this and the plain so far as examined. The lava, strata exposed in the wall near the shore are thin, seldom exceeding three feet, and of a compact dark basalt on the surface, while below phonolitic lava is the common kind. All the coast in the district of Púna is rocky, and destitute of landing-places, except near Kalapànu, where there is a sand-beach. Here the sea often beats with great violence on the loose volcanic sand, and the natives enjoy their remarkable pastime of riding on the surf. The sea is evidently advancing on the shore, as the stumps of cocoa-nuts are standing in the water half buried in the black sand which forms quite a steep slope above them. This place is interesting as exhibiting the effect of a heavy surf on volcanic cliffs and lava-beds where not protected by a fringing coral-reef. Prof. Dana seems to doubt that the ocean has played an important part in the formation of the bays of these islands, and adopts what is doubtless the general rule, that the sea tends to obliterate bays by the removal of projecting headlands. Here is, however, an example of the excavation of a bay by the surf.

Near Kapóho are many cones, and they seem to extend in several nearly parallel lines towards the mountains. One group much broken down contains a pool of stagnant water about twenty feet deep and of a green color. Nothing remarkable was observed in its neighborhood, although the natives believe that its waters become yellow and then black during an eruption of Kilauéa. The water is not warmer than might be expected from its exposure to the sun, and is perfectly sweet. Another cone half a mile from this is about two hundred and fifty feet high, and crowned with an ancient *heiau* or temple, and a clump of cocoa-nut trees. This cone is largely composed of lava, and is doubtless of great age, as the soil upon it is several feet deep in some places. At its base is a large cleft in the rock some three hundred feet long and sixty wide, in which is a remarkably clear pool of warm water, twenty or thirty feet deep and of a temperature of 90°. The water is perfectly fresh and sweet to the taste, but owing probably to its temperature, the dark-colored bodies of the natives bathing in it seem almost white, and a white man resembles marble. The sound of water trickling down within the cliff is distinctly audible after a rain.

Three quarters of a mile from this is a deep narrow cavern into which one may climb, guided by the natives with their bambu torches. It is nearly fifty feet deep to a pool of very warm water which is said to extend more than half a mile under ground.[2] All along the shore for twenty miles, warm springs are common near low-water level. No mineral waters however are found here, nor is there anywhere on the Hawaiian Islands even a carbonated or sulphur spring. The ground is mostly covered with a-a through the whole district of Púna, and of course it cannot retain pools of water. All the rain which is not absorbed by the porous a-a, sinks at once to the sea-level and issues in the clefts on the shore. As there is hardly any soil, it might be supposed that Púna would be a barren region, but the reverse is the case. Groves of cocoa-nut trees extend for miles, growing more thriftily than any-

[1] This formation is quite similar to that of the valley of Thingvellir in Iceland, but unlike that sunken plain, Kalapànu has but one bounding gja or rift.

[2] The writer saw several natives swim nearly that distance holding their torches clear of the steaming water, and the indistinct view thus obtained of the cavern, led to the conclusion that it was a deep crack, over which a subsequent lava flow had formed a roof.

where else on the islands, and the natives have no difficulty in raising pines, bananas, and other fruits. The a-a is often so rough that horses unshod cannot stand on it out of the beaten road, without a carpet of pandanus leaves or sea-weed.

At Nanawálie the flow of 1840 crosses the road in a branching stream a mile wide, and rough with broken caves, clinkers, and a-a. The once high sand-hills of Nanawálie, thrown up where the lava entered the sea, have lost more than half their original height, worn away by the waves which encounter little resistance in the loosely agglomerated black sand of which the hills are composed. The a-a contains a large proportion of olivine, and large granules measuring a third of an inch in diameter are found on the shore. The road is six feet wide, built over the rough lava and covered with the black sand which forms a good bed, and is precisely similar to the sand found in layers near Honolulu and elsewhere on the islands.[1] It is an interesting fact that trees which were encircled by the lava of this flow are still alive, the stream having passed within thirty feet of them on either side. This would indicate an absence of carburetted or sulphuretted hydrogen, or other gases fatal to vegetable life.

The slopes of Kilauéa are quite regular in this district, and many eruptions have flowed down this way. At least twenty may be counted in thirty miles. Tradition declares that formerly Púna was a fertile region surpassing in the productiveness of its soil any district of Hawaii, and that during the absence of the chief of the district, Pélé, the goddess of the volcano, left her abode in Kilauéa to pay him a visit. From the appearance of the streams of lava it is not impossible that many of them were synchronous, and that the larger portion of Púna was overwhelmed by the same eruption of Kilauéa. None of the lavas of Mauna Lòa have ever flowed this way.

Leaving Púna the traveller also leaves the barren pahoehoe and the rough a-a, and enters the beautiful and fertile Hìlo. On the very borders he crosses the first stream of water he has seen since leaving Waiohínu. Fields of high velvety grass, the deep, dark foliage of the ohia-ai (*Eugenia Malaccensis*), the green and wooded slopes on the left and the broad ocean on the right, delight the eye, while before him the majestic, and it may be, snow-capped domes of Kéa and Lòa, every ridge, — almost every rock, — visible through the clear air; the little white village of Hìlo half buried in mango-trees and bananas; — all complete a view seldom equalled, which wholly effaces the weary thoughts of a hundred and fifty miles over roads which wear out the horses' feet and the riders' patience.

The people of Hìlo claim that their village is the most beautiful on the Hawaiian Islands, and few will dispute them. Almost daily showers cool the air, and refresh the rapidly springing vegetation, while the sea and mountain breezes remove all dampness,[2] and prevent the lassitude so commonly attendant upon a moist tropical climate.

The harbor of Waiakéa is, after that of Honolulu, the best on the islands. The town is built on the slopes of Mauna Lòa, which rise regularly with an average slope of 8°–10° to the summit. The soil is deep and loamy, and being well watered is exceedingly productive. Directly back of the town are three cones in line from the mountain towards the sea, about five hundred feet high and containing deep craters, one of which is filled with bambus.

1 Similar black gravel is found among the tufa-cones near Victoria in Australia. See *Transactions of the Royal Society of Victoria*, vol. vii., p. 153.

2 During a rain which continued several days, the writer was able to dry readily papers used in the preparation of botanical specimens, and the latter did not mould at all when exposed to the air in the open verandah.

The Wailùku, the largest river of Hawaii, empties into the sea at Hìlo. Its sources are on the south-eastern slopes of Mauna Kéa, and it forms the boundary between Kéa and Lòa. Occupying such a position, it has received the lavas of both mountains, and exhibits in its rocky bed many a record of conflicts between fire and water. One of these "writings on the wall" discloses the interesting fact that Kéa poured forth lava after the surface was sufficiently decomposed to retain the streams which supply the Wailùku. This is shown in several places, although it may still be one and the same stream, and it must not be inferred that the stream of water which produced the effect on the melted lava was a temporary flood from the snows melted by the eruption. When the snows melt on Mauna Lòa no stream from them reaches the base of the mountain, but the water sinks at once into the porous rock where the snows lie, and to supply the bed of the Wailùku even temporarily, Mauna Kéa must have been subject to the decomposing forces of many ages, unless it be supposed that it was originally built of a more compact material, which certainly is not shown by any examination that has yet been made.[1]

The water has often flowed over heated beds of basalt, and the consequence has been the formation of columns radiating from the bottom of the stream. Often where falls occur, this columnar structure is beautifully exhibited as Gothic archways, from whose apex the torrent pours into a basin surrounded by these curved and broken, half-sunken prisms, black and prominent amid the white foam of the falls. Where the lava has poured into the water, deposits of black volcanic gravel are usually formed from the fracture of the lava, but such deposits are from their nature peculiarly liable to be removed by the action of the water, and it is only where the course of the stream has been changed that they are found *in situ.*

From the much worn condition of the lava over which the river flows it might be supposed that the rock was quite soft, but the great attrition is partly to be attributed to the harder fragments of dolerite brought down from the heights above by the freshets, which scrape and grind the bed of the stream to a great extent, and are themselves rounded when they reach the sea. Under the falls, which are sometimes a hundred feet or more in height, deep pools are worn, into which it is the delight of the Hawaiian youth to jump from the dizzy verge of the fall above.

The Anuenúe, or Rainbow Falls, are about a mile from the sea, and beneath the sheet of water which falls more than a hundred feet is seen another result of the sudden chilling of heated — not melted — basalt. The columns at the point of contact with the water are at right angles to the surface, but curve regularly below, and the surface is much harder than the lower portions, so that while quite perfect near the top where the wearing action of the water is considerable, they are completely washed away below, forming a cave of some depth beneath. It has been suggested that this and similar caves beneath water-falls were simply bubbles in the lava-stream, and that the curved prisms owe their origin to the more rapid cooling of such a cavity, even without the agency of water. But wherever columns of basalt occur around such bubbles, they are always at right angles to the surface of the bubble, that is, in a section, they form radii and not arcs, while in the three or four water-falls examined they exhibited the structure represented in the diagram.

[1] No foreigner seems to have penetrated the ravines which intersect the northeastern slope of Mauna Kéa, so far as to examine the solid core of the mountain. As the summit presents no crater walls, we have only the surface overflows of lava to judge from. The exceedingly compact axe-stone, however, is found in several places near the summit of the mountain.

In several places the Wailùku has pierced the beds of lava, and in one place passes beneath a thick rock-bridge several hundred feet wide. Often where the water flows over beds of compact dark gray basalt, masses of trachyte closely resembling syenite, have formed pot-holes, and by mutual action have been worn to pebbles. A remarkable series of these pot-holes occurs some five miles up the river. These are three circular pools in a bed of columnar basalt, each about fifty feet in diameter, and separated by walls about six feet thick. During high water the river rises sometimes thirty feet and completely hides the pools, filling the ravine in which they occur, but during the low water in the dry season, the upper bed is bare, and after a succession of cascades of various heights the river pours into the first basin (A) from a height of thirty feet, filling it with foam. From this there is no visible outlet, but fern leaves thrown into it soon come out in the second near one side, where a few bubbles alone disturb the tranquillity of the clear deep pool. From this to the third there are two sub-

Fig. 29. Section behind a Fall on the Wailùku.

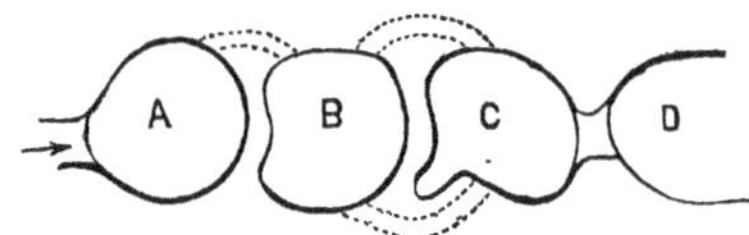

Fig. 30. Plan of Pot-holes in the Wailùku.

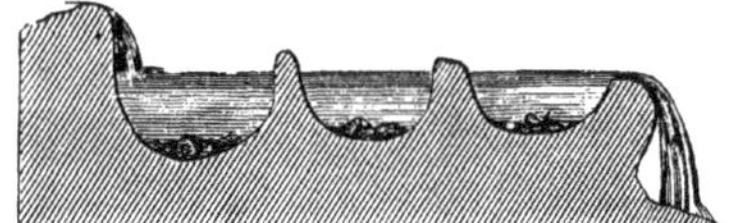

Fig. 31. Longitudinal section of Pot-holes.

terranean passages, one on each side, and the water escapes at last over a fall some forty feet high, nearly covering a perfect Gothic arch which forms the entrance to a shallow cave. The whole series is enclosed by high and almost perpendicular walls, not unlike those of Trenton Falls in New York.

In many places where recent lava-streams have flowed into the river and been broken up, the sand and chrysolite resulting have been washed to the sea, and are there thrown up in the clefts along shore, and such large deposits of the green sand are sometimes found, that it has been used in mortar to lay the furnaces and pans of a sugar-boiler — a purpose for which it seems well suited from its refractory nature. Quartz crystals have been found in masses of lava, but are mostly small, although clear and perfect.

The coast of Hawaii from Hìlo to Laupahòehoe, a distance of thirty miles, consists of a precipice from one to five hundred feet high, and extending to nearly the same depth beneath the water, so that in calm weather, large ships may approach close to the cliff. The road runs somewhat inland, and is one of the most remarkable in the world. Ravines, eighteen hundred or two thousand feet deep, and less than a mile wide, extending far up the slopes of Mauna Kéa, streams liable to sudden and tremendous freshets, must be traversed on a path of indescribable steepness, winding zigzag up and down the beautifully wooded slopes which are ornamented with cascades of every conceivable form. Few strangers, when they come to the worst precipices, dare to ride down, but such is the nature of the rough steps that a horse or mule will pass them with less difficulty than a man on foot who is unused to climbing. No less than eighty-five streams must be crossed in a distance of thirty miles.[1] The amount of water is great, and the soil is often so soft

[1] The following description of a passage over part of this road may convey a better idea of its rugged nature. It is taken from the author's journal: —

"During the night it rained hard, and we were told that the rivers would be impassable early in the morning, but that the water would rapidly subside. We waited until half-past eight, and then rode on, the Road Supervisor, Mr. R., having preceded us more than an hour. We crossed two or three small

from the frequent rains as to be almost impassible, especially near Onomèa, where the soil is deep and fertile, of a yellow loamy nature. Were it not for the ravines, and the impossibility of transportation, many acres of sugar-cane might be cultivated. For twenty miles to Laupahòehoe there is no good landing-place, and during a storm the whole coast is inaccessible except to skilful natives in light canoes.

The strata, as exhibited in the ravines which have been excavated by water, are deep and similar to those described on Kauaì, and bear tokens of as great age. Denudation has been very extensive, and the water-worn valleys extend far up the mountain. The rock is generally a dark gray basalt, sometimes a light colored clink-stone, but scoriæ and a-a are very rare, owing to their more rapid conversion to soil where water is abundant, and not a single deposit was seen during three journeys through this district. Forests cover all the windward side of Mauna Kéa, and extend nearly around it in broken bands.

In Hamakúa the road branches, one continuing along the shore to the beautiful valleys of Waipìo and Waimànu, both of which belong to Mauna Kohála, and exhibit signs of great age; the other turns up the mountain side and soon enters the forest, culminating nearly five thousand feet above the sea on the north-west slopes of Mauna Kéa, and descends into the grassy plains of Waiméa. No streams are met for twenty miles, and the soil is much more scanty than where the rains fall on the other side. The view of Mauna Kéa from the

streams, and then came to one of three large rivers we had been warned against. As we descended the Pali, which makes Gen. Putnam's famous ride down the steps, child's play, we heard the rushing waters several hundred feet below us, and occasionally caught a glimpse of the white foam through the branches. When we at last came to the bank, we found the ford wide and cleared of stones, which above and below this place almost blocked the stream. The water only came half way up our stirrups, and we crossed in safety, rejoiced to have one of the dreadful Jordans behind us. When some two miles up and down almost perpendicular walls brought us to the second of the dangerous streams, our courage was up, and although the river was a hundred feet wide, and much resembling Niagara River in the rapids, I spurred my mule and plunged in. In an instant my poor beast was off his feet, and a native on the other bank screamed to me to go back, for I should be 'make' (dead) if I tried to cross. I of course obeyed, although with some difficulty, and found Mr. R. patiently waiting in the bushes a short distance up the stream where the water was deeper, but free from rocks. He told us that it would be useless to attempt to ford without natives and ropes, and as he had sent for both, we sat down to wait. In the course of an hour the river had fallen a foot, and two young Englishmen, who had passed the night at a neighboring plantation came up, and we were also joined by the United States Minister Resident who was making the tour of Hawaii. Our natives arrived, and the crossing commenced. First my mule was attached to the middle of a long rope, and a native swam across with one end, we retaining the other to prevent the animal from being carried down stream. Thus with great difficulty all the horses and mules were got safely across, and in the mean time a native had been swimming over with all our baggage. He swam with one arm out of water grasping his load, and got every thing over dry, even our heavy Mexican saddles.

"When the animals were all over, a rope was made fast on either bank, and the company stripped and swam, holding to the rope. As the current was very rapid, the swimmers often were whirled around the rope like a water-wheel, and as I did not like the operation, I had been making friends with an old but powerful Kanaka, who seemed to take a fancy to me, and who wished to carry me over on his back, a proposition I emphatically declined, but I made him understand that I would cross on the rocks below if he would go before to show me where to put my feet, as most of the rocks were covered two feet deep with foaming, rushing water. This he thought well, and, armed with a stout guava-stick, I stepped in. Down came the torrents from above, covering the ford more than twelve feet deep, and after rushing by me, almost shaking the great rocks some more extensive freshets had scattered across the channel, went thundering over a fall below, where it was lost in the dense foliage. So strong was the current that had I lost my balance there would have been but little chance for me. The rocks being usually far above water were not slippery, and when I once got a foothold, I was quite firm. I crossed safely, and as I had not taken off my clothes, was in my saddle before the rest of the party were dressed. They stood watching us as we jumped from rock to rock, with such interest, they said, that they forgot to dress!

"Another river was crossed in precisely the same manner, and we rode through many streams that came over our saddles. Mr. R. assures me that from Hìlo to Laupahòehoe, a distance of thirty miles, there are eighty-five water-courses. I believe this to be literally true, and when I add that many ravines occur without streams, some idea of the broken nature of the country may be obtained. . . . The beauty of the scenery is wholly indescribable, and I believe nowhere in the world are collected in so small a territory, so many cascades of every form, of pure, clear, cool, mountain water."

I have since travelled over this road twice, and found no difficulty, owing to the dryness of the season.

road shows several of its terminal cones to great advantage, and they much resemble the lateral cones of Hualalaì.

The district of Waiméa is generally destitute of water, and the vegetation depends wholly on the dews and rain. Nevertheless as a grazing land, Waiméa is perhaps unequalled on the islands, although of late years the introduction of several foreign plants, of which the indigo and verbena are the most troublesome, has much diminished the grass. From its considerable elevation, the climate is cool and salubrious, and is much recommended as a sanitarium. Frosts sometimes occur, and the fruits and vegetables of temperate climes thrive well. Common American potatoes are raised here in large quantities, and in the early days of Californian immigration were exported to the coast.

Many lateral cones have been thrown up on the slopes of Mauna Kéa near Waiméa; and Mauna Kohála has also formed cones of a red ochreous earth covered with grass, and at first resembling tufa-cones, but they seem to be simply decomposed lava or scoriæ, as they do not exhibit the stratification of tufa-cones: those of Kéa are mostly scoriaceous and much furrowed, while these are not at all furrowed, owing to an early growth of grass. Some of them have shallow craters at the top, while others have no depression, but the soil is muddy or soft on the summit. Many large caves are found in the lava-streams which have flowed this way, and some of them, as on the other islands, have been used as sepulchres.[1]

The road from Waiméa to Kohála, the north-west district of Hawaii, crosses the western spur of Mauna Kohála at an elevation of about eighteen hundred feet, and traverses a region of cones, some of them quite perfect and five hundred feet high, while others are broken down. Lava streams have issued from some and flowed down to the coast, a distance of two or three miles. These cones much resemble the extinct craters of Auvergne in France.[2] Kohála is a fertile region, owing to the lengthened period during which its mountain has been in repose. The ridges are broader and smoother, covered with grass or cane-fields, and not rocky. The shore also becomes lower, and affords several good landing-places. Small streams are frequent, although the land cannot be considered well watered through all the district. Mauna Kohála has seldom been ascended, as its summit, although not high, is swampy like Waíaleale on Kauaì, and full of dangerous bog-holes. Its name is said to have been taken from *Kohala* (a whale), and it is not a single dome like the other mountains of Hawaii, but an elongated ridge like Konahuanùi on Oáhu. It is well wooded, and several trees grow there that are not found elsewhere on the islands, and some that grow only on Kauaì. It is quite remarkable that Waíaleale, Kaàla, and Kohála should be so swampy on their summits, while at their base, and on their slopes, the soil is often dry and barren. The three mountains are alike in other respects, in the absence of a single terminal crater, and terminal cones, and in the presence of crateriform marshes, and circular pools. They are probably all of the same age, as they have suffered an equal denudation, allowing for the different exposure to the trade-winds, and consequently to rain.

From Waiméa to Kawaihàe the ground is rocky, and dry. Pahoehoe, and broken beds of lava destitute of vegetation, cover many square miles; and the same is true of most of the

1 The walls of these sepulchral caves are quite porous, and the air within is very dry, converting the bodies into dry mummies without further decomposition. A party which recently visited one of these caves found a body perfectly preserved, which had been dropped near the entrance, the bearers having probably been frightened away, as the two poles between which the body was slung were still attached.

2 See Scrope's *Extinct Volcanos of Central France*.

coast from Kawaihàe to Kailùa, a distance of fifteen miles, except where a few small streams make their way to the surface near the shore and furnish water for kalo-ponds. The natives live principally on fish, which are very abundant and good along the coast. The lava-flow of 1859 has flowed out some distance beneath the sea on the coral-reef, and the same is true of the flow of 1801 from Hualalaì which filled up a large fish-pond and extended the coast some distance. Beyond Kailùa the shore-plain is very narrow, and the sides of Hualalaì rise steeply for several hundred feet to a plain of rich soil forming a belt a mile wide in some places. Between Kailùa and Kaáwalòa the land is fertile and much cultivated, while high up the mountain are extensive forests of koa and ohia.

Having thus hastily sketched the general features of Hawaii along the shores, the mountains next claim attention, and in describing these the author's notes of ascents of Hualalaì and Lòa in 1864 will be chiefly used, while the accounts of several who have ascended Kéa in previous years, must be depended on for that mountain.

Fig. 32. Outline of Hualalaì from the plain on the south-east.

Hualalaì. — On Thursday afternoon, July 28, 1864, Mr. Horace Mann and myself, with a guide, left Kaáwalòa. Our way led at first through open pastures, then through tracts of tall ferns, and finally we came to the forest, where the soil was black and muddy, and the bushes so close as to almost prevent our passage in some places. Gigantic raspberries, with stems two inches in diameter at the base and twenty feet long, hung across our path and often scratched both ourselves and our horses in spite of our precautions. It rained hard, so that we were quite wet, and the clouds prevented our seeing much on either side. After some six miles of forest, we came upon a bed of a-a, fresh-looking and rough, and the trees were thinner and smaller. We were now on a dismal, foggy plain of pahoehoe and gravelly sand, where we could see but little out of our path. This was the elevated plain between the three mountains, and being at least four thousand feet above the sea the atmosphere was cold as well as damp.

A leguminous-tree (*Sophora chrysophylla*) called by the natives Mamáne, was common; the sandal-wood was seen here and there, but of small size, and the ohélo (*Vaccinium penduliflorum*) covered the ground thickly, and was loaded with its large red and purple berries. Twisted lava streams, and masses of scoriæ crossed our path, and so complicated were they that it was almost impossible to trace their course. About sunset we came to the place our guide had selected for our camp, and we soon had a fire at which we dried ourselves and roasted some sweet potatoes, and as the rain had ceased, slept comfortably under some bushes. Our water came from a curious pool in the last place one would think of looking for water, in the midst of a horribly rough bed of scoriæ, porous as pumice, and broken into irregular masses of all sizes. The basin holds about twelve gallons of cold, pure water, and has no evident inlet or outlet, yet is never exhausted; we nearly emptied it, and the next morning it was full again. It was found accidentally, and three columns of stone are piled up to mark the place, which would be most difficult to find without these signals.

At half-past five in the morning we started for the summit, toward which a good path led for some distance, and we galloped over the hard gravel beds, dodging in a zigzag course the clumps of bushes in our way. The morning was clear, and the birds which are scarce near the shore, were abundant, and sang merrily. The path ended after three miles, and we had to slowly pick our way over difficult and even dangerous lava-fields. Our horses occasionally broke through, causing some trepidation to the riders, but no accidents occurred; and after passing nearly round the summit, crossing the flow of 1801, and counting ten flows from the top, and many others almost indistinguishable, we reached the base of the highest plateau at eight o'clock, and left our horses in a little valley where strawberries were abundant, and also American potatoes, planted by some native.

A climb up a steep slope some three hundred feet high, and we were in the midst of a series of large pit craters extending over the whole summit. These craters were very much alike, from three to five hundred feet deep, and from seven hundred to a thousand feet in diameter. The walls were of the solid graystone, seldom capped by cellular basalt in beds, (although the lava was piled in scoriæ near by), and were nearly perpendicular. Vegetation extended to the bottom, and the beautiful Silver-sword (*Argyroxiphium Sandvicense*) was growing in the clefts far down the sides. The bottom was usually flat and gravelly, but in some cases covered with smooth black lava, and in others rough and broken. Fragments of the walls were often seen at their base, and in one crater they were half melted into the lava which covered the bottom, proving that the clinkstone of these mountain summits is fusible by the melted black basalt.

No signs of steam or sulphurous vapors were visible, but on the edge of one of the deepest craters, on the wall which separated it from another less than two hundred feet distant, was a mound of scoriæ some fifty feet high, composed of drops and slightly agglutinated fragments of lava of all sizes and colors, black, red, orange, blue, golden, apparently ejected in a viscid state, and in the centre of this a blow-hole about twenty-five feet in diameter, and, as nearly as we could judge by throwing stones, eighteen hundred feet deep to a ledge, to one side of which we could see a deeper black hole. I was obliged to lie flat on the edge to examine it, the scoriæ were so loose, and the whole cone jarred as we climbed over it. The inside of the blow-hole was of a brown color, smooth as if turned, and grooved horizontally. No vertical striæ could be distinguished, but as these horizontal grooves seem to correspond to the strata of the adjoining crater-walls, I suppose that the projecting ridges mark the more solid substance of these strata, which would be in their centre, while the scoriæ which separate the beds to some extent, would permit the deeper action of the vapors which have formed the hole. Mr. Mann suggests that the column of ascending vapors had a rotatory motion around a vertical axis, but in that case the grooves would be spiral and not circular, and the fragments of lava ejected would have struck the surface obliquely, unless thrown to such a height as to lose the original motion. The wearing force must have been chemical rather than mechanical, as the wall of the crater adjoining, which is not more than twenty-five or thirty feet thick, would have given way to any violent explosion. A similar blow-hole was described by Ellis lower down the mountain. He ascended Hualalaì in 1823, and found on the side of the mountain a large extinguished crater, about a mile in circumference and apparently four hundred feet deep. The sides were regularly sloped, and at the bottom was a small mound with an aperture in its top. By the side of this large crater, divided from it by a narrow ridge of volcanic rock, was another, fifty-six feet in circumference, from which volumes of sulphurous smoke and vapor continually ascended. No bottom could be seen, and on throwing stones into it they were heard to strike against its sides for eight seconds, but not to reach its bottom. There were two other apertures very near this, nine feet in diameter, and apparently two hundred feet deep.[1]

This description corresponds so nearly with the blow-hole we saw on the summit that it cannot be doubted that vapors formed, or at least enlarged, both.

From the vegetation of the summit I should not consider Hualalaì more than 8500 feet high, although some have placed it as high as 10,000.[2] It is covered with lateral cones, and its summit is flat, with many large pit craters. More than one hundred and fifty lateral cones have been counted, and it will be seen from the outline of the mountain (Fig. 32) that they vary much in shape and size.

Fig. 33. The Summit of Hualalaì seen from Mauna Lòa (9000 feet).

In the afternoon we camped about a mile from our last night's resting-place, between two cones. Our guide shot two of the native geese (*Bernicla Sandvicencis*), which were fine eating. The number of these geese has been much underrated. Although they are found only on the highlands of Hawaii and Máui, their number admits of the annual slaughter of several hundred without sensible diminution. They build their nests in the grass, and lay two or three eggs, white, and about the size of a common goose's egg. They are web-footed, but are never seen in the water, indeed there is no water on the uplands, and their food is principally berries and a common species of *Hieracium*. The strawberries (*Fragraria Chiliensis*) were nearly out of season. Trees were comparatively small. The mamáne, a *Dodonæa*, sandal-wood, and an arborescent geranium, were the most common. Of the herbs a *Lythrum*, much resembling our native species, and many compositæ with brilliant yellow blossoms (*Raillardia, Artemisia, etc.*), were seen all through the plain.

I made me a bed of bracken (*Pteris aquilina*) as I might at home on a similar occasion, and with my feet towards a fire of great mamáne logs, went to sleep. The night was clear and cold, — so cold that I awoke and moved nearer the fire. It was strangely silent; the stars were shining brightly, and directly in front of me was the grand Mauna Lòa. At half-past three the moon rose over the slopes of Mauna Kéa, and I fell asleep again. In the morning at sunrise the thermometer marked 46° Fahr. As the sun rose, the lava-flow of 1859 was visible through its whole length from the summit of Mauna Lòa to the sea at Kawaihàe, shining like a river of silver, owing to its glossy black surface. How beautiful a sight it must have presented when it was a river of fire!

All the plain between the mountains, which covers many square miles, is intersected by lava-streams from all three summits, and is wholly rocky and uneven, with caves and beds of

1 Ellis, *Tour of Hawaii*, p. 55.

2 Prof. Dana estimates it at 10,000 feet.

a-a. The vegetation is scanty, but enough to support large flocks of wild goats. A road was attempted some years ago, by government, from Kailùa on the western coast to Hìlo across this plain, but only fifteen miles were ever built, and the natives dislike the cold of the mountain region too much to travel this way often. Caves are the only sources of water here, the surface being too porous to retain pools or streams; but in the caves the water drips from the roof, and is collected in calabashes.

The only recorded eruption of Hualalaì took place in 1800, and was seen by Turnbull.

Ellis gives the following account, taken from the lips of an Englishman and of natives, of this eruption[1]: —

"Stone walls, trees, and houses all gave way before it; even large masses of rocks of hard ancient lava, when surrounded by the fiery stream, soon split into small fragments, and, falling into the burning mass, appeared to melt again, as borne by it down the mountain's side. Offerings were presented, and many hogs thrown alive into the stream to appease the anger of the gods, by whom they supposed it was directed, and to stay its devastating course. All seemed unavailing, until one day the king, Kaméhaméha, went attended by a large retinue of chiefs and priests, and, as the most valuable offering he could make, cut off part of his own hair, which was always considered sacred, and threw it into the torrent. A day or two after, the lava ceased to flow. The gods, it was thought, were satisfied."

To this eruption is referred the sad story, often told to travellers by the natives, of the death of a mother and her infant. In 1800, as now, the base of Hualalaì had many small fishermen's hamlets along its shore. At night, while all were sleeping, the eruption began. The stream of lava came thundering down upon the people on the shore, and while nearly all succeeded in escaping, in one hut only the husband was awakened, and in his terror he fled leaving his wife and child. Before she was aroused by the shrieks of her friends, the lava had encircled the hut and escape was no longer possible. The lava set fire to the house, and the woman sprang into a pandanus-tree near by. But her refuge was of short avail, and the lava-stream, which was flowing into the sea, consumed, as it passed, the two human sacrifices to Pélé.

This latest effort of Hualalaì, besides destroying several small villages, and filling up fish-ponds, ended by changing the coast line for twenty miles from a bay to a headland several miles beyond the old coast. Nevertheless it was not an important eruption, nor equal to the dying effort with which Háleakala rent its vast crater, or Mauna Kéa piled up the monuments on its craterless head.

The remarkable rapidity with which this stream descended indicates great fluidity. It appears to have flowed fifteen miles in two or three hours. Its source was a little below the summit and it issued in two streams, one to the north-west and the other to the north-east. Twenty-three years after this Ellis found a warm spring at Kailùa where Glauber's Salts were formed by the action of sulphurous vapors on sea-water, and warm springs were also found at Kawaihàe at tide level. These are now cooled, and there are no visible signs of volcanic activity anywhere on the mountain. The streams which in former ages flowed at intervals down its sides do not appear to be of so great a volume as those from Mauna Lòa, and this is probably owing to the great number of vents. Their physical structure, however, is identical with that of those from the other craters.

[1] Ellis, *loc. cit.* p. 44.

Mauna Kéa. — In the early part of January 1841, Dr. Charles Pickering made the ascent of Mauna Kéa, and the following facts are taken mainly from his account.[1] On the 10th they left Hìlo, and on the 12th reached the limit of the forest, about six thousand feet above the sea. They passed a small but distinct lava-stream, and found the ground frozen, and the pools of water covered with thin ice. The surface was undulating, broken by ravines, and there were many conical hills varying in height from two to eight hundred feet. On the 14th, they came to a desolate gravelly plain many miles in extent, and an Arctic flora at once succeeded the vegetation of temperate climes. No lava-streams or clinkers were seen, and in the distance rose six peaks whose bases were rough with blocks of lava, while towards their tops scoriæ of a red color with gravel prevailed.

The highest peak is on the south, and near this Rev. Mr. Goodrich describes a lake twenty-five rods in diameter. The terminal peaks are truncated cones with craters within, and the angle of their outer slope is about 30°. The crater of Mokuawéowéo on Mauna Lòa was distinctly visible, being nearly on a level with the base of the summit cones. Caves in the lava were common, and in one of these a gentleman from Honolulu found a few years since a very curious idol, probably left there many years before by some of the natives who ascended the mountain to cut stone adzes and poi pounders, as a large pile of stone-chips was found near by. The stone used for these instruments is a solid phonolite containing much feldspar, and takes a good polish. The kinds most prized are found here and on Mauna Lòa, and, judging from the large piles of refuse, the manufacture from these quarries has been extensive.

Vegetation is more various than on Mauna Lòa and creeps up to the height of twelve thousand feet, while on the latter it extends to ten thousand on the windward and only seven thousand feet on the leeward. In the absence of tracts of pahoehoe and ridges of a-a the slope is comparatively smooth and the ascent to the terminal cones is easily made on horseback from the western side at Waiméa; the usual course being to ride up into the forest in the afternoon, spend the night there, and the next day visit the summit and return to this camp or even to Waiméa. In crossing the mountain to Hìlo through the valley of the Wailùku, it is necessary to proceed on foot, owing to the thickness of the jungle in the latter place. The northern ridges of Mauna Kéa have never been explored; and, as may be inferred from the deep valleys and abundant streams near the coast, are much more difficult of access than any other portion of Hawaii; but doubtless a rich harvest awaits the fortunate botanist who shall penetrate into this region.[2]

Mauna Lòa. — On Tuesday, August 2d, we left the hospitable house of Rev. J. D. Paris, the missionary at Kaáwalòa. The native magistrate, Kupaké, had heard of our intended journey and sent us two large dried fish, a most acceptable present, and a large water-bottle. We secured as a guide an old goat-hunter, Kaákakawaì, and we had also three native bearers and a pack-mule. For the first six or eight miles our road was the same as when we ascended Hualalaì, and, as then, we got wet through in passing the forest, this time by a thunder-storm of short duration. We camped at night on the mountain-plain near Judd's road, and in the morning sent back our horses, and prepared our raw-hide sandals for climbing over the rough lava, as there is no path for horses up the *smooth* dome of

[1] *Narrative of the United States Exploring Expedition*, vol. iv., p. 199.

[2] Mr. Mann and myself found more than thirty new species of plants in a region already partly explored.

Mauna Lòa. We went nearly east until we struck the flow of 1859, and then followed that up more than eight miles. The surface was black and shining and quite brittle, and as we walked over it, it sounded like a hard frozen crust of snow. The outer surface to the depth of half an inch, was very porous and readily separated from the harder interior. In many places the lava had flowed up hill, dammed up behind by its rapidly hardening crust; and it sometimes attained an elevation of twenty-five or thirty feet without breaking from its pipe. Bubbles of great size, some still perfect, others broken in, were very common, and in some of the caves thus formed, ferns were growing in the moist atmosphere. On the surface cracks also we found a *Polypodium*, but lichens were scarce. Here and there we came to a deep round hole, and by its side lay the bleaching tree that had been burned off. The clumps of shrubs often approached within twenty feet of the flow, but in other places they had been killed to a distance of fifty feet, probably by gases, as they were not at all charred.

Immense beds of a-a with almost perpendicular sides, crossed our way, sometimes at the edge, sometimes directly across the flow, but always more or less level on top. The roughness of this a-a was greater than any we had met before; and we needed the raw-hide sandals we had prepared for such places, as well as thick buckskin gloves to protect our hands from the sharp needle-like points. Often the deep canal which the fiery river had burned for itself, was visible through large breaks in the covering crust, and on approaching a hole of this nature, I found myself on the verge of a gulf a hundred feet deep, of unknown length, and, as nearly as I could see, two hundred feet wide. The bottom was rough and cracked, and covered with the fragments from the roof and sides, fallen since the lava had ceased to flow. The crust on which I stood was but a few inches thick, and although I had tested it with my staff before, I thought it safest to lie down and crawl until I had got several rods from the hole, and I did not venture near another.

The roughness of this flow at last turned us aside to the right on to the old pahoehoe, which is covered thinly with grass and small bushes along the numerous cracks. Mauna Lòa remained clear all day, and the summit did not seem very far off. Indeed, at seven o'clock in the evening when we decided to camp for the night, had it not been that we were still within the limit of vegetation, I should have been inclined to push on and reach the summit that night. The whole surface of the mountain is undulating, and as we reached what seemed to be the top, we found a shallow valley and another hill beyond, and so it was all the way. We got the most sheltered place we could find, as we had no tent, and there were not enough bushes to make a hut; Kaákakawaì shot a goat, and we ate our supper. The wind was quite cold, and we were not warm enough to sleep well, and while we were awake we saw a most novel sight,—what I may call an inverted sunset. The clouds had risen rapidly until they quite covered the plain and dashed their misty van against the base of the three giants, quite cutting them off from the rest of the world except Háleakala which towered above the mist. The surface of the clouds was rough and in constant motion, and as the sun sank into it, it seemed to kindle into flames of the most brilliant colors. All the golden canopy we usually see above the sun, was below it here, and above, all was clear. The clouds swept up nearly eight thousand feet, but no higher, and we were soon asleep beyond their limits.

The morning was clear and not very cold, and the view of Hualalaì and Kéa was very grand. At seven o'clock we had eaten our morning meal, put out our fire, and started on our way. The craters of 1859 were just on our left as we went up, and for two miles the crevices were filled with the *limu* or Hawaiian pumice, which is green and very light, and with Pélé's hair. This fine volcanic glass was blown more than sixty miles during this eruption. At three o'clock two of our Kanakas gave out, and we were obliged to leave them, assuming their burdens ourselves. The others were sick, and bound their heads up with leaves, complaining that their heads and stomachs were affected, imputing it all to the wind, which, however, was very light. Mr. Mann and myself felt no inconvenience from the altitude during the journey.

At night we were about half a mile from the terminal crater, and we found a long narrow cave, once the bed of a small lava-stream, and still horrid with projecting points. It was five feet wide, two feet high, and of considerable length. We slept in Indian file, or rather tried to sleep; our bed was a magnified rasp, and although we broke off as many of the teeth as we could, more than enough remained. We needed all our blankets to protect us from the severe cold which froze water solid in the cave at our feet, but we had to push a fold beneath every time we turned. I got up before sunrise, and the air seemed intensely cold; I ran to a little hill and saw the sun come up through the clouds, and then crawled into the cave again and breakfasted. We then covered ourselves well with blankets, and walked up to the crater. Mokuawéowéo is the most perfectly formed crater on the Islands, although not the largest. The walls almost a thousand feet high, are nearly perpendicular and unbroken. When the United States Exploring Expedition ascended Mauna Lòa in 1841, the bottom was rough, and contained eight or ten cones, some of considerable height; now there were only two cones, about two hundred feet high each, near the eastern wall; the whole bottom had been overflowed with fresh black lava, and as examined with a powerful glass was no rougher than an ordinary lava-stream. We were on the highest wall, 13,790 feet above the sea, as determined by the Exploring Expedition, and on the opposite side from the Wilkes Encampment. On a small pile of stones was a sandal with the names of Paris, Alexander, Haskell, 1859. The sandal looked new and fresh as if just cut from the hide. I was told that a cow once strayed up here in search of water, and died, and her body was found dried and retaining its shape completely.

The hard compact gray stone of the summit and walls is much cracked, and exhibits deep strata as elsewhere. Scattered along the edges, and in various places over the great summit plain were large irregular masses of a solid reddish clink stone much used for stone axes, etc. Several immense cracks parallel with the crater walls extended some distance. These sometimes contained ice; and on breaking the surface, which was some two inches thick, we found a large supply of fine water in the ice, with which we replenished our water-bottles. No snow was visible, and it is a mistake to suppose these summits within the limits of perpetual snow, as is sometimes stated. Seldom in the summer is any snow found here except in the caves where it is preserved as in ice-houses. Snow frequently falls on both Mauna Lòa and Mauna Kéa, but, except in winter, it disappears as soon as the sun rises.

At first we did not see any signs of volcanic activity, but at last discovered steam issuing from the northern bank. Mr. Mann advised a descent into the crater, and we attempted it, but after climbing down more than half way gave it up. Mokuawéowéo was partly surveyed by the Exploring Expedition, and the plan given represents its present condition correctly. It is circular, 8000 feet in diameter, and on the northern and south-eastern ends are two semicircular depressions which increase its diameter to 13,000 feet in a north-by-west and south-by-east direction. On the west side the walls were, in 1841, seven hundred and eighty-four feet high, and on the east four hundred and seventy. The bottom of the pit as examined at that time consisted of solid lava, through which there were many fissures and fumaroles emitting steam and sulphurous vapors in large volumes. One of the fissures near the western bank had ejected lava at no very distant period.[1]

Adjoining Mokuawéowéo are two small pit craters on the major axis of the ellipse, and into the southern one a stream of lava has flowed from the main crater. The summit plain is much fissured, and several small cones both north and south, but on the same general line, mark eruptive agencies. The lava of the walls is largely phonolitic.

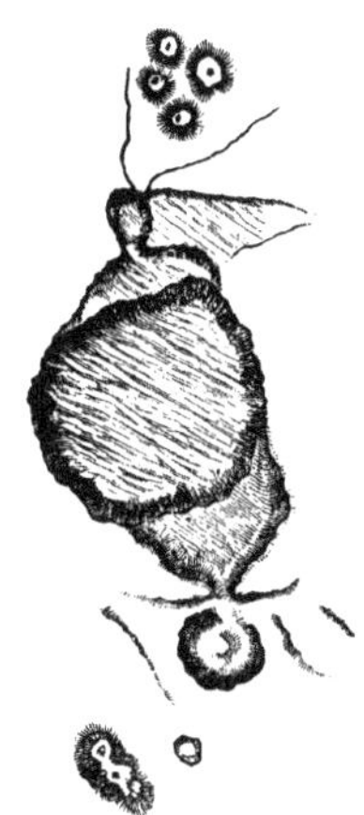

Fig. 34. Plan of Mokuawéowéo.

At nine o'clock we commenced the descent, as our time was limited, and about two in the afternoon a thick misty rain came on, and our guide wished to stop as he could not see the way; we had, however, three compasses, and proceeded without difficulty, although drenched, to the plain, where we found a cave and contrived to light a fire. At nine o'clock the rain ceased, the stars came out brightly, and as the cave still dripped, we rolled ourselves up in our blankets wet through as we were, and with our feet to the fire slept well all night. In the morning we wrung out our clothes, which dried in the course of two hours as we were walking rapidly in the sun, and about noon rested on the edge of the forest, several miles west of where we had come up, at a spring which, as they always are on this island, was in a very improbable place,—the most elevated part of an open plain. Its position was marked by a pile of stones; no stream ran from it, and it was carefully covered to keep the wild hogs out, whose marks we saw near by among the strawberries and on the trees. Striking into the woods we walked down at a rapid rate, although the muddiness of the path, and the many trees that had fallen across the way, made it very laborious. Added to this, it began to rain as we came into the region of ferns, and we were again wet through.

Vegetation on the leeward side of Mauna Lòa only extends to the height of six to seven thousand feet, but on the windward slopes to nearly ten thousand. By various calculations, Prof. Dana gives the average slope of the mountain at 6° 30′, while from Kilauéa to the sea it is but 1° 28′, or one hundred and thirty-five feet to the mile. A lava stream, however, in flowing down the side meets inclinations from 1° to 25°, so uneven is the ground.[2] Eruptions have occurred all over the summit, and although many of these lateral ejections have been of enormous volume, they still compose but a small portion of the solid mass of the mountain. They, however, play a very important part in determining the position of future valleys, should volcanic action ever cease, as in almost all cases they have formed deep chasms in the mountain sides.

History of Mauna Lòa.—The earliest eruption recorded took place in 1832, and it is rather remarkable that no traditions of the natives point definitely to any previous one. On the 20th of June, Mauna Lòa commenced to eject lava from the summit on several sides, and continued three or four weeks, with such brilliancy as to be visible at **1832.**

[1] *Narrative of United States Exploring Expedition*, vol. iv., p. 152.

[2] The slope of Teneriffe is 12° 30′; Ætna, 8°, according to Élie de Beaumont; 10° 15′ according to Von Buch.

Lahaìna, more than a hundred miles distant.[1] Through the summer earthquakes were frequent on Hawaii, although not severe, and finally Kilauéa burst into activity as described in the account of that volcano.

After an interval of eleven years, Mokuawéowéo again broke out. In 1837, Douglass made the first ascent of Mauna Lòa by a foreigner, and describes the crater as being in intense activity, but unfortunately his statements were so evidently false in other respects, that no reliance can be placed on his description. If the crater had been active, doubtless smoke, or the glare reflected on the sky, would have indicated the fact to the residents at the base of the mountain.

1843. The accounts of the eruption of 1843 are as follows, the first by Dr. Andrews in a letter dated February 6th, 1843[2]: —

"Smoke was first seen near the summit of the mountain, on Monday, January 9th. During the succeeding night a brilliant light was emitted from the same spot. The great distance of the mountain from Hìlo — about forty miles — prevented our seeing any thing more than the intense glare sent forth by the boiling mass, which apparently was pouring forth and rolling down the side. . . . During the day vast volumes of smoke were constantly pouring forth, concealing everything beneath. At times the smoke rose in a nearly perpendicular column, not less, as I judged, than one or two thousand feet high. Before the close of the week the light disappeared from the upper part of the mountain, and broke out anew near its base in the valley between it and Mauna Kéa."

The Rev. T. Coan writes under date of February 20th, 1843.[3] After describing the brilliancy of the light he says: "For about four weeks this scene continued without much abatement. At the present time, after six weeks, the action of the fire is greatly diminished, though it is still somewhat vehement at one or two points along the line of eruption. The flow of the lava has probably extended twenty miles." Soon after this he was able to visit the scene of eruption, and ascend the mountain, and writes in a letter dated April 5th: "The eruption has flowed from the summit of Mauna Lòa to the base of Mauna Kéa, where it separates into two broad streams, one flowing towards Waiméa, and the other towards Hìlo. Another great stream has flowed along the base of Mauna Lòa towards Mauna Hualalaì in Kóna. These streams are still flowing, and they have reached a distance of from twenty-five to thirty miles from the crater on the top of the mountain. The quantity of lava is immense, it being many miles wide. There are two great active craters in close contiguity near the summit. Lava does not flow from these craters now; it is conveyed down the side of the mountain in a subterranean duct from fifty to a hundred feet below the surface, at the rate of from fifteen to twenty miles an hour." The flow soon after ceased. Mr. Coan threw stones into the stream as it appeared through the openings in the crust, and they did not sink but were instantly carried along out of sight. Mounds, ridges, and cones were thrown up along the lava-stream, and from the latter, steam, gases, and hot stones were ejected.[4] The angle of descent of the whole distance is 6°, but in many places the stream was continuous at an inclination of 25°. Kilauéa was visited by Mr. Abner Wilcox during this eruption, but it showed no signs of sympathy with the summit crater.

1851. In 1851, a slight eruption took place from the summit of Mauna Lòa, which is thus described by Mr. Coan[5]: —

[1] *Silliman's Journal*, [N. S.] vol. xxv., p. 199.

[2] *Missionary Herald*, vol. xxxix., p. 381.

[3] *Ibid.*, p. 463.

[4] *Missionary Herald*, vol. xl., p. 44.

[5] From a letter to the Rev. C. S. Lyman, by Rev. T. Coan, dated Hilo, Hawaii, Oct. 1, 1851. *Silliman's Journal*, [N. S.]

"On the 8th of August last a new eruption was seen on the western slope of Mauna Lòa, a few miles from its summit. All we could see at Hìlo was a white pillar of smoke by day and a brilliant fiery pillar by night. Owing to a canopy of clouds which much of the time shrouded the mountain, we obtained only occasional views of the eruption. At Ka-ù the view was less obstructed. The rising columns of light and smoke, as seen from some points in that district, were said to be gorgeous and glorious. A gentleman then surveying in Keàwa, of notorious and impressive memory, tells me that the light at that place was sufficient to enable him to read in the night. He also asserted that he heard several distinct detonations from the mountain, during the eruption, like the explosion of gases and the rending of rocks. This would be remarkable, as the distance to the point of eruption must have been thirty or forty miles.

"But the most magnificent scenes were witnessed on the western sides of the mountain in the district of Kóna. Enormous floods of rock in igneous fusion burst from an orifice supposed to be about five miles westward of Mokuawéowéo, the great crater where Capt. Wilkes encamped, and rolled down the western slope of the mountain towards Kaáwalòa in a stream from one to two miles wide, and perhaps ten miles long. You will, however, receive these statements as matters of opinion and conjecture and not of actual observation and exact measurement. The eruption continued but three or four days, and we had hardly time to admire its brilliant coruscations and its rousing demonstrations, before all was hushed in profound silence, and covered with a pall of darkness."

This eruption broke out about a thousand feet below the summit, or two hundred feet below the bottom of the terminal crater. Some observers declare that the smoke proceeded partly from Mokuawéowéo, but no one ascended the mountain. The large masses of ice almost always found in the caves and hollows near the summit may have been converted into steam. No jets were thrown up, and the fissure was soon closed. From the portion of this stream that I visited, I should estimate its dimensions at ten miles in length but less than a mile in average breadth, or in volume one hundred and sixty million cubic yards of lava. The greater part of this lava is the pahoehoe, although some a-a occurs, and the whole flow bears marks of rapid cooling. It followed very nearly the track of an eruption which broke down the western rim of Mokuawéowéo and flowed through Keálakeakùa. The noise of explosions may have proceeded from the bursting of the caves and air bubbles in this ancient flow where they are numerous.

Six months after this, Mauna Lòa broke forth again, and I again quote Mr. Coan's letter.[1] **1852.**

"Old Kilauéa has been quite tame since I last wrote you. Changes have, however, taken place. The keystone of the great dome over Halemáumau (the lake) has parted, the top of the dome has fallen in, an orifice of about one hundred feet diameter has been opened, and an abyss of raging fire may be seen below at the depth of one hundred feet. Small lakes of fire have also broken out here and there in the crater, but the action has been partial and comparatively feeble. No light shines upon us from Kilauéa, and we have no new terrors to record of Mother Pélé at this point, but we have other wonders among the fiery sisterhood.

"At half-past three on the morning of the 17th ult., a small beacon-light was discovered

vol. xi., p. 395. It is said that Mokuawéowéo broke out in 1849.

[1] From a letter to the same correspondent, dated Hìlo March 5th, 1852. *Silliman's Journal*, [N. S.] vol. xii., p. 219.

on the summit of Mauna Lòa. At first it appeared like a solitary star resting on the apex of the mountain. In a few moments its light increased and shone like a rising moon. Seamen keeping watch on deck in our port exclaimed, 'What is that? The moon is rising in the West!' In fifteen minutes the problem was solved. A flood of fire burst out of the mountain, and soon began to flow in a brilliant current down its northern slope. It was from the same point, and it flowed in the same line, as the great eruption which I visited in March 1843. In a short time immense columns of burning lava shot up heavenward to the height of three or four hundred feet, flooding the summit of the mountain with light, and gilding the firmament with its radiance. Streams of light came pouring down the mountain, flashing through our windows, and lighting up our apartments so that we could see to read large print. When we first awoke, so dazzling was the glare on our windows that we supposed some building near us must be on fire; but as the light shone directly upon our couch and into our faces we soon perceived its cause. In two hours the molten stream had rolled, as we judged, about fifteen miles down the side of the mountain. This eruption was one of terrible activity and surpassing splendor, but it was short. In about twenty-four hours all traces of it seemed to be extinguished.

"At daybreak on the 20th of February, we were again startled by a rapid eruption bursting out laterally on the side of the mountain facing Hìlo, and about midway from the base to the summit of the mountain. This lateral crater was equally active with the one on the summit, and in a short time we perceived the molten river flowing from its orifice direct towards Hìlo. The action became more and more fierce from hour to hour. Floods of lava poured out of the mountain's side, and the glowing river soon reached the woods at the base of the mountain, a distance of twenty miles.

"Clouds of smoke ascended and hung like a vast canopy over the mountain, or rolled off upon the wings of the wind. These clouds assumed various hues — murky, blue, white, purple or scarlet — as they were more or less illuminated from the fiery abyss below. Sometimes they resembled an *inverted* burning mountain with its apex pointing to the awful orifice over which it hung. Sometimes the glowing pillar would shoot up vertically for several degrees, and then describing a graceful curve, sweep off horizontally, like the tail of a comet, further than the eye could reach. The sable atmosphere of Hìlo assumed a lurid appearance, and the sun's rays fell upon us with a yellow, sickly light. Clouds of smoke careered over the ocean, carrying with them ashes, cinders, charred leaves, etc.; which fell in showers upon the decks of ships approaching our coast. The light was seen more than a hundred miles at sea, and at times the purple tinge was so widely diffused as to appear like the whole firmament on fire. Ashes and capillary vitrifactions called 'Pélé's hair' fell thick in our streets and upon the roofs of our houses. And this state of things still continues, for even now while I write, the atmosphere is in the same yellow and dingy condition; every object looks pale, and sickly showers of vitreous filaments are falling around us, and our children are gathering them.

"As soon as the second eruption broke out I determined to visit it. Dr. Wetmore agreeing to accompany me, we procured four natives to carry our baggage, one of them, Kekai acting as guide. On Monday the 23d of February, we all set off and slept in the outskirts of the great forest which separates Hìlo from the mountains. Our track was not the one I took in 1843, namely, the bed of a river; we attempted to penetrate the thicket at another point, our general course bearing south-west. In ancient days an Indian trail had been beaten through in this direction, but it was now entangled with jungle so that all traces of it were nearly obliterated. However, we plunged into the forest with a long knife, hatchet, and clubs, and cut and beat our way at the rate of one and a fifth miles an hour. At night we slept in the bush and listened to the distant roar of the volcano. On Wednesday the 25th, we gained a little eminence in the woods, from which we could see the lava-stream which was now opposite us on our left, distant six miles. This fiery flood was now half way through the forest, and more than three fourths of the way from the crater to the shore, sweeping all before it. Apprehending that it might reach the sea in a day or two, and that the ladies at the station might be alarmed, Dr. Wetmore determined to return. Taking one of the natives and leaving three with me, he retraced his steps while I pushed on through jungle and bog and dell, beating every yard of my way out of this horrible thicket. On the 26th, we emerged from the forest but plunged at once into a dense fog more dark than the thicket itself. Pushing up the mountain we encamped for the night on a rough bushy ridge. A little before sunset the fog rolled off, and Mauna Kéa and Mauna Lòa both stood out in grand relief; the former robed in a fleecy mantle almost to its base, and the latter belching out floods of fire from its burning bowels. All night long we could see the glowing fires, and listen to the awful roar of the fearful crater.

"We had now been out four nights, and were within twenty miles of the crater, with the long brilliant river of fusion on our left shining in a line of light down the side of the mountain till it entered the woods. We left our mountain aerie on the 27th, determined if possible to reach the seat of action on that day. Taking the pillar of fire and cloud as our mark, and still having the great river of lava on our left, we pushed on over a rough and almost impassable surface — the attraction increasing as the square of the distance decreased. Our intense interest mocked all obstacles. At noon we came upon the confines of a tract of naked scoriæ so intolerably sharp and jagged that our baggage-men could not pass it. Here I ordered a halt; stationed the two carriers, gave an extra pair of strong shoes to my guide, gave him my wrapper and blanket, put a few crackers and boiled eggs into my pockets, took my compass and staff, and said to Mr. Salt Sea (Kekai), 'Now go ahead, and let us warm ourselves to-night by that fire yonder.' Thus equipped we pressed up the mountain, over fields of lava of indescribable roughness; now mounting a ridge of sharp and vitreous scoriæ (a-a), where the fiery pillar stood full in view, and then plunging into some awful ravine or pit, from which we slowly emerged by crawling upon 'all fours.' But I soon found that my guide needed a leader. He was too slow. I therefore pressed ahead, leaving him to get on as best he could. At half-past three P. M. I reached the awful crater and stood alone in the light of its fires. It was a moment of unutterable interest. I seemed to be standing in the presence and before the throne of the eternal God; and while all other voices were hushed, His alone spake. I was ten thousand feet above the sea, in a vast solitude untrodden by the foot of man or beast; amidst a silence unbroken by any living voice, and surrounded by scenes of terrific desolation. Here I stood almost blinded by the insufferable brightness; almost deafened with the startling clangor; almost petrified with the awful scene. The heat was so intense that the crater could not be approached within forty or fifty yards on the windward side, and probably, not within two miles on the leeward. The eruption, as before stated, commenced on the very summit of the mountain, but it would seem that the lateral pressure of the embowelled lava was so great as to force itself out at a weaker point in the side of the mountain; at the same time cracking and rending the mountain all the way down from the summit to the place of ejection. The mountain seemed to be siphunculated; the fountain of fusion being elevated some two or three thousand feet above the lateral crater, and being pressed down an inclined subterranean tube, escaped through this valve with a force which threw its burning masses to the height of four or five hundred feet. The eruption first issued from a depression in the mountain, but a rim of scoriæ two hundred feet in elevation had already been formed around the orifice in the form of a hollow truncated cone. This cone was about half a mile in circumference at its base, and the orifice at the top may be three hundred feet in diameter. I approached as near as I could bear the heat, and stood amidst the ashes, cinders, scoriæ, slag and pumice, which were scattered wide and wildly around. From the horrid throat of this cone vast and continuous jets of red-hot and sometimes *white-hot* lava were being ejected with a noise that was almost deafening, and a force which threatened to rend the rocky ribs of the mountain, and to shiver its adamantine pillars. At times the sound seemed subterranean, deep, and infernal. First, a rumbling, a muttering, a hissing or deep premonitory surging; then followed an awful explosion, like the roar of broadsides in a naval battle, or the quick discharge of park after park of artillery on the field of carnage. Sometimes the sound resembled that of ten thousand furnaces in full blast. Again it was like the rattling of a regiment of musketry; sometimes it was like the roar of the ocean along a rock-bound shore; and sometimes like the booming of distant thunder. The detonations were heard along the shores of Hìlo. The eruptions were not intermittent but continuous. Volumes of the fusion were constantly ascending and descending like a *jet d'eau.* The force which expelled these igneous columns from the orifice, shivered them into millions of fragments of unequal size, some of which would be rising, some falling, some shooting off laterally, others describing graceful curves; some moving in tangents, and some falling back in vertical lines into the mouth of the crater. Every particle shone with the brilliancy of Sirius, and all kinds of geometrical figures were being formed and broken up. No tongue, no pen, no pencil can portray the beauty, the grandeur, the terrible sublimity of the scene. To be appreciated it must be felt. . . . During the night the scene surpassed all power of description. Vast columns of lava at a white-heat shot up continuously in the ever-varying forms of pillars, pyramids, cones, towers, turrets, spires, minarets, etc. While the descending showers poured in one incessant cataract of fire upon the rim of the crater down its burning throat, and over the surrounding area,—each falling avalanche containing matter enough to sink the proudest ship. A large fissure opening through the lower rim of the crater gave vent to the molten flood which constantly poured out of the orifice, and rolled down the mountain in a deep, broad river, at the rate, probably, of ten miles an hour. This fiery stream we could trace all the way down the mountain until it was hidden from the eye by its windings in the forest, a distance of some thirty miles. The stream shone with great brilliancy in the night, and a long horizontal drapery of light hung over its whole course. But the great furnace on the mountain was the all-absorbing object.

"*March* 6. The fire has not yet reached the shore, and it may not. It is winding in the woods, filling our atmosphere with smoke, and sending down showers of ashes, charred leaves, etc. The great furnace in the mountain is still in terrible blast. No decrease of activity, but rather an *increase*."

In a letter dated September 27th, 1855, Mr. Coan says: "On the evening of the 11th of August, a small point glowing like Sirius, was seen at the height of twelve thousand feet on the north-western slope of Mauna Lòa. This radiant point rapidly expanded, throwing off coruscations of light, until it looked like a full-orbed sun."[1] 1855.

Sixty-five days after, the fissure which permitted the escape of the lava was still open, and in awful activity. The stream was flowing directly towards Hìlo and there were no valleys or ridges of sufficient size to turn its course. The inhabitants of this beautiful village were exceedingly anxious, and made frequent excursions to the scene of the lava-flow. On the 2d of October, Mr. Coan with a party of friends passed through the thick forest, following the course of the Wailùku, and on the fifth reached the lava-stream early in the morning, at a narrow point where it was about three miles wide. "In some places it spread out into wide lakes and seas, apparently from five to eight miles broad, enclosing, as is usually the case, little islands not flooded by the fusion." Mr. Coan continues in this letter, which is dated Oct. 15th, 1855[2]: —

"Early on Saturday, the 6th, we were ascending our rugged pathway, amidst steam and smoke and heat which almost blinded and scathed us. At ten we came to open orifices down which we looked into the fiery river which rushed furiously beneath our feet. Up to this we had come to no open lake or stream of active fusion. We had seen in the night many lights like street-lamps, glowing along the slope of the mountain at considerable distances from each other, while the stream made its way in a subterranean channel, traced only by these vents. From ten A. M. and onward, these fiery vents were frequent, some of them measuring ten, twenty, fifty, or one hundred feet in diameter. In one place only, we saw the river uncovered for thirty rods and rushing down a declivity of from ten to twenty-five degrees. The scene was awful, the momentum incredible, the fusion perfect (a white-heat), and the velocity forty miles an hour. The banks on each side of this stream were red-hot, jagged and overhanging, adorned with burning stalactites and festooned with immense quantities of filamentose, or capillary glass, called 'Pélé's hair.' From this point to the summit crater all was inexpressibly interesting.

"Valve after valve opened as we went up, out of which issued 'fire and smoke and brimstone,' and down which we looked as into the caverns of Pluto. The gases were so pungent that we had to use the greatest caution, approaching a stream or an orifice on the windward side, and watching every change or gyration of the breeze. Sometimes whirlwinds would sweep along, loaded with deadly gases, and threatening the unwary traveller. After a hot and weary struggle over smoking masses of jagged scoriæ and slag, thrown in wild confusion into hills, cones, and ridges, and spread out over vast fields, we came at one P. M. to the terminal or summit crater (not Mokuawéowéo).

"This we found to be a low elongated cone, or rather a series of cones, standing over a great fissure in the mountain. Mounting to the crest of the highest cone, we expected to look down into a great sea of raging lavas, but instead of this the throat of the crater, at the depth of one hundred feet, was clogged with scoriæ, cinders, and ashes through which the smoke and gases rushed up furiously from seams and holes. One orifice within this cone was about twenty feet in diameter, and was constantly sending up a dense column of blue and white smoke which rolled off in masses and spread over all that part of the mountain,

[1] *Silliman's Journal*, [N. S.] vol. xxi., p. 144.

[2] *Ibid.*, p. 139.

darkening the sun, and obscuring every object a few rods distant. So toppling was the crest of this cone, so great the heat, and so deadly the gases, that we could find no position where we could look down the throat or orifice; and could we have done so, it is not probable that we should have seen the deep fountain below us, as the lavas were forced up its horrid chimney from the burning bowels of the earth. I have no doubt that the point at which the igneous river flowed off in its lateral duct was at least five hundred, perhaps a thousand feet below us.

"The summit cone which we ascended was about one hundred feet high, say five hundred feet long and three hundred broad at its base. Several other cones below us were of the same form and general character, presenting the appearance of smoking tumuli along the upper slope of the mountain. As you descend the mountain these cones become lower and less frequent, but here they are the rims or jagged jaws of those orifices through which we look into that subterranean tube of angry fusion which hurries with such fearful speed down the side of the mountain. The molten stream first appears some ten miles below the fountain crater, and as we viewed it rushing out from beneath the black rocks, and, in the twinkling of an eye, diving again into its fiery den, it produced indescribable feelings of awe and dread.

"This summit crater I estimate at twelve thousand feet elevation; the principal stream (there are many lesser and lateral ones) including all its windings, sixty miles long; average breadth, three miles; depth, from three to three hundred feet, according to the surface over which it flowed. The present eruption is between those of 1843 and 1852, and from our high tower we could see them both and trace their windings.

"Early on Monday we decamped and set our faces for Kilauéa, distant some thirty-five miles, hoping by a forced march to reach it at night. At eight A. M., we passed the seat of the grand eruption of 1852, and travelled for miles on its cinders. A little steam only issues from that cone whose awful throat, in 1852, sent up a column of glowing fusion to the height of a thousand feet. We explored Kilauéa, and on Thursday reached Hìlo.

"Hìlo is now in a state of solemn and thoughtful suspense. The great summit fountain is still playing with fearful energy and the devouring stream rushes madly down towards us. It is now about ten miles distant, — nearly through the woods, following the right bank of the Wailùku, and heading directly for our bay.

"*October* 22. It is now seventy-two days since the eruption commenced, and the fountain is in full force. The matter disgorged is of the same general character as in former eruptions. We saw nothing new. Among the salts, sulphur, and sulphate of lime are the most abundant. They are scattered freely at several points along the line of flow."

Mr. Coan, it will be seen, struck the flow at a point above the terminus and followed it to its source. On his return he determined to cut through the forest and meet the stream. Following a branch of the Wailùku in a drenching rain which made the stream almost impassable, he thus describes the scene:[1] —

"So soon as we entered this stream we found it discolored with pyroligneous acid from burning wood, whose odor and lustre became more and more positive the further we advanced up the stream. The discoloration also became more apparent as we proceeded, until the water was almost black. This showed that the lava flow had crossed the head waters of the stream and its small tributaries, consuming the forest and jungle, and sending down what could not be evaporated of the juices to mingle with the stream.

1 *Silliman's Journal*, [N. S.] vol. xxi., p. 237. The letter is dated Nov. 16, 1855.

"A little before sundown our guide led us at right angles from the stream we had been threading for six hours, and in a few minutes the fires of the volcano glared upon us through the woods. We were within six rods of the awful flood which was moving sullenly along on its mission towards Hìlo. Thrusting our poles into the lava, we stirred it, and dipped it up like pitch, taking out the boiling mass, and cooling all the specimens we desired. We were on the right or southern verge of the stream, and we also found that we were about two miles above its terminus, where it was glowing with intense radiance and pushing its molten flood into the dense forest which still disputed its passage to the sea.

"We judged the stream to be two or three miles wide at this point, and over all this expanse, and as far as the eye could see above, and down to the end of the river, the whole surface was dotted with countless fires, both mineral and vegetable. Immense trees which had stood for hours, or for a day, in this molten sea, were falling before and below us, while the trunks of those previously prostrated were burning in great numbers upon the surface of the lava.

"You are aware that the great fire-vent on the mountain discharges its floods of incandescent minerals into a subterranean pipe which extends, at the depth of from fifty to two hundred feet, down the side of the mountain. Under this arched passage the boiling lava hurries down with awful speed until it reaches the plains below. Here the fusion spreads out under a black surface of hardened lava some six or eight miles wide, depositing immense masses which stiffen and harden on the way. Channels, however, winding under this scorified stratum, conduct portions of the lava down to the terminus of the stream, some sixty-five miles from its high fountain. Here it pushes out from under its mural arch, exhibiting a fiery glow, across the whole breadth of the stream. Where the ground is not steep, and where the obstructions from trees, jungle, depressions, etc., are numerous, the progress is very slow, say one mile a week.

"On the evening of our arrival we encamped within ten feet of the flowing lava, and, as before stated, on the southern margin of the stream, some two miles above its extreme lower points. Here under a large tree, and on a bank elevated some three feet above the igneous flood which moved before us, we kept vigils until morning. During the whole night the scene was indescribably brilliant and terribly sublime. The greater portion of the vast area before us was of ebon blackness, and consisted of the hardened or smouldering flood which had been thrown out and deposited here in a depth of from ten feet to one hundred.

"Not only was the lava, as aforesaid, gushing out at the end of this layer, but also at its sides. These lateral gushings came out before and behind us, and two thirds surrounded our camp during the night, so that in the morning, when we decamped, the fusion was just five feet, by measurement, in front of us, six feet in our rear, and three feet, or the diameter of the trunk of our camp-tree, on our left. The drenching rain and our chilled condition induced us to keep as near the fire as we could bear it. Evening and morning we boiled our tea-kettle and fried our ham upon the melted lavas, and when we left, our sheltering tree was on fire."

Mr. Coan made several attempts to cross the lava-flow, "but the hardened surface of the stream was swelling and heaving at innumerable points by the accumulating masses and the upraising pressure of the lava below; and valves were continually opening, out of which the molten flood gushed and flowed in little streams on every side of us. Not a square rod could be found on all this wide expanse, where the glowing fusion could not be seen under our feet through holes and cracks in the superincumbent stratum on which we were walking. The open pots and pools and streams we avoided by a zigzag course; but as we advanced, these became more numerous and intensely active, and the heat becoming unendurable, we again beat a retreat after having proceeded some thirty rods upon the stream. It may seem strange to many, that one should venture on such a fiery stream at all, but you will understand that the greater part of the surface of the stream was hardened to the depth of from six inches to two or three feet; that the incandescent stream flowed nearly under this crust like water under ice, but showing up through ten thousand fissures and breaking up in countless pools. On the hardened parts we could walk, though the heat was almost scorching, and the smoke and gases suffocating. We could even tread on a fresh stream of lava only one hour after it had poured out from a boiling caldron, so soon does the lava harden in contact with the air."

Although the stream of lava continued to move for more than a year after in parts of its course, its front became cold and fixed on the banks of the river, and a Merciful Providence listened to the prayers of the people of Hilo.

Prof. Dana considered it most probable that a fissure had extended completely down the mountain-side, and that the lava issued from many vents along this line.[1]

March 7th, 1856, Mr. Coan writes[2]: "The great fire-fountain is still in eruption, and the terminus of the stream is only five miles from the shore. The lava moves slowly along on the surface of the ground, and at points where the quantity of lava is small, we dip it up with an iron spoon held in the hand. During the last three weeks the stream has made no progress towards Hilo, and we begin to hope that the supply at the summit-fountain has diminished. There is, however, still much smoke at the terminal crater. You will understand that the molten flood is all poured out of the fissures on the summit and for a few miles down the slope of the mountain. At first this disgorgement flowed down and spread wide on the surface of the mountain, as blood flows down a punctured limb. This phenomenon continued until the stream had swept down some thirty miles, which it did in about two days. It now came upon a plane where the angle of slope was small, say one degree. Here its progress became slow, it spread more widely, and refrigeration was more rapid. The surface of course hardened first. But this refrigerating process went deeper and deeper like the congelation of water, and extended higher and higher up the mountain until at length all the lava was covered, except at occasional vents — as heretofore described — for the escape of steam and gases.

"The process of breaking up vertically and spreading out afresh upon the hardened crust, was occasioned by obstructions at the end of the stream, damming up the liquid, and thus obliging the accumulating lavas to force new passages and outlets for disgorgement. In this way the stream was widened by lateral outgushings, divided into several channels, swayed to the right and left, and raised to great heights by pushing up from below, and heaping mass after mass upon what *had been* its upper stratum. Often when the stream had been flowing briskly and brilliantly at the end, it would suddenly harden and cool, and for several days remain inactive. At length, however, immense areas of the solidified lava, four, five or six miles *above* the end of the stream, are seen in motion — cones are uncapped — domes crack — hills and ridges of scoriæ move and clink — immense slabs of lava are raised

1 *Silliman's Journal*, [N. S.] vol. xxi., p. 241. 2 *Ibid.*, vol. xxii., p. 240.

vertically or tilted in every direction, while a low sullen crash is heard from below. While you gaze in mute amazement, and feel the solid masses of rock, often thirty, fifty, or seventy feet thick, moving under your feet, the struggling lava oozes out through ten thousand orifices and fissures over a field of some four or five square miles. More than once have I been on such a field, and heard, and seen, and felt more than is here or can be described. And yet the action of the lava is so slow, in the conditions described, that there is no fear, and little danger to one well acquainted with such phenomena.

"During the night of the 29th of January, the molten stream poured continuously over a precipice of fifty feet, into a deep, dry basin half filled with flood-wood. The angle down which this fire cataract flowed, was about seventy-five degrees: the lava was divided into two, three, and sometimes four channels from one to four yards wide, and two or three feet deep. The flow was continuous down the face of this precipice from two P. M. until ten the next morning, when we left. During the night the immense basin under the fall was filled, the precipice converted into an inclined plane of about four degrees, and the burning stream was urging its way along the rocky channel below. But the scene on the night of the 12th of February was, in some respects, more gorgeous still, as it combined the element of water with that of fire. A stream of lava from twenty to forty yards wide had followed the rocky and precipitous bed of a river, until it was two miles in advance of the main lava-flow, which was nearly two miles broad. Beating our way through the thicket we came upon the terminus of this narrow stream of lava, near sunset. It was intensely active, and about to pour over a precipice of thirty-nine feet (by measurement), into a basin of deep water, large enough to float a ship. Before dark the lava began to fall into the water, first in great broken masses, like clots of blood; but in a short time in continuous, incandescent streams, which increased from hour to hour in volume, in brilliancy, and in rate of motion. The water boiled and raged with fearful vehemence, raising its domes and cones of ebullition ten feet high, and reflecting the red masses of fusion like a sea of fire mingled with blood.

"We encamped on the bank of the river, about fifty feet below the fiery cataract, and exactly opposite the basin of water into which the lava was flowing, twenty feet only from its rim. The face of this precipice was an angle of about eighty degrees, and the lava flowed down it briskly and continuously, in streams from one to four feet deep, during the night. Before morning this whole body of water, some twenty feet deep, was converted into steam, and the precipice became a gently inclined plane.

"I have seen continuous lava-streams flow rapidly down the sides of the mountain from ten to probably fifty feet deep. Lava flows at any depth, or any angle, and at any rate of progress from twenty feet an hour to forty miles."

To make the fact that the fissure did not extend to the base of the mountain more clear, Mr. Coan again writes under date of October 22d, 1856; he had then visited the flow seven times.

"A fracture or fractures occurred near the summit of the mountain, which extended in an irregular line from the terminal point, say five miles down the north-east slope of the mountain. From this serrated and yawning fissure, for two to thirty yards wide, the molten flood rushed out and spread laterally for four or five miles, filling the ravines, flowing over the plains, and covering all those high regions, from ten to one or two hundred feet deep. Along this extended fissure, elongated cones were formed at the points of the greatest activity. These cones appear as if split through their larger diameter, the inner sides being perpendicular or overhanging, jagged and hung with stalactites, draped with filamentous vitrifications, and encrusted with sulphur, sulphate of lime, and other salts.

"The outside of these cones are inclined planes, on an angle of forty to sixty degrees, and composed of pumice, cinder, volcanic sand, tufa, etc. You will not, however, understand that these semi-cones were once entire, and that they have been *rent*. They are simply masses of ridges of cinder and dross deposited on each side of the fractures where the action is greatest. *It is all a new deposit.* After you leave the region of open fissures, near the summit of the mountain all below *appears to be a flow on the surface.*

"1st. We can *see* no chasms or fractures except those always found in the surface flows. There is no visible evidence that the old substrata had been fractured, except on the higher regions of the mountain.[1]

"2d. Where there is a throat extending down to the fiery abyss below, there will, we think, always be a column of smoke and gaseous vapor ascending to mark the spot, so long as action continues. This is true of Kilauéa, and it is also true of *all* the eruptions I have noticed. Now if you were at Hìlo, you would see a continuous volume of smoke ascending from the terminal point, and another from the terminus of the stream — separated in a direct line forty miles, and by route of the flow seventy miles — while between these extreme points you see no smoke and have no evidence of fire beneath,[2] except the radiation of heat as you pass up. The smoke at the fountain is mineral, that at the end of the stream is from vegetation, and only here the fusion now makes its appearance, having come, as I believe, all the way from the mountain under cover, without showing itself at a single point. I do not mean that it has tunnelled the mountain, or melted a lateral duct through its mural sides. The process is this: lavas flowing on the surface and exposed to the atmosphere, unless moving with great velocity, as down steep hills, soon refrigerate on the surface. This hardened surface thickens, until it extends downward from one to two hundred feet, as the case may be. Under this superstratum the lava remains liquid; consequently at the termini and sometimes along the margins of the hardened streams, you see the fusion gushing out in red lines and points, and in irregular masses. When lavas refrigerate through the whole stratum, and thus rest upon an ancient or previous formation, they form dams which divert the stream of lava from above, unless this obstruction is broken up, tilted, or overflowed by fresh lava. Down the steep sides of the mountain such obstructions occur more rarely; consequently the lava ceases to reach the surface either at the fountain or down the sides of the mountain, but is confined to channels, mostly covered with fresh, solidified lavas, where it finds a free and rapid passage to the plains below. Here the movement is slow, the obstructions more numerous, and the force to overcome them less patent. This accounts for the spreading laterally, the upliftings, and the ten thousand irregularities which diversify the ever-changing surface of lava-streams. I have seen a dome, some three hundred feet in diameter at base, raised one hundred feet high, and split from the summit in numerous radii, through which the red and viscid fusion was seen; and I have mounted to the top of such a dome in this state, thrust my pole

1 A careful examination of the line of eruption resulted in the conviction that the fissure was originally very small, not exceeding three or four feet, and did not extend below the point where the lava first reached the surface.

2 This has been the case for some eight months. At first the whole ridge of the mountain was lighted with fusion on the surface; afterwards no fire was seen except at the end of the stream near Hìlo. — *Note by Mr. Coan.*

into the liquid fire and measured the thickness of its shell, which was from two to five feet.

"Wherever vegetable matter is being consumed there is smoke; when this is exhausted there is none. Consequently I argue that there are no fissures extending to the central fires of the earth, except for a few miles near the summit of the mountain.

"3d. Again, and what is more reliable, I have surveyed the ground upon which lava-streams have been approaching, for distances of five to twenty miles, and have seen the burning flood move on, covering to-day the ground on which I travelled yesterday, and consuming the hut where I slept; and the process is so familiar that it is difficult to see how I can be mistaken.

"I *think* that this stream of lava is *now flowing* more than sixty miles longitudinally under its own refrigerated cover; but I may be mistaken. No fire is *seen* anywhere except at the end of the stream. Here it still pushes out and spreads and heaps with little abatement, while the great mountain furnace sends up large and continuous volumes of smoke."[1]

To this exceedingly full and minute account, I need only add that I visited the terminus of the stream, where it ceased to flow, in 1865, and found the whole appearance of the stream in strict accordance with Mr. Coan's account. The surface was horribly rough and piled with slabs of hardened crust in vast ridges extending for miles. I slept on the fresh lava and examined the structure minutely, and found nothing to distinguish this stream from other eruptions, except its broken condition, arising from the wet soil over which it passed, which raised the surface into huge blisters. Where the lava fell into the water it was shivered into coarse sand like the deposit near Honolulu, and as the water was evaporated the pahoehoe covered the ground almost entirely and even penetrated its mass. The angles down which the continuous stream of lava fell were as large as Mr. Coan mentions, and the lava does not seem much more cellular here than on level ground.

At the lowest edge of the lava flow, I found, on the more ancient rock beneath, rounded masses of red earth of the consistency of putty, and as large as a man's head. They were in considerable number, and seemed to have been pushed along by the lava; their softness was owing to the rain, as when dried they became as hard as dried potter's clay.[2] The surface of the lava was covered with a minute lichen on which vast numbers of succineas had been feeding.

A letter from Prof. R. C. Haskell of Oáhu College, gives the following very full account of the important eruption of 1859:— **1859.**

"Our party consisted of Prof. Beckwith, Prof. Alexander, myself, and twenty students of the College. Twelve of us went to the source of the flow. . . . The eruption broke out on the 23d of January. No earthquake was felt in any part of the island at the time, but dead fish were noticed on the 21st and a few days afterwards, to the east of Molokaì, and between Molokaì and Oáhu. The fish gave no evidence of disease but seemed to have been parboiled. At Honolulu, two hundred miles from the eruption, the atmosphere was exceedingly thick and hazy. So much was this the case that it caused considerable excitement, before the news of the eruption arrived.

"Rev. Mr. Lyons of Waiméa states that on Sunday afternoon, January 23d, smoke was

[1] *Silliman's Journal*, [N. S.] vol. xxiii., p. 435.

[2] These masses were mostly composed of ferruginous oxides, as will be seen below.

seen gathering on Mauna Lòa. In the evening, lava spouted up violently near the top of the mountain on the north side, and apparently flowed both towards Hìlo and towards the west side of the island. This continued but a few minutes, when at a point considerably farther below the top, and farther west, another jet spouted up.

"Accounts from Hìlo say, that on the night of the 23d, it was so light there that fine print could be read without difficulty. After the 23d, the light was much less. At Lahaìna, more than one hundred miles distant, the whole heavens in the direction of the eruption were lighted up.

"Our party started from Honolulu, February 1st, and reached Keálakeakùa on the 3d. Here we learned that the stream from the eruption had reached the sea on the 31st of January, at Wainanalíi, about forty [sixty] miles from the place of eruption. This makes the average progress of the stream above five [seven] miles per day. After procuring guides, natives, pack-oxen, and mules, we started for the source of the flow on the 5th. About noon we had a view of the source, distant from us, probably, twenty-five miles in an air-line. The crater was about one hundred and fifty feet high, and two hundred feet in diameter (as we afterwards estimated). From within this crater, liquid lava was spouting up to the height of three or four hundred feet above the top. In shape and movement it resembled a mighty fountain or jet of water, though more inconstant. At one moment it was uncommonly high and quite narrow at the top, at the next not as high but very broad. At night, and from a good position near, the view of the jet, according to Mr. Faudrey (the only man who reached the crater while the jet was spouting) was grand beyond all description.

Fig. 35. Views of the Lava Fountain seen February 6th and 7th, 1859.

"Owing to an accident which befell one of our party, and the failure of water where it was supposed to be abundant, we were delayed two days and induced to divide our party into two divisions. One part returned to visit the flow at a point some twenty miles below, by another and easier route. The party who went on, consisting of twelve white persons and thirty kanakas, reached the crater Wednesday evening February 9th, and encamped about two miles from it. Here all fears about water were at an end, for we found snow in abundance within half a mile of our camping-ground. In the evening the view was magnificent. The jet had ceased to play; but two craters, about eighty rods apart, were sending up gas and steam, with appearances of flame. This apparent flame, however, we afterwards ascertained was only fine particles heated to redness. The noise attending this action was like that of an ascending rocket, very much increased of course, but quite irregular. About half a mile below the lower of the two craters, the stream first made its appearance. For five or six miles its course was well defined, and there were no side streams. From this point the main stream divided more or less, and on the plain, between the three mountains Hualalaì, Kéa, and Lòa, the branches extended over a breadth of three or four miles. Some of these streams were very broad and sluggish and partially cooled, some were narrow and running, as it seemed, at the rate of two or three miles per hour, burning the jungle and trees before them, and vying with each other in their work of destruction.

"For the first few miles the stream appeared to be a succession of cataracts and rapids. As it approached the plain between the two mountains, it gradually changed into a network of streams, or a lake of fire, embracing numerous islands and sending out streams on all sides. The color of the stream upon its first appearance was a light red approaching to white; on the plain a deep blood-red. From the plain towards Wainanalii the stream was narrow, varying from half a mile to a mile in width, and showing only a dull reddish light. . . . The next morning we were able to make some explorations about the craters. On the windward side we could ascend them and look in, though the heat was so great that we could look for a moment only, before turning our faces away. The sulphurous gases also were so strong that we were obliged to close our mouths and noses as we approached to look in. The craters were both very irregular in shape not only on the outside but on the inside. No liquid lava was seen in either at the time. In each there were two or three separate holes where gases and steam were issuing. The sides of these holes, and indeed the entire bottom of the craters, were at a white heat. The lava-stream appeared to be running underneath these craters, and the holes within seemed to be merely vents for the escape of gases. The craters were formed of fragments of light scoriæ and lava combined. The lower of the two (the one from which the jet was thrown up for fifteen days) was now open on the lower side. This was not the case while the jet was thrown up, according to Mr. Faudrey. . . . The upper crater was closed on all sides.

"Above these two craters we visited a third not then in action, but still hot. This was smaller and open on the lower side, and broken down somewhat on the upper side. This was formed not so much of scoriæ as of old lava. Above this we could see others of the same kind, and it is probable that they extend to the place where the lava first spouted out. From that place to the craters then in action, the stream appears to have flowed under the surface mostly, but to have been forced up to the surface, where these craters, now inactive, appear, by hydraulic pressure, or by the pressure of gases; or by both combined.

"The next morning we visited the point where the stream first made its appearance. Here we found the lava rushing out of its subterranean passage, and dashing over cataracts and along rapids at such a rate that the eye could scarcely follow it. The lava was at a white heat, and apparently as liquid as water. Only a few feet from where the stream issued, small masses of lava were thrown up from ten to fifty feet into the air, which cooled in falling. The cause of this was without doubt the escape of gas, and we then thought that the gas might come from the stream itself. But about three hours afterward we returned to the same place, and found that the action had greatly increased. Gases were escaping at two other points (Fig. 36 *b* and *c*) a few rods below the point first seen. Pieces of lava were thrown as high as one hundred and fifty feet, and at the lowest of the three points (Fig. 36 *a*), there was a fountain twenty-five feet high. The bits of lava thrown up cooled as they fell, and had already

Fig. 36. Lava fountain of February 10th, 1859.

formed craters ten feet high around two of the points where gases were escaping. It was now evident that the escaping gases were not derived from the stream simply, but issued from a vent, which reached to the common reservoir within or under the mountain. From a friend of mine who visited the spot three or four days afterwards, I learn that the fountain had ceased, and that the crater increased only a few feet after we left.

"Descending by the stream, we were able to follow it on its south side, as a strong wind was blowing from that direction. Here we found good walking, and could with safety approach within a few feet of the channel. The width of the stream was from twenty to one hundred feet, but its velocity almost incredible. Some of our party thought it one hundred miles per hour. We could not calculate it in any way, for pieces of cold lava thrown into it would sink and melt almost instantly. The velocity certainly seemed as great as that of a railroad car. For eight or ten miles the stream presented a continued succession of cascades, rapids, curves, and eddies, with an occasional cataract. Some of these were formed by the nature of the ground over which it flowed, some by the new lava itself. The stream had built up its own banks on each side, and had added to the depth of its channel by melting at the bottom. The stream flowed more gracefully than water. In consequence of its immense velocity and imperfect mobility, its surface took the same shape as the ground over which it flowed. It therefore presented not only hollows but ridges. In several places for a few feet the course of the stream was an ascent of five to ten degrees, in one instance of twenty-five. Where the turns in the stream were abrupt, the outside of the stream was much higher than the inside. So much was this the case, that the outside sometimes curved over the inside, forming a spiral.

"After arriving at the plain between the mountains, we had so much fog and rain that we could explore but little. We however saw pahoehoe or solid lava forming, and also a-a or clinkers.[1] Pahoehoe was formed mostly by small side streams, and always by shallow streams, which flowed freely but slowly. They were derived generally from the overflowing of the main stream. After flowing for some distance they became cooled at the end, and as there was little pressure from behind, gradually stopped. The little ridges which give the pahoehoe a ropy appearance, were caused by the flowing on of the stream for a little after it had cooled forward, and these are circular because the sides of the stream cool first, while the centre moves on a little further. These streams become solid in a short time, cooling through, and not simply coating over. At a subsequent time during the same flow, another layer of pahoehoe may be formed upon the first, as we saw in several instances.

"The clinkers are always formed by deep streams, and generally by wide ones, which flow sluggishly, become dammed up in front by the cooling of the lava, and in some instances cooled over the top, forming as it were, a pond or lake. As the stream augments beneath, the barriers in front and the crust on the surface are broken up, and the pieces are rolled forward and coated over with melted lava which cools and adheres to them more or less. Then from the force of the melted lava behind and underneath, the stream rolls over and over itself. In this way a bank of clinkers ten to forty feet high, resembling the embankment of a railroad, is formed. Often at the end of the stream no liquid lava can be seen, and the only evidence of motion is the rolling of the jagged rocks, of all sizes, down the front of the embankment. Sometimes the stream breaks through this embankment

1 Prof. Haskell does not distinguish between a-a and clinkers; they are, however, quite different formations. See above, p. 371.

and flows on for a time until it gets clogged up again, and then the same processes are repeated." [1]

In another letter Prof. Haskell writes under date of June 22d, 1859 : —

"I have just returned from a second visit to the scene of the lava-flood on Mauna Lòa. There is one fact which I observed that I desire to communicate to you. The real source of the flow is about four miles above the two craters, which in February seemed to be the source. From this point down to the two craters, a crack in the mountain can be traced nearly all the way. At first it is no more than two inches in width, but gradually increases to about two feet. At the present time heat can be perceived in the crack within a few feet of the highest point. But little lava has issued from this crack above the two craters. During the first quarter of a mile lava has oozed out in different places a few rods apart, to the amount of three or four cubic feet. Below this point there is a stream, now cold of course, a few rods in width. In this flow, therefore, there is no doubt that there is a continuous crack in the side of the mountain for four miles. How much farther this crack extends down the mountain cannot be ascertained, now at least, for the craters are still sending forth immense volumes of sulphurous vapors, and the stream of lava is still flowing below them. This stream, however, is much smaller than it was in February, and is entirely subterranean for the first twenty-five or thirty miles, except that there are a few holes where the running lava can be seen. In some instances this stream is as much as forty feet below the surface.

"During this trip I went to the top of Mauna Lòa. There is no perceptible action in the crater of Mokuawéowéo. The source of the present flow is probably about 11,000 feet above the level of the sea." [2]

On the 30th of December, 1865, a light was discovered on the summit of Mauna
Lòa which rapidly increased in brilliancy, and the whole upper region of the 1865.
mountains was bathed in light. The action was wholly confined to the terminal crater of Mokuawéowéo, and although it continued for four months no lateral outbreak took place. During this period the intensity of the volcanic fires varied considerably, sometimes being apparently nearly extinct, and again breaking out with such violence as to illuminate the whole island. As it was winter no one ascended the mountain, and we do not know as yet what the condition of the crater may be since this outburst. It is most remarkable that no lateral streams escaped, and it is probable that the crater has been more or less filled, as is the case in Kilauéa when no stream escapes from the encircling walls.

No sympathy was exhibited in Kilauéa, and although the fires seemed constantly increasing for the last two years, no extraordinary developments took place until some weeks after the summit crater had become extinct. It must not be inferred from this, however, that there is no connection between the two vents. An exactly simultaneous action seldom or never takes place in the adjacent fiery pools of Kilauéa although there is an undoubted connection at a probable depth of less than four hundred feet. [3]

History of Kilauéa.—At what period in the history of Hawaii, Kilauéa first broke forth,

[1] *Silliman's Journal*, [N. S.] vol. xxviii., p. 66. President W. D. Alexander has described this eruption in the "Volcano Supplement to the Pacific Commercial Advertiser," Honolulu, March 26, 1859.

[2] *Silliman's Journal*, [N. S.] vol. xxviii., p. 284.

[3] From letters of Rev. T. Coan to the author.

it is impossible to say. Dana seems to incline to the opinion that some vast rending of Mauna Lòa, similar to that of Háleakala, gave birth to this lateral crater, and accounts for its lasting operation by supposing the rent of immense depth. The other theory, that Kilauéa is coeval with the other members of the Mauna Lòa chain of volcanic peaks, supposes its sides to be too weak to sustain the pressure of a column of lava high enough to overflow the upper rim, and thus increase the height of the mountain by successive discharges. An examination of the lava-streams in the valley between Kilauéa and the slopes of Mauna Lòa, gives the following result: the valley is deeper than the ancient black ledge of the crater, narrow, and the wall towards Kilauéa is much broken by rents, some of which have taken place in the last two years, and the layers which have run over Kilauéa pass under those from Mauna Lòa, although the latter seem of equal antiquity. Again, in looking for traces of a rupture like that on Máui, or like the smaller one on the south-western side of this same mountain, mentioned in the description of Ka-ù, no signs of dislocation can be found at all commensurate with the supposed size of the fissure; the mountain is quite as even and regular on this side as on the others.

Whether Kilauéa was formed before or after Mauna Lòa its action has been generally independent of the summit crater, and while an eruption has been taking place on the top, Kilauéa, ten thousand feet below, and only sixteen miles distant, exhibited no signs of sympathy. A history of the recorded eruptions will make this independent action of the two volcanoes more evident. The first of which any authentic account has been

1789. preserved took place in 1789, and was observed by many natives who were marching to battle under the chief Keoùa. On their way from Hìlo to Ka-ù they encamped by the volcano.[1] "In the night a terrific eruption took place, throwing out flame, cinders, and even heavy stones to a great distance." Thunder and lightning accompanied this outburst, and the terrified natives dared not proceed. But on the second and third night similar disturbances took place, and they resolved to move on, separating for safety into three companies. The party in advance had not proceeded far, "before the ground began to shake and rock beneath their feet, and it became quite impossible to stand. Soon a dense cloud of darkness was seen to rise out of the crater, and almost at the same instant the electrical effect upon the air was so great that the thunder began to roar in the heavens, and the lightning to flash. It continued to ascend and spread abroad until the whole region was enveloped and the light of day was entirely excluded. The darkness was the more terrific, being made visible by an awful glare from streams of red and blue light variously combined, that issued from the pit below, and being lit up at intervals by the intense flashes of lightning from above. Soon followed an immense volume of sand and cinders which were thrown in high heaven and came down in a destructive shower for many miles around. Some few persons of the forward company were burned to death by the sand and cinders, and others were seriously injured. All experienced a suffocating sensation upon the lungs and hastened on with all possible speed.

"The rear body, which was nearest the volcano at the time of the eruption, seemed to suffer the least injury, and after the earthquake and shower of sand had passed over, hastened forward to escape the dangers which threatened them, and rejoicing in mutual congratulations that they had been preserved in the midst of such imminent peril. But what was their surprise and consternation, when on coming up with their comrades of the centre

[1] *History of the Sandwich Islands*, by Sheldon Dibble, Lahainalùna, 1843, p. 65.

party, they discovered them all to have become corpses. Some were lying down, and others were sitting upright, clasping with dying grasp their wives and children, and joining noses (their form of expressing affection) as in the act of taking a final leave. So much like life they looked, that they at first supposed them merely at rest, and it was not until they had come up to them and handled them, that they could detect their mistake. Of the whole party, including women and children, not one survived to relate the catastrophe that had befallen their comrades. The only living being they found, was a solitary hog. In these perilous circumstances the surviving party did not even stay to bewail their fate, but leaving their deceased companions as they found them, hurried on, and overtook the company in advance."

On their return after a week or ten days, they found the bodies entire and exhibiting no signs of decay except a hollowness of the eyes. They were never buried, and a missionary who collected a part of the account from the natives who marched with Keoùa, saw a human skull lying in the black volcanic sand of this neighborhood. It is said by some who saw the corpses that, although never deeply burned, they were thoroughly scorched, and this will perhaps account for their preservation for so many days.

This eruption surpassed any subsequent one, and was of a totally different nature. No lava is mentioned, but an immense amount of sand and scoriæ, with volumes of steam and sulphurous vapor. The description at once reminds us of the eruption of Vesuvius in 79; the same black, lofty column of smoke, lightnings, and destructive showers of sand such as overwhelmed Pompeii and Herculaneum. Could it have marked a renewal of activity after a long rest, and were the scoriæ the remains of the long-cooled crust at the bottom of the crater? South and west of Kilauéa where the sand deposits are quite extensive, the whole ground is cracked with earthquake throbs. These rents are sometimes filled with the black sand, and sometimes, especially near Ponahohòa, with lava.[1] It seems probable that from these cracks came the steam and vapor so destructive to the army, as those nearer the crater did not suffer from them. The prevailing trade-winds have carried all the ejections of this eruption to the south-west of the crater, and no sand of similar appearance is found on the windward side. The Ponahohòa region seems to overlie some fissure, or at least a weak part of the volcanic dome, as the earthquakes are usually quite severe here, cracks are frequent, and even lava has been ejected, although there are no signs of the existence of a volcano distinct from Kilauéa. More probably it is over the line of a subterranean lava-stream, and the facts mentioned by the Rev. William Ellis, who visited the place in 1823, seem to corroborate this view. He saw a deep chasm which had opened several months before, and was still emitting vapors. Black lava was spattered on the bushes and rocks in the neighborhood, and at the same time there is every reason to believe that the lavas of Kilauéa were finding an outlet.

1823.

The appearance of Kilauéa itself as described by Mr. Ellis, who was the first to publish an account of it, was quite different from its present condition.[2] It was evidently in an unfilled state, and we must infer that it was emptying itself, as the action was much diminished the next year. It may be allowable then to consider 1823 as the date of an eruption although no stream of lava, if we except the traces at Ponahohòa, appeared above ground. The volcano discharged as usual by a lateral rent, the side walls

[1] See plate in *A Tour through Hawaii*, by Rev. William Ellis. London, 1827, p. 203.

[2] Mr. Ellis visited Kilauéa, August 1, 1823.

of the dome yielding before the pressure of the enclosed lava, and quietly allowing the passage of the molten torrent to the sea. Ellis's description is as follows: —

"Immediately before us yawned an immense gulf, in the form of a crescent, upwards of two miles in length, about a mile across, and apparently eight hundred feet deep. The bottom was filled with lava, and the south-west and northern parts of it were one vast flood of liquid fire, in a state of terrific ebullition, rolling to and fro its fiery surge and flaming billows. Fifty-one craters of varied form and size rose like so many conical islands from the surface of the burning lake. Twenty-two constantly emitted columns of gray smoke, or pyramids of brilliant flame, and many of them at the same time vomited from their ignited mouths streams of florid lava which rolled in blazing torrents down their black indented sides into the boiling mass below.

"The sides of the gulf before us were perpendicular for about four hundred feet, when there was a wide horizontal ledge of solid black lava of irregular breadth, but extending completely round. Beneath this black ledge the sides sloped to the centre, which was, as nearly as we could judge, three or four hundred feet lower. It was evident that the crater had been recently filled with liquid lava up to this black ledge, and had, by some subterranean canal, emptied itself into the sea, or inundated the low land on the shore. . . . Between nine and ten [in the evening], the dark clouds and heavy fog that since the setting of the sun had hung over the volcano gradually cleared away. The agitated mass of liquid lava, like a flood of melted metal, raged with tumultuous whirl. The lively flame that danced over its undulating surface tinged with sulphureous blue, or glowing with mineral red, cast a broad glare of dazzling light on the indented sides of the insulated craters whose bellowing mouths, amidst rising flames, shot up at frequent intervals with loudest detonations, spherical masses of fusing lava, or bright ignited stones. . . . [In passing along the eastern edge of the crater], we entered several small craters that had been in vigorous action but a short period before, marks of very recent fusion presenting themselves on every side. Their size and height was various, and many which from the top had appeared insignificant as mole hills, we now found to be twelve or twenty feet high. The outsides were composed of bright shining lava, heaped up in piles of most singular form. The lava on the inside was of a light or dark-red color with a glazed surface, and in several places, where the heat had evidently been intense, we saw a deposit of small and beautifully white crystals. . . . In the neighborhood we saw several large rocks of a dark gray color weighing probably from one to four or five tons, which although they did not bear any marks of fire, must have been ejected from the great crater during some violent eruption, as the surrounding rocks in every direction presented a very different appearance. They were hard, and exhibited, when fractured, a glimmering and uneven surface.[1] . . . As we travelled on from this spot, we unexpectedly came to another deep crater, nearly half as large as the former. The native name of it is Kilauéa-iki, or Little Kilauéa. It is separated from the large crater by an isthmus nearly one hundred yards wide. Its sides were covered with trees and shrubs, but the bottom was filled with lava, either fluid or scarcely cold, and probably supplied by the great crater, as the trees on its sides showed that it had remained many years in a state of quiescence."[2]

The next year Kilauéa is described as follows: —

[1] Similar rocks are now found in ridges through the crater. Their composition is given below.

[2] Rev. William Ellis, *loc. cit* p. 224.

"From the time we arrived within two miles of the crater, we had the smoke arising from it directly in our faces, attended with a sulphureous stench. The wind 1824.
was very strong and brought along with it fine particles of sand so that I found it necessary to draw my hat as close as possible over my eyes in order to preserve them, carrying my head at the same time pretty low. The travelling was also difficult from the sand which covered the smooth stones on which we had before walked. Into this sand our feet sunk six or eight inches at every step. We however sometimes found the sand sufficiently hard and compact to bear us up. . . . We reached several large crevices from which smoke was issuing at a distance of five miles from the crater. Continuing to advance towards the crater our attention was arrested by a hissing noise like that of the blowing of a furnace, except that it was irregular, the noise being sometimes very low, and then again exceedingly loud. The smoke in which we were now enveloped became so dense that we could see only a small distance before us. . . . We had made the volcano at the south-west end, and we now proceeded round the eastern side hoping to be soon freed from the steam or smoke, which, being condensed by the wind, was falling upon us like rain. . . . At the distance of two hundred and fifty or three hundred feet below us was a level platform which appeared to have been formed by the falling in of the bank of the crater. This platform, I believe, extends nearly around the whole of the crater which is supposed to be nearly six miles in circumference. I had little difficulty in descending to this platform. From the side where I descended it extends nearly fifteen rods towards the centre of the crater, where there is another descent of two hundred and fifty or three hundred feet. Down this I proceeded, though not without danger, it being in most places perpendicular, and nearly so where I descended. Many of the stones also on which it was necessary to step were loose. . . . I had now reached the ancient bed of the volcano, having, as I supposed, descended six hundred feet. The surface of the lava was smooth though not level, sometimes rising in heaps like cocks of hay, and broken by innumerable fissures crossing each other in various directions.

"This lava was of a deep black color, exceedingly porous, and as light as a pumice-stone. The steam was constantly issuing from the crevices, and was so hot that I could not hold my hand in it for a moment. On this bed of lava I walked eight or ten rods towards the centre of the crater, when I came to another descent of two or three hundred feet, the volcano having sunk thus far below its ancient bed. The lower bed appeared much like the one on which I stood, but from various parts of it not only smoke, but flames of fire were issuing. The appearance of these small craters where the fire was bursting out, attended with a horrid noise, was indeed awfully grand, but I was disappointed in not finding this lower bed a mass of liquid fire. About a year since, when several of our brethren were making the tour of this island, this lower bed of lava was in a liquid state. The surface has now become hard, and I have no doubt would have supported my weight could I have descended to it. This I wished to do, but I looked in vain for a place where I might descend, the sides being in most places shelving over or perpendicular. . . . I proceeded along to the base of the sulphur mountain to collect specimens to carry home. It was in those places from which the smoke was issuing that I found the sulphur most pure, and formed into beautiful crystals." [1]

[1] The writer has been permitted to extract the above account from an unpublished *Journal* of E. Loomis, who was connected with the American Mission, and visited the volcano on the 16th of June 1824.

1825. The next year, July 28th, 1825, Kilauéa was visited by the Rev. C. S. Stewart, who describes its appearance as follows:[1] —

"About midway from the top a ledge of lava, in some places only a few feet, in others many rods wide, extends entirely round, at least so far as an examination has been made, forming a kind of gallery to which you can descend in two or three places, and walk as far as the smoke settling at the south end will permit. . . . The gulf below contains probably not less than sixty, — fifty-six have been counted, — smaller conical craters, many of which are in constant action. The tops and sides of two or three of these are covered with sulphur of mingled shades of yellow and green. With this exception, the ledge and every thing below it are of a dismal black. The upper cliffs on the northern and western sides are perfectly perpendicular, and of a red color, everywhere exhibiting the seared marks of former powerful ignition. Those on the eastern side are less precipitous, and consist of entire banks of sulphur of a delicate and beautiful yellow. The south end is wholly obscured by smoke which fills that part of the crater and spreads widely over the surrounding horizon. . . . Two or three of the small craters nearest to us were in full action, every moment casting out stones, ashes, and lava, with heavy detonations, while the irritated flames accompanying them glared widely over the surrounding obscurity. . . . The great seat of action, however, seemed to be at the south-western end. . . . Rivers of fire were seen rolling in splendid corruscations among the laboring craters, and on one side a whole lake whose surface constantly flashed and sparkled with the agitation of contending currents. . . . At an inconsiderable distance from us was one of the largest of the conical craters whose laborious action had so impressed us during the night. On reaching its base, we judged it to be one hundred and fifty feet high — a huge, irregularly shapen, inverted funnel of lava, covered with clefts, orifices, and tunnels, from which bodies of steam escaped with deafening explosion, while pale flames, ashes, stones, and lava were propelled with equal force and noise from its ragged and yawning mouth. . . . Leaving the sulphur banks on the eastern side behind us, we directed our course along the northern part to the western cliffs. As we advanced, these became more and more perpendicular, till they presented nothing but the bare and upright face of an immense wall, from eight to ten hundred feet high, on whose surface huge stones and rocks hung — apparently so loosely as to threaten falling, at the agitation of a breath. In many places a white curling vapor issued from the sides and summit of the precipice; and in two or three places streams of clay colored lava, like small waterfalls, extending almost from the top to the bottom, had cooled evidently at a very recent period."

Lieutenant Malden, who accompanied Mr. Stewart, made a sketch of the crater,[2] and calculated the height of the upper cliff from the black ledge, at nine hundred feet, making the whole depth of the crater fifteen hundred feet; and the circumference of the crater at its bottom, from five to seven miles, and at its top from eight to ten miles. On the evening of the 29th, after terrific noises and tremblings of the ground, "a dense column of heavy black smoke was seen rising from the crater directly in front of us — the subterranean struggle ceased — and immediately after, flames burst from a large cone, near which we had been in the morning, and which then appeared to have been long inactive. Red-hot stones, cinders, and ashes, were also propelled to a great height with immense violence; and shortly after the molten lava came boiling up, and flowed down the sides of the cone, and over the

[1] *Journal* by C. S. Stewart, p. 374.

[2] See the plan of Kilauéa, Plate XV.

surrounding scoriæ, in two beautifully curved streams." At the same time a whole lake opened over an extent two miles in circumference.

In December of the same year Rev. A. Bishop found the crater much fuller than when he visited it with Mr. Ellis in 1823. There were many cones from fifty to one hundred feet high on a surface about four hundred feet higher than the bottom of the crater two years before. There were lakes boiling actively, and "every now and then sending forth a gust of vapor and smoke with great noise.[1] The natives remarked that after rising a little higher the lava will discharge itself, as formerly, towards the sea, through some aperture underground."

1829. In the early part of October 1829, the Rev. C. S. Stewart again visited the crater. He found the lower pit filled up more than two hundred feet; many of the cones had disappeared, and there was much more fire at the northern end. He thus describes two cones which he examined. "They were in the neighborhood of each other — each about twenty feet in height, not more than sixty in circumference at the base, and tapering almost to a point at the top — being in fact two immense hollow columns formed by successive slight overflowings of lava, cooling as it rolled down, into irregular flutings, ornamented with rude drops and pendants, and long tapering stalactites. Though the ragings beneath must have been intense, from the tremendous roar within, the irresistible force and deafening hiss with which the steam rushed from every opening, and from the flames which flashed up, followed by lava white with an intensity of heat, still the incrustation of scoriæ immediately around seemed firm, and was less hot, than in many other places; admitting not only of our coming close to the sides of the cone, but also of clambering some feet up them, till we could run our canes into the orifices at the top, and withdraw, with their burning ends, red-hot lava, on which we readily made impressions. Pélé did not seem well pleased with this familiarity, however; even the slightest touch with our sticks against the molten lava, produced an increased rush and roar from below, with an angry spitting of the fiery matter high in the air around us."[2]

1832. Four years after, an eruption took place simultaneously with one from the summit of Mauna Lòa. Unfortunately we have no account from any eye-witness. In September 1832, the Rev. J. Goodrich visited Kilauéa, and describes the appearance of the emptied crater. "The lavas had previously risen fifty feet above the black ledge, but were now more than four hundred feet below this level, and the action seemed confined to the Halemáumau at the south end. In January an earthquake had rent in twain the wall between Kilauéa and Poli-o-Keàwe,[3] the large crater on the east, producing seams from a few inches to several yards in width, from which the region between the two craters was deluged with lava."[4]

This outbreak on the wall was very remarkable, rising as it did in a strip of land four hundred yards wide bounded on either side by precipices between two and three hundred feet high. Before this time, Poli-o-Keàwe had long been free from volcanic action, and its sides were wooded to the bottom. The stream issued from several rents south of the centre of the isthmus and above the lowest part, flowed toward the north a few yards to the lowest part, and then ran east and west into the two craters in a stream a hundred feet wide but quite shallow; indeed the quantity of lava was so small, that its eruption is hardly more

[1] *Missionary Herald*, vol. xxiii., p. 53.

[2] *A Visit to the South Seas*, vol. ii., p. 93.

[3] The same called by Ellis Kilauéa-iki.

[4] *Silliman's Journal*, [N. S.] vol. xxv., p. 199.

wonderful than the action of slender cones as described by Mr. Stewart. Where the subterranean discharge which emptied the crater, reached the sea, is not known.

1834. Mr. David Douglass was at Kilauéa in January 1834, and measured the depth of the pit at one thousand feet. A lake of boiling lava at the north end was three hundred and nineteen yards in diameter. The Halemáumau was much in the condition as described by Mr. Ellis.[1]

1838. On the 8th of May 1838, Captains Chase and Parker visited Kilauéa, and their description has been published with a sketch of the crater.[2] The lavas had again nearly reached the black ledge, and all over a surface of four square miles were cones and lakes of fire; twenty-six of the former were counted, eight of which were ejecting cinders and red-hot lava. Six small lakes were boiling violently, becoming crusted over, cracking, and again boiling. On the Halemáumau was an island which the lava was not seen to overflow. The remarkable oscillations in the heat, remarked by all visitors, seem to have taken place on this occasion with more than the usual rapidity. As they were looking at one of the lakes which was boiling violently, they say: "After a few minutes, the violent struggle ceased, and the whole surface of the lake was changed to a black mass of scoriæ; but the pause was only to renew its exertions; for, while they were gazing at the change, suddenly the entire crust which had been formed, commenced cracking, and the burning lava soon rolled across the lake, heaving the coating on its surface like cakes of ice upon the ocean surge." As they left the crater, nearly a quarter of the floor gave way, forming a vast pool of liquid lava.

Count Strzelecki, in the same year, estimates the size of five of the lakes at about five thousand seven hundred square yards, and they were almost at the level of the great area. The Halemáumau was encircled by a wall of scoriæ fifty yards high, and covered an area of three hundred thousand square yards.[3]

1839. Captain John Shepherd was at the crater September 16th, 1839. The Halemáumau was estimated at a mile in length and half a mile in breadth, and flowed over in some places "leaving ridges of scoriæ on the northern side."[4]

It took nine years for Kilauéa to fill up after the eruption of 1823; and for eight years the process had been continued until the lava had reached a point nearly a hundred feet above the black ledge which seems to be about the limit of pressure the walls of the mountain will bear. The force tending to rupture the mountain may be readily calculated, assuming the pressure of every twelve feet of lava to be fifteen pounds to the square inch; and as the crater is usually emptied to a depth of four hundred feet we have a pressure of five hundred pounds to the square inch. It must be remembered that the mountain wall is by no means solid and compact, and although successive discharges may strengthen some volcanic mountains, here the effect seems to be quite the contrary, owing to the extreme fluidity of the lava which runs off, leaving tunnels and caverns instead of solid interlacing dykes; consequently the discharges usually follow the same direction.

Kilauéa, then, was ready to break out, and in 1840 the most extensive eruption recorded took place.

1840. Rev. Titus Coan thus describes the eruption of 1840 in a letter dated September 25th, 1840.

1 *Journal of the Royal Geographical Society*, vol. iv.

2 *Silliman's Journal*, [N. S.] vol. xl., p. 117.

3 *Hawaiian Spectator*, vol. i., p. 435.

4 *Athenæum*, November 14, 1840.

"For several years past the great crater of Kilauéa has been rapidly filling up by the rising of the superincumbent crust, and by the frequent gushing forth of the molten sea below. In this manner the great basin below the black ledge, which has been computed from three to five hundred feet deep, was long since filled up by the ejection and cooling of successive masses of the fiery fluid. These silent eruptions continued to occur at intervals, until the black ledge was repeatedly overflowed, each cooling and forming a new layer from two feet thick and upwards, until the whole area of the crater was filled up, at least fifty feet above the original black ledge, and thus reducing the whole depth of the crater to less than nine hundred feet. This process of filling up continued till the latter part of May 1840, when, as many natives testify, the whole area of the crater became one entire sea of ignifluous matter, raging like old ocean when lashed into fury by a tempest. For several days the fires raged with fearful intensity, exhibiting a scene awfully terrific. The infuriated waves sent up infernal sounds, and dashed with such maddening energy against the sides of the awful cauldron, as to shake the solid earth above, and to detach huge masses of overhanging rocks, which, leaving their ancient beds, plunged into the fiery gulf below. So terrific was the scene that no one dared to approach near it, and travellers on the main road, which lay along the verge of the crater, feeling the ground tremble beneath their feet, fled and passed by at a distance. I should be inclined to discredit these statements of the natives, had I not since been to Kilauéa and examined it minutely with these reports in view. Every appearance however, of the crater confirms these reports. Every thing within the cauldron is new. Not a particle of lava remains as it was when I last visited it. All has been melted down and recast. . . . I will now give a short history of the eruption itself.

"On the 30th of May, the people of Púna observed the appearance of smoke and fire in the interior, a mountainous and desolate region of that district. Thinking that the fire might be the burning of some jungle, they took little notice of it until the next day, Sabbath, when the meetings in the different villages were thrown into confusion by sudden and grand exhibitions of fire, on a scale so large and fearful as to leave them no room to doubt the cause of the phenomenon. The fire augmented during the day and night; but it did not seem to flow off rapidly in any direction. All were in consternation, as it was expected that the molten flood would pour itself down from its height of four thousand feet to the coast, and no one knew to what point it would flow, or what devastation would attend its fiery course. On Monday, June 1st, the stream began to flow off in a northeasterly direction, and on the following Wednesday, June 3d, at evening, the burning river reached the sea, having averaged about half a mile an hour in its progress. The rapidity of the flow was very unequal, being modified by the inequalities of the surface, over which the stream passed. Sometimes it is supposed to have moved five miles an hour, and at other times, owing to obstructions, making no apparent progress except in filling up deep valleys, and in swelling over or breaking away hills and precipices.

"But I will return to the source of the eruption. This is in a forest, and in the bottom of an ancient wooded crater, about four hundred feet deep, and probably eight miles east of Kilauéa. The region being uninhabited and covered with a thicket, it was some time before the place was discovered; and up to this time, though several foreigners have attempted it, no one, except myself, has reached the spot. From Kilauéa to this place the lava flows in a subterranean gallery probably at the depth of a thousand feet, but its course can be distinctly traced all the way, by the rending of the crust of the earth into innumerable fissures, and by the emission of smoke, steam, and gases. The eruption in this old crater is small, and from this place the stream disappears again for the distance of a mile or two when the lava again gushes up and spreads over an area of about fifty acres. Again it passes underground for two or three miles, when it reappears in another old wooded crater, consuming the forest and partly filling up the basin. Once more it disappears, and flowing in a subterranean channel, cracks and breaks the earth, opening fissures from six inches to ten or twelve feet in width, and sometimes splitting the trunk of a tree so exactly that its legs stand astride at the fissure. At some places it is impossible to trace the subterranean stream on account of the impenetrable thicket under which it passes. After flowing underground several miles, perhaps six or eight, it again broke out like an overwhelming flood, and sweeping forest, hamlet, plantation, and every thing before it, rolled down with resistless energy to the sea, where, leaping a precipice of forty or fifty feet, it poured itself in one vast cataract of fire into the deep below, with loud detonations, fearful hissings, and a thousand unearthly and indescribable sounds. Imagine to yourself a river of fused minerals, of the breadth and depth of Niagara, and of a deep gory red, falling in one emblazoned sheet, one raging torrent, into the ocean. . . . The atmosphere in all directions was filled with ashes, spray, gases, etc.; while the burning lava as it fell into the water was shivered into millions of minute particles, and, being thrown back into the air fell in showers of sand on all the surrounding country. The coast was extended into the sea for a quarter of a mile, and a pretty sand beach, and a new cape were formed. Three hills of scoriæ and sand were also formed in the sea, the lowest about two hundred, and the highest about three hundred, feet.

"For three weeks this terrific river disgorged itself into the sea with little abatement. Multitudes of fishes were killed, and the waters of the ocean were heated for twenty miles along the coast. The breadth of the stream where it fell into the sea, is about half a mile, but inland it varies from one to four or five miles in width, conforming itself, like a river, to the face of the country over which it flowed. The depth of the stream will probably vary from ten to two hundred feet, according to the inequalities of the surface over which it passed. During the flow night was converted into day on all eastern Hawaii; the light was visible for more than one hundred miles at sea; and at the distance of forty miles fine print could be read at midnight.

"The whole course of the stream from Kilauéa to the sea is about forty miles. The ground over which it flowed descends at the rate of one hundred feet to the mile. The crust is now cooled, and may be traversed with care, though scalding steam, pungent gases, and smoke are still emitted in many places. In pursuing my way for nearly two days over this mighty smouldering mass, I was more and more impressed at every step with the wonderful scene. Hills had been melted down like wax; ravines and deep valleys had been filled; and majestic forests had disappeared like a feather in the flames. On the outer edge of the lava, where the stream was more shallow and the heat less vehement, and where of course the liquid mass cooled soonest, the trees were mowed down like grass before the scythe, and left charred, crisp, smouldering, and only half consumed. As the lava flowed around the trunks of large trees on the outskirts of the stream, the melted mass stiffened and consolidated before the trunk was consumed, and when this was effected, the top of the tree fell, and lay unconsumed on the crust, while the hole which marked the place of the trunk remains almost as smooth and perfect as the calibre of a cannon. These holes are innumerable, and I found them to measure from ten to forty feet deep, but, as I remarked before, they are in the more shallow part of the lava, the trees being entirely consumed where it was deeper. During the flow of this eruption the great crater of Kilauéa sunk about three hundred feet, and her fires became nearly extinct, one lake only out of many being left in the mighty cauldron. This open lake is at present intensely active, and the fires are increasing, as is evident from the glare visible at our station, and from the testimony of visitors. During the early part of the eruption slight and repeated shocks of earthquake were felt, for several successive days, near the scene of action. These shocks were not noticed at Hìlo. Through the directing hand of a kind Providence no lives were lost, and but little property was consumed during this amazing flood of fiery ruin.

"During the progress of the descending stream, it would often fall into some fissure, and forcing itself into apertures, and under massive rocks, and even hillocks and extended plats of ground, and lifting them from their ancient beds, bear them with all their superincumbent mass of soil, trees, etc., on its viscous and livid bosom, like a raft on the water. When the fused mass was sluggish, it had a gory appearance like clotted blood, and when it was active, it resembled fresh and clotted blood mingled and thrown into violent agitation. Sometimes the flowing lava would find a subterranean gallery diverging at right angles from the main channel, and pressing into it would flow off unobserved, till meeting with some obstruction in its dark passage, when, by its expansive force, it would raise the crust of the earth into a dome-like hill of fifteen or twenty feet in height, and then bursting this shell, pour itself out in a fiery torrent around. A man who was standing at a considerable distance from the main stream, and intensely gazing on the absorbing scene before him, found himself suddenly raised to the height of ten or fifteen feet above the common level around him, and he had but just time to escape from his dangerous position, when the earth opened where he had stood, and a stream of fire gushed out."[1]

The small crater where the lava first appeared is called Ararè, and is about six miles east of Kilauéa, in the dense forest. The natives say that the lava rose in this crater about three hundred feet, and then sunk again when the fissure opened below, and at the present time there are evident proofs of this on the crater walls. The line the stream seems to have followed passes through a high hill (seen in the view of the Deep Crater Fig. 44) thus just avoiding this large pit where it might be supposed the resistance would be least, but the hill is undoubtedly hollow, being a cone from which the lava has been emptied, and the cavity beneath it was perhaps larger than that of the pit crater.

The elevation of the place where the lava finally reached the surface is given by Wilkes at 1244 feet, and it is twenty-seven miles from Kilauéa, twenty-one from the first outbreak, and twelve from the shore at Nanawálie. The sand-hills thrown up at this place were found to be one hundred and fifty, and two hundred and fifty feet high, eight months after their formation. At present they are not a third of this height, as the sea has rapidly removed the loose material of which they are composed. There seems to be no reason for supposing that any fissure beneath these hills opening to the interior reservoirs of lava existed, as the height from which the lava reached the sea is amply sufficient to account for their formation, and they do not at present correspond with the other tufa cones on the islands.

In November of the same year, when visited by Prof. Dana, the lava was still hot in many places, a few feet below the surface. Small sulphur-banks, with deposits of alum and other salts, were met with in several places.[2]

1 *Missionary Herald*, vol. xxxvii., p. 283.

2 *Geology United States Exploring Expedition*, p. 190

The lava of this eruption closely resembles that in the walls of Aliapaakaì on Oáhu, and like that contains a very large proportion of chrysolite, in some places nearly one half, and in quite large grains. No similar lava is found in Kilauéa, but chrysolitic lava has issued in several streams from Mauna Kéa in ancient times, and also perhaps from Mauna Lòa, if we suppose the large deposits of this lava occasionally found along the coast near Hìlo to have proceeded from this mountain.

In November of the same year, when visited by Prof. Dana, the lava had fallen three hundred and forty feet below the black ledge, or nearly one thousand feet below the highest wall, and only three pools of lava were in action. The Halemáumau was fifteen hundred feet long and a thousand feet wide. The black ledge, three hundred and forty feet from the bottom, was from one to three thousand feet wide, and extended completely around the crater. No flames were visible, and there was but little noise.[1]

1841. In December, and January 1841, Dr. Pickering describes several considerable variations in the surface of the Halemáumau, a hundred feet or more. On the 17th of January, two of the pools discharged large quantities of lava over the bottom of the crater.[2]

1842. The next February, Mr. Coan writes as follows: "When within four or five rods of the great lake, unaware of our near proximity to it, we saw directly before us a vast area of what we had supposed to be solid lava moving off to the right and left. We were at first a little startled, not knowing but all was about to float away beneath us, especially as the lavas for a mile back were almost insupportably hot, and gases and steam were escaping from numerous openings. On looking again, we perceived that the whole surface of the lake was from six to fifteen feet above the level of the surrounding lava, although at my last visit, it was from sixty to seventy feet below. Within six feet of this embankment we could see nothing of the lake, and in order to examine it we climbed the precipice some fifty feet. The explanation of this strange condition of things, is this: When the liquid contents of the lake had risen to a level with the brim, there was a constant and gradual boiling over of the viscid mass, but in quantities too small to run off far. Consequently, it solidified on the margin, and thus formed the high rim which confined the lavas. Twice, or at two points while we were there, the liquid flood broke through the rim, and flowed off in a broad, deep channel which continued its flow until we left the volcano. The view was a new one, and thrilling beyond description."[3]

1844. In July, Mr. Coan saw the large lake overflow on every side, spreading over the whole southern end of the crater to the base of the black ledge on either side, and wholly concealing the outlines of the cauldron. Two deep fissures opened under the ledge on either side, nearly encircling that part of the crater, and one of these was two hundred feet deep. Soon these yawning gulfs were filled with the overflow of the Halemáumau, and in one place the lava "fell in a cascade of fifty feet, producing a scene of terrific sublimity."

1846. In a letter dated June 25th, 1846, Mr. Coan states that "the great lake is intensely active most of the time. The repeated overflowings have elevated the central parts of the crater four or five hundred feet since 1840, so that some points are now more elevated than the black ledge."

The Rev. C. S. Lyman visited Kilauéa twice this year, and we find from his description

[1] *Loc. cit.* p. 171. [2] *Narrative of the United States Exploring Expedition*, vol. iv., p. 178. [3] *Loc. cit.* p. 178.

that several changes of importance had taken place. The long ridge of blocks of compact lava, like the upper wall which extends at intervals nearly around the northern edge of the crater, had then formed. He says: "This ridge rose on its outer or eastern face often to the height of fifty or one hundred feet, especially towards the south, where it approached the great lake; and generally it left a space or canal as it has been called, between it and the ledge [black ledge of Prof. Dana] several rods in width, and in some places forty or fifty feet in depth." The canal mentioned is the same one into which Mr. Coan saw the lava flow in 1844. The lake at the southern end was still surrounded by a rim of lava, and bounded on the north-east by a high plateau, — the raised floor of the crater. There was no other lake or pool of lava visible. A curious dome, corresponding to the "hornitos," described by Humboldt in the malpays of Jorullo, was observed about a mile north of the great lake. It was ten or twelve feet high, its walls not "more than a foot thick, and through two openings, the one a foot and the other half a foot in diameter, the interior was revealed of a glowing white heat, and by throwing pieces of lava into these orifices they were seen to fall into the pasty semifluid mass ten or fifteen feet below. This furnace was in full blast six weeks after."[1]

Mr. Coan, in a letter dated December 7th, 1846, says: "Visited the volcano a few days ago. Found the lake full and active. Dipped up the molten lava with our canes." So that the lava must have risen ten or twenty feet in the few months since Mr. Lyman's visit, when the lava was that depth below the rim.

Mr. Coan again writes in a letter dated January 1851: "My next visit to the crater 1847.
was in July 1847, in company with Captain (late Admiral) Dupont and several officers of the United States ship Cyane. No essential changes had occurred in the bottom of the volcano during this interim, except that the great lake had filled up, had overflowed a considerable area around its rim, was still full and in an active state. The boiling of the lava was intense around most of its circumference, and at many points over its surface. Access to the red-rolling fusion was comparatively easy, so that by carefully watching and dodging its fiery jets we could dip up its viscid matter with sticks or ladles. Silent and successive overflowings took place from time to time during this year, considerably elevating all the area in the vicinity of Halemáumau, but not affecting the other and larger portions of the crater. I think it was about the beginning of 1848, that the great lake was first 1848.
noticed as crusted over with a thick stratum of lava, and this stratum was soon raised into a dome some two or three hundred feet high over the whole lake; traversed here and there by rents and fissures, and studded by an occasional cone. Occasionally the visitor, or the passing traveller, would descry, through these fissures, the glowing of the subterranean fires, and now and then the gory mass would be pressed sluggishly through these chasms or driven up with more force through the several chimneys, apertures, or orifices of the dome. These eruptions rolled in heavy and irregular streams down the sides of the dome, spreading over its surface or cooling at its base. Thus the dome as it now exists, has been formed by the compound action of upheaving forces from beneath, and of eruptions from its openings forming successive layers upon its external surface. During most of this year, however, an extraordinary *inactivity* prevailed throughout the crater. During the summer and autumn when I was at Kilauéa, there was no fire to be seen even in

[1] *Silliman's Journal of Science* [N. S.], vol. xii., p. 75. From a manuscript map prepared by Mr. Lyman, I find the "ridge" occupied the same position as at present. See the Plan of Kilauéa, Plate XV.

the night. Old Vulcan seemed to have forsaken his furnace, buried his fires, and retired to his deep, dark caverns, leaving his awful forge surrounded with smouldering masses of scoriæ and slag. At the time of my visit in August, the great dome was so elevated as almost to overtop the lower parts of the outer walls of Kilauéa and look out upon the surrounding country.

1849. "In April and May 1849, travellers upon the borders of Kilauéa were startled by explosions and detonations from cones on the great dome. A party lodging in the hut on the upper banks were greatly terrified during one whole night, by hissings, bellowings, and sharp and loud detonations, sometimes like the discharge of whole ranks of musketeers, sometimes like field artillery, and sometimes like awful deep-toned thunder, roaring and reverberating around the adamantine walls of the dark cavern. These bellowings were repeated hourly through the night, and were attended by a brilliant column of red-hot lava thrown perpendicularly from an orifice in the apex of the dome to the height of some fifty or sixty feet. At other times red-hot stones were projected with great force into the air and sent whizzing like fiery meteors through the gloom of night. As the glow of this scene a little abated, a stream of burning lava was disgorged from the orifice of a lateral cone on the ridge of the dome, flowing down to its base and winding along upon the dark substratum like a fiery serpent. Fire was seen through some of the fissures in the dome, and nearly the whole bottom of Kilauéa was quivering and cracking with heat; so much so, that travellers feared to descend into any part of the crater.

"Since the time just mentioned no remarkable phenomena have been noticed in the crater. It has been for the most part in a quiescent state, with more or less steam and smoke, and occasionally opening a small red eyelid, or letting loose a few fire-flies upon the wings of the night.[1]

1850. "During December of 1850, the smoke and steam are said to have much increased; and the occasional throe of an earthquake indicates that all subterranean action has not ceased. The sulphur beds remain much as formerly, except, perhaps, that the bank within the crater has less heat and activity, and the one above, or near the hut, has a little increase of heat.

1851. "There is now one cone feebly active at a little distance from the dome in the crater. Those *on* the dome are inactive."[2]

1852. Mr. Coan, after a visit to Kilauéa the next year, writes under date of July 30th: "I had visited Kilauéa in March and found the action in the crater much increased. On this occasion the action was still more intense. The great dome, one mile and a half in circuit and several hundred feet high, has now lost its keystone, and the massive arch is fallen in. The orifice on the summit is two hundred feet in diameter, and through this orifice you look directly upon the raging fire below. On one side the dome is rent from the base to the summit, and through this fissure smoke and lava pass off from the boiling cauldron.

"This fiery lake, so long concealed by the ponderous dome, is gradually rising and lifting and rending the superincumbent strata of which the great dome is composed, and threaten-

[1] In a letter from Lieut. Henry Eld who accompanied the United States Exploring Expedition in 1840, and again revisited the crater this year, we find that the bottom was much raised, the lava had subsided in the great lake and seemed nearly extinguished. *Silliman's Journal* [N. S.], vol. ix., p. 362.

[2] *Silliman's Journal* [N. S.], vol. xii., p. 80

ing at no distant day to engulf the whole overhanging mass within its burning bowels. Aside from this increased action within the dome, no important changes have occurred in the crater for two years past." [1]

Under date of January 30th, 1854, he continues: "Changes have been slowly taking place within the crater. A gradual rising is going on in the whole floor of the crater. This is effected by two causes, — first, by the uplifting forces below, as gases, igneous fusion, etc., — and second, by repeated overflowings. The former is more uniform and general, the latter irregular and partial. You are aware that all the central part of the floor of the crater, embracing nearly one half of its area, is an elevated plateau, the highest points of which are now some six hundred feet above what was the floor after the eruption of 1840. This central elevation rises in some places gradually, in others abruptly, from the surrounding floor. On the east and south-east its mural walls are perpendicular, presenting a dark, lofty, and frowning rampart which no human foot can scale. Of course the black ledge is now a lower plane than this central table, at its highest point, by about two hundred feet. Many parts of the black ledge have also been elevated by subterranean forces. From repeated agitation of the sea around our shores,— instances of which have recently occurred, — we are led to think that submarine eruptions are occasionally taking place on the submerged portions of Hawaii, or from volcanic mountains and cones covered by the waters of the Pacific." [2]

1854.

July the 18th, 1855, Mr. Coan writes: [3] "For months past this awful furnace has been brightening and glowing, and raging and roaring with fearful intensity. The action, however, is all confined to the great dome and the girdle between the central table and the crater walls; while the elevated interior is unaffected, and even begins to produce plants and ohelo-berries. But it is surrounded by the burning streams of Phlegethon, and stands as a burnt island in a sea of fire. The great dome (over Halemáumau) is thundering and throwing up columns of dashing fusion from its horrid throat to a height of two hundred feet, while its walls tremble at the fury of those waves which rage and dash within. Occasionally a burning river bursts through the rent chasm near its base, and rolls in glaring waves over all that region, flooding the heavens with light, and filling the spectator with mingled emotions of delight, of awe, and of terror. But this is not half. The whole of the surrounding belt, from its periphery at the base of the great walls of Kilauéa, to the elevated central platform, and even eight miles in circumference by half a mile in diameter, is in a state of intense activity. Over this surface I could count sixty lakes of fusion. The whole of this surface is not, of course, broken and fused at once; but it is everywhere rent with fissures, studded with burning cones, and dotted with boiling lakes; and even the solid portions of the surface are so hot as almost to crisp the sole of one's shoes, while the smoke and the pungent gases render it difficult to travel in some parts and impossible in others.

1855.

"During the last week in May and the first in June, visitors and passing travellers reported a fiery girdle around the whole circumference of Kilauéa, along the base of her lofty walls, — and so intense was the heat, so suffocating the gases, so fearful the hissings, so awful the surgings, and so startling the detonations, that horses wheeled and plunged with panic, and men retired from the old Ka-ù and Hìlo road which, as you may recollect, lay

[1] *Silliman's Journal* [N. S.], vol. xvi., p. 46. [2] *Ibid.* vol. xxi., p. 46. [3] *Ibid.* vol. xxi., p. 100.

near the upper precipice, and passed the great fissure at a respectful distance. And I have been told by those who observed and felt it, that so great was the heat on the road above the western precipice, seven hundred feet above the fires, that they were obliged to hold their hats between their faces and the crater and pass rapidly along to avoid it. The upper banks also of the crater are smoking and steaming intensely.

"For twenty years I have watched the movements of the great crucible of Nature — this Hawaiian volcano — with intense interest, and never, perhaps, have I seen the fires more extensively distributed over the crater, or more active and vivid in their play."

Under date of October 22d, 1855, he continues: "After this the action gradually moderated until the summit crater [eruption of 1855 on Mauna Lòa] broke out, and it remains now much as it was then. There are now about a dozen open lakes of raging lava in Kilauéa, extending in two semicircular lines from the great fountain lake, Halemáumau, along the eastern and western sides of the crater, and evidently forming vents to igneous subterranean canals which are carrying the incandescent floods from this great active vent to the northern parts of the crater, sometimes overflowing this region and sometimes heaving up the ponderous superincumbent strata, like the surface of an agitated ocean. The great dome over Halemáumau is swept away, and a raised and jagged rim from twenty to sixty feet high, now encircles it. The fusion may be one hundred feet below. The movement of the streams northward is distinctly seen through the valves or vents mentioned above. The encircling belt has been raised from one to two hundred feet since last April, first, by uplifting forces; second, by successive overflowings." [1]

1856. Under date of October 22d, 1856, he writes: "During the whole of the past year Lua Pélé has been getting more and more profoundly asleep. A little sluggish lava is found in the great pit of Halemáumau, and the steam issues from a thousand vents. But there is no subsidence of the floor of the crater. This vast area of hardened lavas keeps its elevation some six hundred feet above the level of the floor that was formed at the eruption of 1840." [2]

1857. September 1st, 1857, Mr. Coan writes: "I was at Kilauéa in June last. Pélé was rather quiet. All the area of Halemáumau is now a deep basin encircled by a rim consisting, in some places, of a bold perpendicular precipice, and in others of an inclined plane of unequal angles rent into numerous yawning fissures, and strewed with burnt masses of scoriæ. The bottom of this basin is rent and smoking, and studded with a few cones near the centre and enclosed by a jagged rim from twenty to fifty feet high, is the lake of fire which has burned from time immemorial. It is about one hundred feet below the rim, and some five hundred feet in diameter." [3]

1859. During the eruption of Mauna Lòa, Kilauéa was visited to see if any extraordinary action was visible, but it was comparatively quiet. The fires showed no sympathy with those being poured out ten thousand feet above.

Visitors to Kilauéa were more numerous after the grand eruption of Mauna Lòa of this year, but for several succeeding years they had little to report, but the ordinary activity of the crater. The Halemáumau always exhibited fire, and the cracks poured out steam and vapor, and the accounts of the action varied with the impressibility of the various reporters. Although no marked change took place, the vast abyss was slowly filling up, and its surface became more and more uneven and broken. The very slight shocks of earthquakes, not

1 *Silliman's Journal* [N. S.], vol. xxi., p. 144. 2 *Ibid.* vol. xxiii., p. 438. 3 *Ibid.* vol. xxv., p. 136.

uncommon on the islands, were not noticed particularly for two or three years on Hawaii, while on Oáhu several were perceived. An eruption was almost desired, as those from Kilauéa usually reach the sea through an uninhabited part of the island. It almost seemed as if the crater was at last strong enough to hold its weighty contents, and would once more empty itself over its rim, and even raise its outer walls.

Fig. 37. The Crater of Kilauéa from the northern bank.

In visiting Kilauéa in 1864, with Mr. Horace Mann, we approached it from the south-west on the Ka-ù path. For ten miles we had seen the cloud of smoke over the crater, and for more than half that distance we had traversed beds of pahoehoe, and large tracts of sand, deep and difficult for our horses. No a-a was visible from the path, and but little scoriæ. The eruption of 1789, is said to have thrown out most of the sand, but the winds have entirely changed its original location. It is dark, fine, and uniform, and it now lies covering the solid pahoehoe in places to the depth of several yards. Soon after one o'clock we came upon the brink of the crater. From below us steam and sulphurous vapors rose in a sluggish column, but we saw no fire and heard no noises. The great sunken plain before us, covering six or eight square miles, looked bright in the clear sunlight, and even the walls on which we stood were of a light gray color. The whole circuit of the walls on the northern and western sides is much cracked and interrupted. We rode along over several cracks, one of which, a little more than a yard wide, had opened about a year since, accompanied by an explosion heard distinctly at a distance of twenty miles. Some of the cracks were parallel with the edge of the abyss, others were at right angles to these, and in one place the small cracks were so numerous as to resemble a geometric spider's web. 1864.

Passing over the high cliffs on the north-west, which are the highest part of the circuit. the road leads down by a steep descent of fifty feet to a plain a mile long and three quarters of a mile wide, gravelly and covered thinly with dwarf ohia and ohelos, and thickly dotted with small oval or circular fumaroles, from which steam was issuing, not as at the Geysirs in California with great noise, but as a quiet, respectable tea-kettle pours out its vaporous offering. The steam had no odor, and ferns and other plants grew luxuriantly over the openings. On the leeward side of these steam-holes the muddy and tenacious red soil retained pools of excellent water condensed from the steam. There was no trace of sulphur or acid in it that could be detected by test papers or the taste. The rock through which these cracks passed was completely decomposed from a hard gray clink stone to a red loamy earth, soft and worn smooth by the ascending vapor. It was quite evident that these fumaroles were not originally formed by the vapor, but were simply cracks, through which the steam escaped, and the circular shape resulted from the falling in of the surface gravel and soil. The steam was quite hot, and we saw the remains of several cattle who had gone too near in search of water.

On the northern edge of this plain are extensive sulphur banks, that is to say, they cover a large space although containing but little sulphur, under a perpendicular ledge of clink stone nearly a hundred feet high. They are simply great piles of the decomposed lava, through which steam and sulphurous vapors constantly escape through a thousand apertures, depositing beneath the crust the most beautiful, almost acicular crystals of sulphur The soil formed by the decomposition of the rock by sulphurous vapors is quite unlike that resulting from the action of steam alone; it is light gray or yellow, and does not form a plastic mud as easily as the latter, which is red and smooth to the touch. In some places the sulphates of oxides of copper, iron, sulphates of soda, lime, and alumina were forming within minute fissures, and the silica thus set free was gradually consolidating the earth into a firm crust whenever the action of the steam ceased, and we could often raise large slabs of this curious conglomerate. Metamorphism was progressing rapidly under the combined influence of heat and moisture. Twigs and leaves were fast passing into the condition of fossils in this hardening earth. All the sulphur found here is deposited from the vapor, and seems to be tolerably pure and is of a light yellow color, indicating the absence of selenium. There would seem at first to be no doubt that this plain has sunk to its present position, as it is surrounded, except towards the crater, by a wall of the same material; but this is not the case. Where the lava-beds of this portion adjoin the other walls of the crater, there is no fault, the strata are continuous, and this plain was once the bed of Kilauéa, — a black ledge.

As soon as our men came up with the blankets, we engaged guides and went down into the crater. The descent was steep and winding, and we passed over several terraces, which were the result of a sinking or falling in, as their strata were inclined and much broken, and came under the grand pali of compact lava figured in the "Narrative of the United States Exploring Expedition."[1] A descent of more than four hundred feet brought us to the bottom, and we stepped from a gravelly shelving bank on to a black lava which had broken out last year under the north bank, and overflowed this end of the crater. Where it touched the gravel bank it had glued to its under surface the small fragments of stone, but had not altered their appearance, and all along the edge it was cracked, and laid up on the bank as

[1] *Narrative of United States Exploring Expedition*, vol. iv., p. 171.

if, on cooling, the lava had fallen about a foot. The surface was covered with a thin scaly vitreous crust, which crumbled beneath the tread, sounding like snow on a cold morning, and thus a very distinct path was made to the Halemáumau, the enduring house of the goddess Pélé. The lava beneath this crust, however, was so hard as to give out abundant sparks as the steel-nails in my shoes scraped upon it. When hard it was often iridescent, like some anthracite coal, and so closely resembling this mineral that the difference would hardly be detected on a cursory examination. The fresh lava exactly resembled that from Mauna Lòa in the flow of 1859. Three quarters of a mile over this uneven lava, and we came to a long wall of lava composed of fragments of all sizes and shapes, very solid and heavy and full of small grains of olivine; and this wall, which is concentric with the main wall of Kilauéa, is said to rise and fall and sometimes disappear, which seems to be a fact. although no one has ever seen it in motion. It is the fragments broken from the edge of the crater by an eruption and floated out to its present position. An unpractised eye would see no marks of fire on the rough granite-like masses. Caves, cracks, and ridges make the surface very uneven, and after walking two miles we came to several large cracks

Fig. 38. Halemáumau.

of great depth, but not more than a yard wide, and then a wall enclosing an amphitheatre down which we climbed on the loose slabs of lava.

The whole bottom of the crater is above what Prof. Dana describes as the Black Ledge, and although no fire is visible over the northern and eastern portion, steam constantly rises from many cracks, and the caves are often uncomfortably warm. When we were near the Halemáumau, we came to a cone formed of spattered lava and cemented scoriæ, some twenty-five feet high, with a bright light at its apex. This was the first fire we had seen, but we passed by, eager to reach the great lake. This we reached after ascending a gradual incline. It was about eight hundred feet in diameter, and the lava was fifty feet below the cliff on which we stood, covered with a dark crust which was broken around the edges, and there the blood-red lava was visible, surging against its walls with a dull, sullen sound. The smoke was blown away by the wind so that we were able to stand on the very verge of the pit; but the heat was so great that we were obliged to hold our hands before our faces.

The walls on which we stood, and where we intended to sleep, were thickly covered on the side towards the pit, with waving wooly Pélé's hair, which we saw forming continually. The drops of lava thrown up drew after them the glass thread, or sometimes two drops spin out a thread a yard long between them, and the "hair" thus formed either clings to the rough sides or is blown over the edge where it catches on any projecting point. The drops are always black, or a very dark green on the surface, but light green within, porous and excessively brittle, and the thread is transparent, and when first formed, of a yellow or greenish color. Occasionally a crack would open across the lake, and violent ebullition commence at various points along its surface. There were two small islands in the lake which the lava seemed seeking to destroy. The current would often set in toward the banks, and it appeared as if the whole lake was about to be drawn in, as cake after cake broke off from the surface and disappeared. But it would soon cease, and then run towards another point of the wall, and I could not see that it was oftener on one side than another. As a cake of lava parted from the crust the red lava rose above the crack, running on the surface, and as the crack grew wider, cooling rapidly, and being drawn out much like molasses candy. While white hot, the lava was as liquid as water, but it rapidly assumed the viscid condition, and then the solid. I threw a stick of dry wood on the surface the instant it became fixed after a violent bubbling, and it was ten minutes before any smoke was made, and it was only when a crack opened under it that it was consumed. The motion was always from the centre, except when the lava was thrown back in spray from the caverns which extended under much of the wall.

We laid down in our blankets on the eastern edge where the walls were highest, and the wind drove away the smoke, and soon fell asleep. About nine o'clock I got up and moved to the very edge of the pit to view the molten mass to better advantage, and warm myself, as the wind was quite cold. The moon was up and almost full, but her orb was pale beside the fires of Pélé. Finding the place quite comfortable, I lay down and went to sleep. At twelve I awoke with a start, and found myself in the midst of a shower of fiery drops, some of which were burning my blankets. I shook myself and jumped back, looking at my watch to note the time, for I thought a great eruption at hand, and then stood gazing at the strange scene for some time before I thought of calling my companions. The whole surface of the lake had risen several feet and was boiling violently and dashing against the sides, throwing the red-hot spray high over the banks, causing the providential rain of fire which awoke me to see this grand display. There was no noise except the dash and the sullen roar. When I could think of anything else, I called the others, who were asleep several rods from the edge, but only succeeded in awakening the guides, and just then a drop came plump on to a greasy paper we had brought our supper in, and it blazed up so suddenly that one of the kanakas thought a new jet was opening at our feet, and ran off to some distance. Failing to arouse my companions by calling, I threw a handful of small stones at them but without effect, and I had to climb down and shake them roughly. When they had got to the edge the action had greatly diminished, and in a few minutes more the dark crust again covered the central portion, and we all went to sleep.

I was glad to see such distinct flames, as it has been denied that they exist in Kilauéa. They burst from the surface and were in tongues or wide sheets a foot long and of a bluish-green color, quite distinct from the lava even when white-hot; they played over the whole surface at intervals, and I thought they were more frequent after one of the periodical risings of the surface in the pit.

In the morning we found it very misty, and the mist soon turned to rain, but we went to the cone we had seen the evening before, and climbing its sides looked into its red-hot mouth. It was nearly full of melted lava, but although we tossed in scoriæ we could not excite it. Another cone with several pinnacles called the "Cathedral" we did not visit, as no fire was visible, although smoke poured from it copiously. The rain caused steam to rise from the cracks over the whole surface of the crater, and we got quite wet, and our views were wholly cut off. At half-past seven we were in the saddle on the way to Hìlo, which was only twenty-nine miles distant, but the road was so rocky in some places and so muddy in others that we were obliged to walk our horses all the way, and it was twelve hours before we dismounted at the house of the excellent missionary who has done more than all others to record the volcanic phenomena which have taken place on Hawaii during the last thirty years. Kilauéa lies in Mr. Coan's district, and he passes its brink at least twice a year.

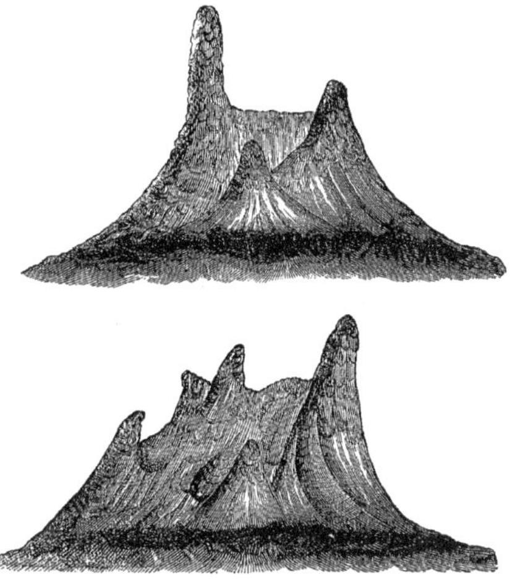

Figs. 39–40. The Cathedral in Kilauéa (——> West and North-east.)

On the second of August, 1865, I again visited Kilauéa, this time with Mr. C. W.
Brooks of San Francisco,[1] to make arrangements for a survey. The appearance was 1865.
much the same as last year, although the bottom had evidently risen, and several new cracks formed, while others had closed. The banks of the Halemáumau had changed considerably. The platform on which I slept before was gone, and the diameter was now at least a thousand feet. The islands had disappeared, and the lava was not more than thirty feet below the top of the bank. We went down in the crater in the evening, and fell asleep with the usual resolve to wake up now and then to enjoy the fire-works; but we were so weary with our tiresome ride from Hìlo, that we slept until after midnight, when a puff of sulphurous vapor from a crack under our heads, waked us up choking, and we beat a hasty retreat. In a few minutes, however, the gas ceased to blow, and after enjoying the changing fire of the lake for half an hour, we slept until five in the morning, when our guide advised us to return, as we were to breakfast on the upper bank some three miles distant. We went round by a new lake, which had opened during the winter on the northern side, near the bank. It was small, hardly two hundred feet long and fifty wide, but the melted lava was not more

[1] I was particularly glad to secure the company of Mr. Brooks, as he had visited the volcanic regions of Italy, and other parts of the world, and was well acquainted with their phenomena.

than a foot below the surface, so that we could work it with our sticks. It was blood-colored and very viscid, and exhibited the same motions as the larger lake, — the currents to the sides, and the cracking and bubbling, but on a much smaller scale. Fire was visible at night at various points between this and the Halemáumau. Near this lake my kanaka picked and brought me a poor *Rumex* which was growing in a steam crack on the hard black lava which had run over from this lake last winter.

The next night I slept on the upper bank, while several of our party spent the night in the crater. They could not approach the place where we had slept the night before, owing to the change of wind, and during the night the whole shelf fell in with a loud noise. This formed a small island which was soon broken and melted by the boiling lava.

August 22d, I returned to Kilauéa from Hìlo, having since my last visit explored the district of Púna, and the pit craters on the flow of 1840. I brought with me surveying instruments and a photographic apparatus, and after spending a day in selecting stations and drilling my kanakas in chaining, commenced the survey from the house on the northern bank. Going eastward the ground was covered with bushes and full of steam cracks which made chaining very difficult. Waldron's Ledge, so called after the purser of the United States Exploring Expedition, is a continuation of the wall which bounds the plain near the northern sulphur banks, and on meeting the crater's edge it turns to the east towards a large lateral crater called *Poli-o-Keàwe*,[1] enclosing this with a circular wall four thousand feet in diameter

Fig. 41. Poli-o-Keàwe from the Western bank of Kilauéa.

and deeper than the main crater at present. Descending the steep precipice we came upon the gravelly isthmus which connects the two craters. In the midst of this a lava stream issued in 1832, and ran down into both. Its appearance is still fresh, and where it descended into Kilauéa over a precipice of 60° and more than two hundred feet high, it has formed a fine lava-fall perfectly continuous, although for a short distance it is nearly perpendicular. It is hollow, and of small volume.

The ascent from this isthmus is not so steep on the southern side, and above, the soil is gravelly and barren, supporting but few plants. The wall of Kilauéa is much cracked and broken on this side and is also much lower. The second lateral crater, *Kilauéa iki*, on the

[1] This is the crater called Little Kilauéa on Wilkes' chart.

south-east is much smaller than Poli-o-Keàwe. Its walls are quite perpendicular on tne side towards Kilauéa, and the depth is greater than that of the main crater. The bottom is gravelly, level, and a small mound rises near the northern side. Near the edge of Kilauéa was a ledge of sandstone much split into parallel vertical plates, and evidently formed by the cementation of the volcanic sand common on the banks on this side. There were many curious circular depressions in the hard gravelly soil, about three feet in diameter and from six to eight inches deep, which I did not at first understand. I soon found that they were over cracks in the subjacent rock, and the sand, which is quite loose a foot below the surface, had settled into these small fissures, causing the depression in the sandstone above, which is almost as flexible as Itacolumite. There were evidences of severe showers over this plain, as the torrent channels were numerous and deep, and always emptied into the crater.

At the edge of Kilauéa iki, as it was late in the afternoon, my kanakas built a stone house to shelter the instruments, and we decided to cross Kilauéa as the easiest way home. We climbed down a steep gravel bank formed by the action of sulphurous vapors on the rock of the walls, crossed a small sulphur bed from which steam was issuing, and continued our way over the portion of Kilauéa which was overflowed the year before. It was very disagreeable walking, as the crust was quite thin and brittle, and we constantly cracked through, only a foot perhaps, but there was a constant feeling of insecurity, for we could not know but that the breaking crust covered a deep crack in the harder lava beneath. Half way across we found a cone three or four feet high covered with spatters of lava of various colors. Crossing the crater again the next morning in the rain we found it difficult to find our way owing to the steam, but finally reached the bank. It was two o'clock before the mist cleared away enough to permit the use of the theodolite. The large sulphur bank near this side of Kilauéa was of a bright green color owing to a large proportion of sulphate of protoxide of iron which seemed to be constantly forming. The sulphur is much of it in large amorphous masses, as if melted.

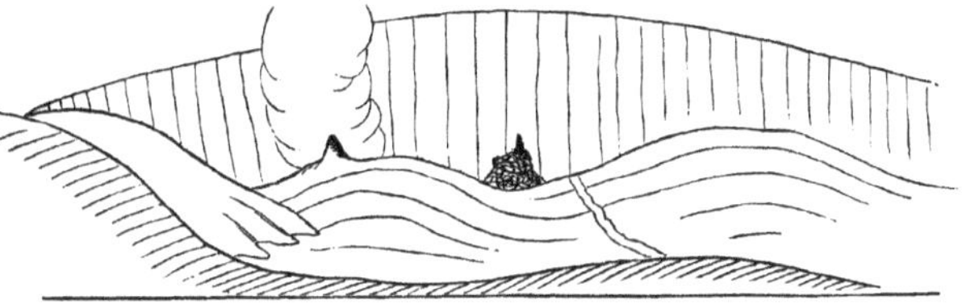

Fig. 42. Outline of the south end of Kilauéa.

The ground on this side of the crater is smooth, free from stones, and so terraced and sloped that it is difficult to define the boundaries of Kilauéa. As no rock is visible it is impossible to determine the direction of the disturbing forces, but the present condition of the bank seems to indicate a falling in of the wall in several places, probably over one or more of the subterranean streams that have deluged Púna. The soil of the mountain is thinner here than elsewhere, and most of the subterranean eruptions have forced their way through it, forming a line of craters to the sea. One of Wilkes' signal posts was found rotted off at the base, but otherwise sound.

On the south-west side the smoke from the Halemáumau was very suffocating, and I was obliged to pass through it with a wetted handkerchief to my face which was quickly dried by the smoke, which was wonderfully free from aqueous vapor. The ground was covered with Pélé's hair which collected on the leeward side of the ridges and stones, and also extensive beds of the Hawaiian pumice or "limu." This limu is identical with that seen on

Mauna Lòa, and is the froth of the burning lake. As the chain was drawn through it, the steel became completely polished. It was so loose that in one place I sank up to my waist in it. Stones and fragments of scoria were lying about apparently loose, but we found it almost impossible to break them off, so firmly were they cemented to the gravel rock below. The action of the sulphurous atmosphere soon dissolves the Pélé's hair, and this with the silica in the gravel itself makes a solid cement. There is an easy descent into the crater at the south-west end, and beyond this the nearly perpendicular rock wall again begins.

I reached the highest point on the Ka-ù road about dark, and sent home the instruments, while I followed slowly along the bank, watching the fires which were gleaming brightly seven hundred feet below. The new lake close beneath the bank was exceedingly beautiful, as it emitted but little smoke, and constantly cracked and broke up its crust, forming an everchanging network of fire. A line of fires was burning all the way between the two lakes, but the level of the new one is more than fifty feet below the old.

Saturday it was rainy and impossible to obtain sights with the instruments, so I went into Kilauéa to explore the caves. The Halemáumau was not in a very lively condition, and passing beyond that, I went into a cave of considerable extent, where the curious siliceous tubes had formed on the rock roof, and obtained many of these fragile specimens some of which were coated with beautiful white crystals. This cave was more than fifty feet below the level of the melted lava in the lake, and the walls did not seem very secure. A lava stream had recently poured into the mouth of the cave, but there were no vapors, nor any uncomfortable heat. Taking advantage of a change of wind, I passed around the lake, and ascended a cone with two peaks formed by lava spatters, but completely closed on the top, as nearly all the others in the crater were, and found steam hissing from many apertures. On breaking off the crust beautiful crystals of various salts were found thickly coating the under surface, and in one place we found much nitrate of potassa. I went from cave to cave, from cone to cone, collecting various kinds of lava and several salts, and finished by a bath in a steam cave, where the steam issued from the floor at an agreeable temperature, and condensed on the roof, falling in rain. The water was quite sweet, and no smell of sulphur was noticeable in the cave. On the roof the little tube stalactites were constantly forming by the solution of the silica in the rock above, and I broke off the brittle, twisted tubes sometimes a foot long. On the floor the drops have made stalagmites of various forms.[1] This steam bath was most delightful after the smoking I had just experienced in a cave where the end was red-hot, and into which my natives did not dare to go.

Sunday was the first bright day I had had, and the pulu[2] pickers from the neighboring region came to my hut after the morning service, and told me the names of the various parts of the crater, and legends of ancient eruptions. Monday was again rainy, but I completed my measurements, and in the evening made a series of observations to determine the declination of the magnetic needle. The electric currents in the lava and the large quantity of iron in the rock, made strange work with the compass ; I have seen the needle suddenly turn through an arc of forty degrees. The variation of declination will be

[1] I shall refer more particularly to these stalactite caves, when describing the minerals.

[2] Pulù is the silky covering of the opening fronds of several species of tree ferns, and is exported in large quantities to California for beds, &c.

seen in the table on another page. The remainder of the week was too cloudy to take photographs, and I was reluctantly obliged to send back my instruments, and return to Hìlo.

In May, 1866, Kilauéa commenced a series of discharges all over the surface of the crater which were still in operation in August. New lakes of fire opened along a **1866.** curve north-west to north of the great lake of Lua Pélé, flooding all that portion of the crater with fresh lava, and reaching even to the sulphur-banks on the southern side of the plain, in a stream about four miles long and from an eighth to half of a mile wide, cutting off for much of this time the usual entrance to the crater. This whole portion of Kilauéa now flooded was about fifty feet below the central area; it is now at least a hundred feet higher than it was last year, but the central plateau has also risen, and the relative height is about the same. The whole appearance of the crater has however changed. The ledge of compact broken lava, which swept around the eastern end of the crater, marking the limits of Dana's Black Ledge, is nearly covered with the successive overflowings, and the caves which formed so interesting a feature of this portion of the crater are filled and obliterated.

The throes and detonations caused large blocks to fall from the outer walls, and the heaving of the intensely active flood at their base soon removed the débris, thus showing the method in which pit craters may be enlarged horizontally. Travellers who visited Kilauéa while this eruption lasted, speak of the hissings and spoutings, the subterranean rumblings and detonations, as terrific. In August the force of the eruption seemed to be spent, but no subterranean outflow was perceived, and the crater remains full of broken and hard lava. A few more such eruptions will raise the bottom to a level with the upper walls, and Kilauéa will cease to exist as a Pit Crater.

Craters south-east of Kilauéa.[1] The cone craters near Kapóho on the coast of Púna have been described. The same line of volcanic action extends to Kilauéa, and seems to mark the position of an extensive rent in the side of the mountain. No foreigner has well explored this region of craters, as the jungle is almost impenetrable; and the Rev. T. Coan was the first who discovered the craters near the eruption of 1840. Dr. Charles Pickering extended his explorations to a greater distance, and mapped out some of the craters which were afterwards verified by Captain Wilkes. More than fifty cones and pit craters, some of the latter of remarkable size, have been seen, and the number will probably exceed a hundred when the whole district shall be well explored.

The passage through this way has been exceedingly difficult, until the last few years, when the business of picking and exporting pulu has become so important, that paths have been cut by the pulu-pickers, and several stations established for their convenience. The great similarity of the cones and craters in this region, and the fact that they are all formed in the same lava-beds, renders a particular description unnecessary, and I will content myself with a brief account of a journey through the part of the forest where the largest are placed.

Here and there on the way from the coast at Panaù we passed lava streams. Ohia-trees were growing on these, thin and tall, suggestive of Alpine regions; indeed, I have seen precisely such forests on the Swiss mountains, and there was a peculiar grace, which, while pleasing the eye, yet conveyed the idea of a struggle for existence amid the storms which

[1] There is a fine chart of the Púna craters among the maps of the Exploring Expedition.

sweep the rocky slopes of Mauna Lòa. At the height of eighteen hundred feet we entered the fern forest. The fruit of the *Physalis* and *Vaccinium* was abundant, and sandal-wood was occasionally met with at an elevation of two thousand feet. As we came to the fern region, we turned into a path cut through the jungle, and, as the soil was a soft black mould, it had been paved with the stems of tree ferns, which are about six inches in diameter. This "corduroy road" was constructed with great labor by the natives, and we calculated that forty thousand pieces of fern were used to build it. The ferns are cut in lengths of six feet, and many of them sprout and make a green edging to the roadway. This path led through the most tropical region I had seen on Hawaii. Tree ferns whose stems were fifteen feet high to the base of the fronds, and eight to twelve inches in diameter, were mingled with *Myrsine*, *Byronia*, *Pelea*, *Ilex*, and *Metrosideros*, while over all, the long leaves of the *Ié* (*Freycinetia arborea*), the dark glossy green *mailé* (*Alyxia olivaeformis*), and mosses in great abundance covered the stems and branches, and hung in long graceful festoons.

Nearly two miles through this, and we came to a tract of pahoehoe, and here was the pulu station to which the roads had been cut. This is the present residence of a remarkable native who has leased this whole district for the pulu business, — Kaina, the district judge. His house was directly on the line of craters, and only a few rods from steam cracks where his men cooked their food. It was well built, and surrounded with a substantial stone wall. The interior was furnished with bedsteads, rocking-chairs, and other conveniences; and our supper-table was supplied with fresh wheaten bread, milk, butter, eggs, and delicious berries.

West of the house was a large open field where the silky golden fibre of the pulu is dried before packing, and beyond, in the woods, I found curious tubes of lava on an ancient flow, one of which was seven feet high, eighteen inches external diameter, and with a bore of eight inches. It was brittle, and on breaking it off, I found the hole was six feet deep, making its whole length thirteen feet. Others of the same height were near by, and their sides were always thicker towards the source of the flow. Externally they are rough, and look spattered, but the top was smooth, and sometimes projected like an umbrella. Where several were in close proximity, a slab of lava was supported like a roof on columns. The lining of the tube was smooth, and much more compact and vitreous than the exterior. The trees which served as cores have entirely decayed, and were mostly tree ferns, although I think that I detected some ohias. I followed the stream down some distance to ascertain the cause of its subsidence, which must have been rapid, and found that a fissure had opened and swallowed most of the lava. Judging from the great size of the trees over its surface the flow must be quite ancient.

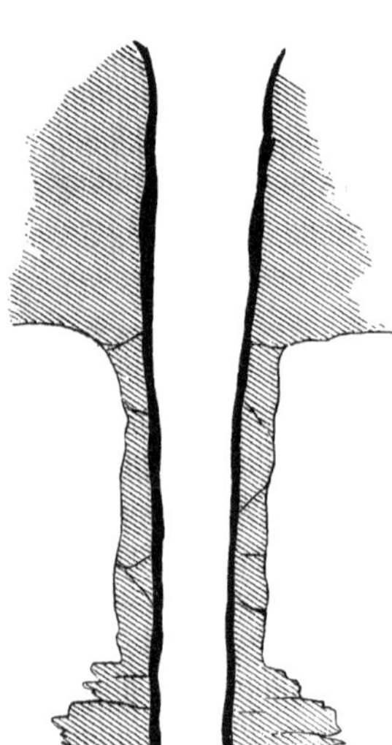

Fig. 43. Tree-casts in a lava stream.

Tuesday I went with my boy Ioane to explore the woods. As I followed a path made by the pulu-pickers through the dense forest, I came upon a large hole on the edge of the path which proved to be the entrance to a cave of great depth. The path had been turned to one side to avoid it, and in the dark it would be exceedingly dangerous. Such holes are common in this part of Púna, and natives occasionally disappear mysteriously. Brushing through the bushes I came to a precipice forming the edge of a crater nearly three quarters of a mile in diameter and seven hundred feet deep. The sides were quite perpendicular, and in

Fig. 44. Pit Crater in Púna.

most places impassable. The bottom was level and gravelly, with a thin growth of ohia, and at the western end, directly under the wall, was a much deeper pit, indeed the deepest I have seen on Hawaii. Beyond this was a cone of some size, near which the eruption of 1840 reached the surface first, passing under the cone; (see Fig. 44). Half a mile beyond this is another pit crater, smaller, and covered on the bottom with black lava. Following the line down in a south-easterly direction, I came to the steam cracks, which extend for several hundred feet, and since tradition existed have furnished the natives of the neighborhood with the means of cooking. The pahoehoe has been decomposed into a soft red muddy soil, covered with a hard crust, which may be raised in slabs. Under these are most beautiful crystals of sulphur in clusters, but of too fragile a nature to be removed.

Beyond these cracks was a much larger crater, being elliptical, with a major axis a mile long, and about five hundred feet deep. The perpendicular walls were prismatic in various places, and at the west end were rent asunder, affording an easy descent to the bottom, which was gravelly, level, and free from cracks or holes. The walls of all the craters were compact gray clinkstone in deep strata, like the walls of Kilauéa, and no recent lava was visible. Several dykes were seen at right angles to a line from Kilauéa to Kapóho.

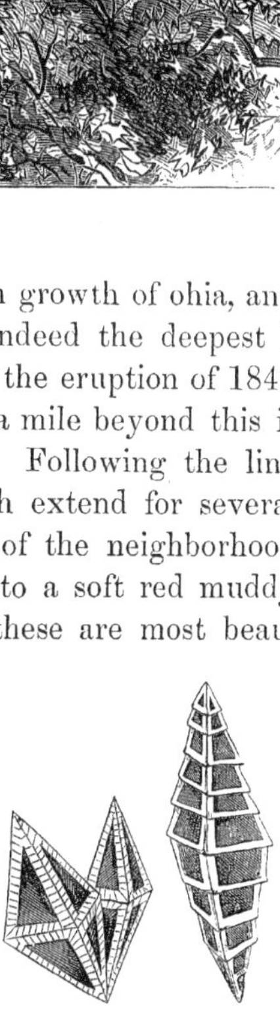

Fig. 45. Sulphur crystals.

Periodicity of Eruptions on Hawaii.

Our knowledge of the Hawaiian volcanoes covers too short a period of their history to determine with any certainty the laws which regulate the discharges. The following table contains all the eruptions that have occurred since the discovery of the Islands: —

Kilauéa.	Mauna Lòa.	Mauna Hualalaì.
1789.		
1798? No record.		
		1801.
1806? No record.		
1814? No record.		
1823.		
1832.	1832.	
1840.		
	1843.	
1849? Subterranean.		
	[1851. 1852.]	
	1855.	
1858? Subterranean.		
	1859.	
1866.	1866.	

It will be seen that while Kilauéa fills up and breaks out in about eight years, Mauna Lòa has poured out lava streams at intervals of eleven, eight, three, four, and seven years. The action of Kilauéa indicates a constant and regular supply of lava, which accumulates to about the same height and then flows off. In Mauna Lòa the action is nearly as regular, if we consider the different elevations from which the discharge takes place. At Kilauéa it is always about three thousand feet above the sea, as the reservoir of lava subsides to this level, but on Mauna Lòa the discharges have been at thirteen thousand feet or a little below the bottom of the summit crater, nine years after at the same elevation, which afterwards changed to ten thousand feet, thus draining the mountain three thousand feet lower than the last, and requiring three years to fill up to twelve thousand feet, the height of the next outbreak, which continued to flow eighteen months; four years after at the height of eleven thousand five hundred feet, and finally after seven years of repose, at the height of twelve thousand five hundred feet.

Usually the eruptions from the several vents have been quite independent, and only twice, in 1832 and 1866, have they been simultaneous. The intervals of neither mountain seem to be increasing, and we learn from native tradition that since the island was peopled by the Hawaiians, some two thousand years since, eruptions have taken place with about the present frequency at Kilauéa.

Volume of Lava ejected.

1823	Kilauéa		27,000,000,000	cubic feet.
1840	"	Exploring Expedition	15,400,000,000	" "
1843	Mauna Lòa	These are estimated roughly, as the flows have never been surveyed or measured.	17,000,000,000	" "
1852	" "		18,000,000,000	" "
1855	" "		38,096,000,000	" "
1859	" "		28,560,000,000	" "

The other eruptions were either subterraneous, or no sufficient data exist for an estimate. The volume of a discharge of Kilauéa is probably pretty constant.

Review of the Hawaiian Eruptions.

The eruptions that have been recorded on the Hawaiian Islands are then as follows: —

I In 1789 an eruption from Kilauéa, not seen by any foreigner. It was accompanied by ejections of black sand and great volumes of hot sulphureous gases, both from the crater itself, and from fissures on a south-east line between Kilauéa and the sea. The earthquakes were violent in the neighborhood, and nearly a hundred men lost their lives by the hot and poisonous gases.

II. In 1801 Mauna Hualalaì poured forth from near the summit a torrent of lava which filled up a deep bay, and changed the whole aspect of the coast.

III. In 1823 Kilauéa emptied itself by a subterranean outlet which reached the surface some miles south of the crater, and poured a torrent of lava through the district of Ka-ù. The stream is nearly five miles wide where it entered the sea near Kápapala.

IV. In 1832 both Kilauéa and Mokuawéowéo were active. In Kilauéa the lava broke out on the narrow neck of rock between the main crater and Poli-o-Keàwe, in the spot where Lord Byron had encamped some years before, and flowed down into both craters. The amount of lava ejected here was small. The lavas were previously fifty feet above the Black Ledge of Ellis, and between June and September had fallen some hundred feet. It is not known where the lava reached the sea. June 20th, Mauna Lòa was pouring forth lava from the summit in every direction, and continued in action for two or three weeks. The light was visible at Lahaìna.

V. In 1840 Kilauéa emptied itself in a south-east direction through the district of Púna. The stream of lava reached the sea at Nanawálie, a distance of forty miles, in four days. Owing to the exceeding roughness of the country the depth varied from twelve to two hundred feet, and the width from five hundred feet to three miles. For two weeks the light was so brilliant, that at Hìlo and places forty miles distant, the finest print could be easily read at midnight.

VI. In 1843 Mauna Lòa broke out near the summit. Two large craters were formed, and two streams of lava poured out from fissures, one flowing westward, towards Kóna, and the other and larger one towards Mauna Kéa on the north a distance of nearly thirty miles, when it divided, one branch turning towards Waiméa, and the other towards Hìlo. This eruption continued nearly four weeks.

VII. In 1852 an eruption broke forth on the north side of Mauna Lòa, shooting up great jets from two to five hundred feet high.

VIII. In 1855 an eruption took place from the same vicinity. It continued for about thirteen months, pouring a stream of lava down the mountain slopes for sixty miles and covering nearly three hundred square miles.

IX. In 1859 another eruption took place from Mauna Lòa, throwing up fountains of lava as in 1852, and, after flowing some forty miles, poured into the sea at Wainanalíi.

X. In 1866 both Kilauéa and Mauna Lòa were active, the latter pouring out several small streams of lava.

Theoretical Formation of the Hawaiian Group.

In describing the various islands of the group, slight allusion has been made to the theory of their formation, because it was necessary to compare each with all, and especially to examine the active formative processes now going on in some portions of Hawaii. The external appearance of all the islands and their physical history in recent times, so far as known, have been carefully though rapidly reviewed, and it now remains to trace back the history of this group as completely as may be from the record referred to.

Formative and destructive agencies have worked in succession, and together, to bring the islands to their present condition, and are both still at work on Hawaii. On the other islands the volcanic forces which raised their mountains have ceased to act, and only the destroying forces of the atmosphere alter the external features of the land. It is with the formative processes we have to deal principally, and we may first consider the phases of volcanic action here exhibited.

The linear direction of volcanic action has long been a recognized fact in geology, and the Hawaiian Islands are fine examples of the result of such action, but it is difficult to determine the extent of the original fissures from which their lines of volcanoes were ejected. According to one theory there are two fissures extending from north-west to south-east, one commencing with Waíaleale, and including Konahuanùi, Olokùi, Háleakala, Kohála, and Kéa; the other closely adjacent, reaching from Kaàla to Kilauéa, including the remaining peaks. The other and more probable theory supposes a west-north-west main fissure, with lateral subordinate fissures.

Prof. Dana considers "that there were as many separate rents in the origin of the Hawaiian Islands as there are islands. That each rent was widest at its south-east portion. That the south-easternmost rent was the largest, the fires continuing there longest to burn. That the correct order of extinction of the great volcanoes is therefore nearly as follows: —

"1. Kauaì.
"2. Western Oáhu, Mauna Kaàla.
"3. Western Máui, Mauna Eéka.
"4. Eastern Oáhu, Mauna Konahuanùi.
"5. North-eastern Hawaii, Mauna Kéa.
"6. South-eastern Máui, Mauna Háleakala.
"7. South-eastern Hawaii, Mauna Lòa."[1]

A more extended exploration than Prof. Dana had the opportunity of making, completely confirms this view, enlarging the series as follows: —

1. Western Kauaì, Napàli, (Púuokapélé region).
2. Western Oáhu, Mauna Kaàla.
3. Eastern Kauaì, Waíaleale.
4. Western Molokaì.
5. Western Máui, Mauna Eéka.
6. North-western Hawaii, Mauna Kohála.
7. Eastern Oáhu, Mauna Konahuanùi.
8. Eastern Molokaì, Mauna Olokùi.

[1] *Geol. United States Exploring Expedition*, p. 282.

9. North-eastern Hawaii, Mauna Kéa.
10. Lanai, Kahooláwe.
11. Eastern Máui, Mauna Háleakala.
12. Western Hawaii, Mauna Hualalaì.
13. Eastern Hawaii, Mauna Lòa, which with Kilauéa is still burning.

These have been arranged in both lists in accordance with the extent of degradation exhibited, and they comprise the whole series of volcanic vents which have formed the group. Niihau, I believe to have been a portion of Napàli on Kauaì, and Kahooláwe and Molokìni are but subordinate coast craters, or possibly the former is a portion of Lanai.

Kauaì. — In describing Kauaì, I mentioned the remarkable similarity in structure and appearance, between the western precipice of Napàli and the eastern cliffs of Niihau. The strata, so far as examined, correspond, and I cannot but consider the two islands parts of the same.[1] Some vast disruptive force has torn it from its original position and moved it twenty miles without any considerable disturbance of its strata. I own that the force seems improbably great, but we know that Háleakala, a mountain of much greater bulk, was rent asunder, and a segment moved more than two miles, and even greater breaks are supposed to have occurred on Oáhu.

The history of the Kauaì group I suppose to have been this: The original vents from two centres of action poured forth their lava until two mountains were formed in close proximity; the double axis of Oáhu, Molokaì, and Máui, was here also, but instead of ceasing to eject lava when the mountains were completed, there succeeded a period of intense activity, — possibly prior to the formation of a new vent on some of the other islands, — the mountains were broken up forming the ridges of Maunas Kalaléa, Nóunou, Kápu, and the Kolòa Ridge, — a gigantic Somma, — while the lavas again piled up two mountains on the ruins, the eastern one being the larger, as on the other biaxial islands. This will be rendered clearer by reference to the diagram, which is drawn in proportion. The line *a d* in No. I. will represent the base of the two mountains as originally formed, while *xx* will denote the lava ducts. No. II. is a section of the island after the first mountains have been broken up and the shore ridges formed; and No. III. is the present section, L representing the coast of Napàli, and N that of Niihau. In the second section the base line *a d* is represented as equalling that at present plus the distance L *a* which is the breadth of Niihau. The circumference has increased but little since the shore ridges were formed.

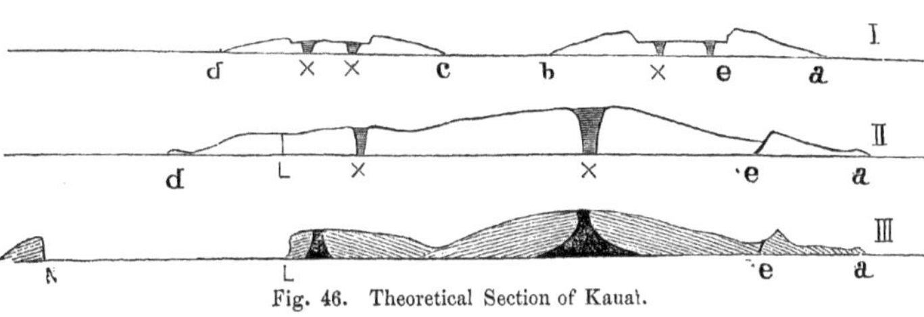

Fig. 46. Theoretical Section of Kauaì.

The strata of these shore ridges all exhibit a dip towards the sea from the mountain, exceeding that of Waíaleale, and are undoubtedly older, as lava beds from the latter have penetrated their cracks. Dykes occur in the ridges in various places, always radial from the

[1] The natives have a tradition that two of their gods were once fishing on the two extremes of Oáhu, and that their lines and hooks became entangled on the west coast of Kauaì, and the gods pulled so hard as to drag Niihau some distance before the lines broke.

centre Waíaleale, and numerous breaks, so extensive as to divide the chain into several apparently distinct ridges, have the same direction.

The lavas did not reach the surface in a single vent over each axis, as on Háleakala, Mauna Lòa, Kilauéa or Kéa, but were distributed in a number of craters, several of which were simultaneously active as on Hualalaì and Kohála.

The solid, unstratified axis of Waíaleale is a cone with a greater diameter in proportion to its height than that of either Kaàla, Konahuanùi or Eéka, indicating either an intenser heat or a longer period of activity. From the greater horizontal extent of this solid core, Kauaì retains more moisture on the surface and has thus become more decomposed through the superficial strata that mark the successive overflows of lava; and its compact summit, almost constantly bathed in clouds, collects and retains enough water to form swamps and springs, the sources of large and constant streams whose rapidly descending currents are still enlarging the ravines and valleys they have hollowed out on all sides of the mountain. Vegetation has been promoted, and in turn has decomposed the rock, forming earth which will retain water, so that now, from the base to the summit, Waíaleale is clothed with verdure, and its middle slopes are covered with large and ancient forests. In taking denudation as an index of age, regard must of course be had to the material acted upon. The greater the height, and the steeper the slope, the more transporting and wearing power will the water have; the more compact the rock the more water will be retained to form streams; and if the rock in the upper regions is easily detached in blocks, a grinding and cutting machine is supplied of which water is only the motive power. As the hard boulders cut out the pot-holes in the bed of a stream, so the rough, freshly broken masses of hard basalt from which the rounded boulders are formed, cut and tear away the softer strata which have been in succession the surface of the mountain, and even cut deeply into the very core which is composed of their own material. The rock of the summit of Waíaleale is a very hard clinkstone, which is brought down in the numerous torrents, and is found in rounded boulders blocking the bed in the mile or so of nearly level course near the shore. The erosion is almost visible from day to day, clearly from year to year. On Mauna Lòa the rock is porous, the core is not proportionally thick, and the rains form no single stream, and of course there are no water-worn valleys.

The beach sandstones near Hanaleì are buried from eighteen to twenty-four inches beneath the surface by the deposit of the river which extends over many square miles, but this is the only case on the island where anything like a delta is formed by fluvial deposits. Even during the storms, when the streams are swollen and the bed is worn away to a considerable extent, the waters are not remarkably muddy, and they become quite clear as soon as the freshet begins to subside.

The evidences of elevation on Kauaì are by no means so satisfactory as on Oáhu. The so-called *raised reef* near Kolòa, I am satisfied, is only a consolidated dune of coral sand; and all the sandstones on the shores may easily have been formed in their present positions. The fact that the water near the shores is becoming shallower, only shows that the deposits washed down from the mountains are not removed by the waves as fast as they form. I did not see any marks of subsidence.

The interior elevated regions of Kauaì will doubtless reveal to the future explorer many interesting geological facts; no other island of the group promises so much, but like northern Hawaii the rank vegetation and difficult ridges and ravines make the exploration no easy task. From the reports of natives, we learn that there is much very fertile land on the plateaus which might be rendered accessible by roads cut through the thicket. Should the islands ever be annexed to the United States, American enterprise, with American capital, will doubtless utilize these now savage and deserted tracts.

Oáhu. — As on Kauaì, the lava has issued from two centres, but the vents were not clustered around two points, thus forming a symmetrical peak, but are arranged in two lines parallel to the general trend of the group; resulting in two mountain chains.

At some period of its history Oáhu must have suffered from vast forces tending to rend its mountains, which however acted in a quiet way as when Mauna Lòa is broken to admit the passage of lava. The result has been a detachment of a portion of the northern slope of the eastern or Konahuanùi ridge, and this fragment has wholly disappeared. I cannot with Prof. Dana consider the missing portion so large that the remaining mountain is but a small part of the original mass. He had never seen the line of craters extending through fifteen miles along the centre of the Konahuanùi Range. Kaneóhe Point was perhaps the immediate result of the great rupture; the engulfed portion has made shoal water to the distance of a mile and a half from the shore, and the lavas from the crack piled up the craters of Kaneóhe and the various islands along the coast.

Sinking Oáhu two hundred feet makes a very great change in its topography, and seems to explain many puzzles. There are then two islands; the cliffs almost perpendicular on the Koolaù side are washed by the waves that drive against them on the windward side; the rounded cones of Kóko are under the waves, and Leáhi is an island half a mile from shore; the currents and winds strike its tufa walls, and it is slowly washed away on the windward side. On the south of the island of Konahuanùi is a series of deep bays from Palòlo valley to beyond Kalìhi, on the west. Puawaìna is on the shore, while Aliapaakaì is almost submerged, its material being swept away by the currents to form the extensive shoal of Laelóa. The Kaàla mountains form an island similar in most respects to the Konahuanùi, but being on the lee side are less exposed to marine erosion.

What are the indications that this picture of Oáhu is outlined from fact? The rounded cones of Kóko are perhaps a more striking proof than even the raised coral reef which extends nearly around the island. That tufa cones are sometimes thrown up on land with a rounded summit I do not deny; but a crater is always present in such cases. Even the winds and meteoric influences generally do not obliterate it; submarine currents alone do that when the cone is growing, or at least before it has become cemented by meteoric influences. The plain between the two ridges is however the most conclusive proof. Fine natural sections are exhibited in the bed of the several streams which traverse it in very winding courses, and there we see broad beds of alluvial deposit of uniform thickness, which were undoubtedly formed beneath the water. Above these however are irregular bands of varying thickness extending to the surface, evidently subaërial in their formation. Indeed, every severe storm adds to their number, when the mountain torrents invade the plain and tear away from one portion to pile upon another, or break down from the mountains by other than their usual routes, carrying with them earth and rocks. The upper level of the submarine beds is from a hundred to a hundred and seventy-five feet above the sea. Fragments of coral are found in them, and a careful search would probably reveal shells.

The erosion of the sea-walls of Puawaìna and Leáhi, the former now some distance from the shore, can hardly be due to pluvial influences alone; the material of Puawaìna is too evenly spread over the elevated reef which forms the foundation of the city of Honolulu. I am much inclined to the belief that Oáhu has been elevated nearly two hundred feet since the coast craters were formed.

Whether this elevation was gradual and long continued, or spasmodic and extensive, is not easily determined, for the steps in the ancient elevated reef which would seem to indicate the latter, may have been formed by subsequent earthquakes, and there are no distinct terraces or ancient beaches to be traced around the island. Molokaì is the only other island which bears evident signs of elevation, and on examining these two islands, it seemed as if the axis of Konahuanùi was not vertical but inclined towards the north-north-west; or that the island of Oáhu had been raised at the south-eastern end nearest Molokaì much higher than at the opposite side. On Molokaì the appearance was still stronger, but owing to the removal of nearly the whole of the windward slope on both islands it is perhaps impossible to determine by measùrement whether this inclination of the mountain axis really exists. Certainly one shore appears to have been elevated more than the other. Possibly the eruption which cracked Konahuanùi and opened the Nuuánu and Manóa craters, formed Leáhi and the other coast craters, and inaugurated the elevation of the island.

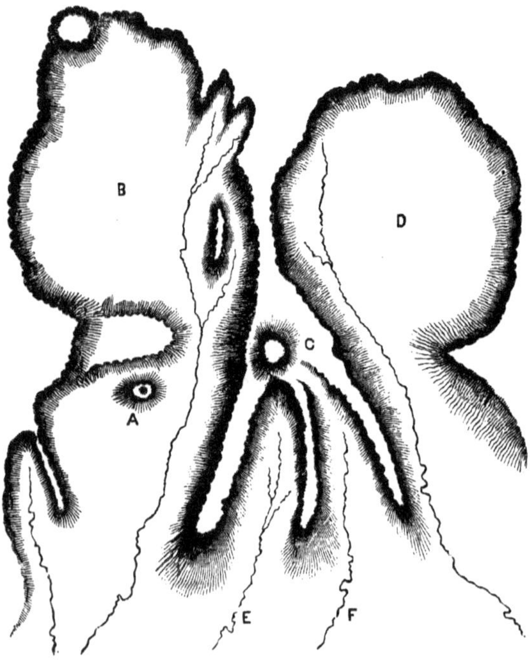

Map of the Valleys near Honolulu.

A, small cone in Nuuánu; B, circus of Nuuánu Valley; C, smooth conical peak; D, Manóa Valley; E, stream from Pauóa Valley; F, stream from Makiki Valley.

The lineal arrangement of craters has not been before noticed on Oáhu; indeed, few explorers have had the time required to scale the sharp ridges and penetrate the dense jungle of the valleys. Manóa and Nuuánu have already been referred to as craters, and their shape will readily be seen from the sketch-map (Fig. 6), where B represents Nuuánu, D Manóa. Precisely similar to these are the valleys west of Kalìhi, and at Punalúu a complete cone crater is found. The nature of the Konahuanùi Range precludes the possibility of a longitudinal path, and the explorer must ascend every lateral ridge, a toilsome journey.

On the Kaàla Ridge many of the ancient craters are now marshes or ponds, and the same is true of Konahuanùi to a less extent.

Earthquake throes usually vibrate from the mountains to the sea on all sides of Oáhu, perhaps indicating a solid axis over a fissure not yet wholly cut off from internal commotions.

Molokaì. — This island was formed much in the same way as Oáhu, by the union of the overflows of two linear vents. The western part never attained the dimensions of a mountain, and bears many tokens of having been wholly formed beneath the sea, while the eastern Mauna Olokùi has suffered a fracture similar to Konahuanùi. The precipice left by the rending apart of the mountain is steep and like that of Koolaù, and at the bottom is a plain of pahoehoe containing many cones and craters of comparatively recent origin. Like Oáhu, Molokaì has been elevated above the sea considerably, probably from three to five hundred feet.

Lanai. — While Oáhu, Molokaì, and Hawaii present high precipices to the windward side, Lanai slopes from a vertical wall on the lee side, that is to say, a break has occurred nearly parallel with that on Oáhu, but in this case the opposite side has fallen. No series of soundings have been made off these islands, but the water is deep, and the break seems to extend some distance below the surface; but this is mere conjecture.

Máui. — Much like Kaàla at its western end, Máui in its great Háleakala closely resembles Mauna Lòa. Eéka is much broken through, and its ancient craters are now extensive valleys. The whole mountain is so pierced that a tunnel a quarter of a mile in length would connect the two sides.

Hawaii. — The formation of this island has been traced in the successive outpouring of its lava-streams, and we may turn at once to the consideration of the action of lava as exhibited in the volcanoes of this group.

Lava as a formative Agent.

The lava rises to the surface and overflows, forming a bed of lava of a thickness proportionate to the level of the ground; the action is always intermittent, and as it diminishes the lava cools; another discharge increases the thickness of the layer, and where following the first without the intervention of scoriæ, ashes, or decomposition, may unite completely with it, forming one bed. Where scoriæ intervene, the two deposits are separated by a distinct line. In this way we may have beds of eighty or a hundred feet in thickness, and as the surface around the discharge is at first tolerably level, or has been made so by subsequent eruptions, the lava will flow in all directions slowly, and form such uniform beds as are seen in many places on the islands. Discharge succeeds discharge, and the mountain is raised up around the orifice from which the lava flows. As the lavas are liquid, they will flow away from the central opening, forming a gentle slope quite unlike the cinder cones, where the material must remain nearly where ejected, until the angle of its sides becomes too steep to retain additions. Consequently while cinder cones may have an angle of 40°, lava cones seldom exceed 10°. The specific gravity of the lava exercises a considerable influence in determining the angle at which its streams will consolidate, and thus the slope of the mountain. The Hawaiian lavas contain much iron and augite, and the dome formed is quite flat.[1]

Each succeeding stream melts into the previous ones, unless a bed of cinders or soil interposes their non-conducting properties, and in some cases I have seen recent flows so united with the beds through which they pass, as to render it quite impossible to detect the point where one ended and the other commenced. The more rapid the motion of a lava-stream,

[1] See Scrope *on Volcanos*, p. 131.

the deeper it burns into the subjacent rock, acting, if I may use the comparison, like a soldering iron which may often be held against a stick of solder for some time without melting it, when the motion of rubbing would liquefy the metal at once. Examples have been mentioned where this action of a rapidly moving stream has melted into the lava beds over which it passed, to the depth of even two hundred feet. This was the case in the long-continued flow of 1855 from Mauna Lòa, and the apparent fissures are often as much the result of this action as of a forcing apart of the mountain side, and they often mark the site of a future valley.

Each overflow from the central vent will form a rib or buttress covering a segment of the mountain more or less extensive, imparting a vast strength to the walls and permitting the rise of the lava within, until its pressure breaks through the walls and escapes in a lateral eruption. These side outflows are of frequent occurrence in various volcanic domes, and may arise from a rending of the whole mountain, — or the opening of a small fissure; in the former case strengthening the wall by an interlacing dyke, in the latter usually rendering it cavernous. All the recent discharges from Mauna Lòa have been of the latter kind, and occur at nearly the same elevation. A small fissure opens, which gradually widens as the flow progresses, until the stream leaps forth in its full strength. It is a noticeable fact, that never has the rending of the mountain been perceived by earthquakes or tremblings. "A small beacon fire" announces the opening of a *small* crack, which opens as gently as the cracks in drying clay.

The eruption of 1840 from Kilauéa made a more extensive crack, and no subsequent eruption has taken the same direction.

Within the mountain the tube of lava which supplies the summit crater, protected in great measure from a loss of heat by the outer wall, melts during its periods of activity into the sides of the mountain, becoming a conical reservoir of lava which will have a greater or less diameter at its base in proportion to its activity.

It is probable that a mass of melted lava, fluid and comparatively quiet, will experience a change in composition at different levels, by a separation of the different minerals mechanically united in its mass, according to their different specific gravities. Thus trachyte and the feldspar lavas, will, owing to their low specific gravities, rise to the top, and the heavier augitic lavas fall towards the bottom. The specific gravity of trachyte is 2.4 – 2.62, while that of augite is 3.23 – 3.5, a difference quite sufficient to cause a separation if other circumstances admit.[1] That the top of the cone will be all trachyte and the bottom all basalt must not be supposed, for the constant currents prevent a complete separation, and all varieties and all proportions of admixture will be found at different heights. This is the view taken by Mr. Darwin,[2] as well as by Prof. Jukes and Mr. Scrope.

After a separation of this nature, which doubtless requires time, if the lavas rise and overflow the edge, trachytic streams will be poured out; and in support of this view we find that all the summits of the Hawaiian volcanoes are more or less trachytic, or at least feldspathic.

1 See Scrope *on Volcanos*, p. 110.

The specific gravity of volcanic minerals is as follows: —

Mineral		Specific gravity
Orthoclase	Feldspar	2.4 — 2.62.
Albite	Feldspar	2.59 — 2.65.
Oligoclase	Feldspar	2.58 — 2.69.
Leucite		2.483 — 2.49.
Quartz		2.5 — 2.8.
Mica (hexagonal)		2.7 — 3.1.
Hornblende		2.9 — 3.4.
Augite		3.23 — 3.5.
Garnet		3.15 — 4.3.
Olivine		3.33 — 3.5.
Hæmatite		4.5 — 5.3.

2 Volcanic Islands, pp. 118–124.

If a break occurs near the base the lavas will contain more augite, as the lava-stream which formed Aliapaakaĭ on Oáhu, where crystals of augite are quite common. Intermediate vents will pour out a lava of a mixed composition, and of this nature are most of the Hawaiian lavas. But this is the rule only when an eruption has been preceded by a long period of rest.

It is a mistake to adopt the theory that formerly trachytic, and now basaltic lavas are ejected. In many volcanoes basaltic underlie trachytic, and lavas of all gradations between the two are found at different ages of the same volcano.

There is another cause of the variety of eruptions from the same mountain, in the separation of minerals of different fusibility. Ferruginous minerals may be volatilized, leaving in one place a lava destitute of iron, while in another the lava is highly ferruginous; or they may line the cavities of the upper mass with specular iron ore, as at Elba.

M. Daubrée has shown that the concurrent influence of heat and pressure will form crystals of augite, feldspar, quartz and mica from water containing alkaline silicates in solution with common clay;[1] and it is not at all improbable that the frequent melting and hardening, the great heat and pressure on the mass of lava, may cause the crystallization of its elements into new mineral forms. It is certain that such crystals are formed in the interior of the mountain and ejected in an undecomposed condition. Mr. Darwin saw in Albemarle Island a stream of black lava thickly studded with large fractured crystals of albite, many of them half an inch in diameter, which he says were evidently enveloped and penetrated by the lava and rounded by friction as the stream flowed on. MM. Monticelli and Covelli describe a lava ejected from Vesuvius in 1822 as containing leucite in the proportion of six to one of the other ingredients. The granules were melted on the surface.[2]

The Hawaiian lavas contain much olivine, a very refractory mineral; and where the stream has issued from a considerable depth, as in the eruption from Kilauéa in 1840, it is in large granules and very abundant. Its specific gravity, it will be remembered, is 3.33 – 3.5. In the ejections from the summit it is in minute particles, as if broken and carried up by the currents in the melted mass. M. Von Buch has remarked of the basaltic lavas of Lancerote (and Mr. Scrope has observed the same in those of the Eifel and the Vivarais), that while the nodules of olivine are large near the source of the current, they dwindle away towards the extremity so as to be scarcely visible.[3]

In the lava-stream of Aliapaakaì, before mentioned, the eruption took place after a long period of rest, and from a considerable depth; and the lava contains large nodules of olivine five or six inches in diameter. The same is seen in the lava of Kóko, a similar formation, where crystals of augite also occur.

The separation of the less fusible portions of melted lava is well shown in the formation of a-a which is simply a sort of imperfect crystallization of the parts of the lava first cooled, from which the mother liquor, the still liquid lava, has been suddenly drained by the removal of the dam which blocked the stream.

When the volcanic action ceases or becomes extinct, the conical mass of lava cools slowly, and forms a mass wholly destitute of stratification. This fact was noticed in the volcanic islands of the Pacific by Prof. Dana, and it is in these islands that the inner core of the

1 See Daubrée, *Études sur le Métamorphisme*, Paris, 1859.

2 *Monticelli e Covelli. Storia de' Fenomeni del Vesuvio*, Napoli, 1823.

3 Scrope *on Volcanos*, p. 119, (2d ed.)

mountain may be best examined, as the denudation has exposed it in all the deep valleys so common on these high islands.

In these valleys I have been able to examine the solid nucleus of Mauna Kéa on Hawaii, Eéka and Háleakala on Máui, Olokùi on Molokaì, Konahuanùi on Oáhu, and Waíaleale on Kauaì, and I find the general appearance of all these cones to be the same, compact and unstratified; but the kind of rock at the summit varies slightly. On Waíaleale it contains less feldspar, and is more uniform, as if no opportunity had been allowed for it to settle: Konahuanùi has more feldspar, and portions of its rock much resemble syenite: Olokùi and Eéka almost the same; while Háleakala and Kéa are quite feldspathic, and the former has streams on its flanks of highly feldspathic lava. Olokùi contains much iron on its summit overflows (not in its core), as does also Konahuanùi, while on Waíaleale there are said to be large deposits of ferruginous lava. The base of the cones in all cases is basaltic, so far as exposed. It may be added that the summits of Maunas Lòa, Hualalaì, and Háleakala are all largely composed of trachyte or a phonolite closely approaching it.

In Waíaleale, Eéka, Konahuanùi and Olokùi then, the composition of the cone is tolerably uniform, while on the other mountains various gradations between trachyte and basalt may be traced. The mass of these mountains is not sufficiently different from each other to lead us to suppose that a different period of cooling after the action ceased has caused the different distribution of elements which seem to be the same in all; and we cannot believe that the different lavas have been produced at different times, for it is impossible to draw any line of demarcation, so closely do the intermediate greystones connect the trachytes with the basalts. I infer from this that the mountains which produce the most uniform discharges, are the most active ones, and that when a volcano enjoys a long period of rest, its lavas will present greater variety. Kilauéa and Mauna Lòa are at present in a constant state of activity, and their lavas have comparatively no rest, and the eruptions are nearly uniform. Vesuvius is exceedingly irregular, sometimes bursting forth after a repose of nearly two centuries, and its lavas are more composite than those of any other known volcano.

Angle at which Lava flows.

M. Dufresnoy declares that lavas, to be compact and crystalline, must have cooled on a slope of less than 3°.[1] This statement has been proved incorrect by Sir Charles Lyell in his valuable "Memoir on the Lavas of Etna,"[2] and on the Hawaiian Islands slopes of every degree of inclination occur. I have measured streams that have consolidated on angles of from 10° – 90°, and in all cases they were continuous. Rev. Mr. Coan has done even more, and I quote his own words: "On the mountain and in Kilauéa I took the angles of several lava-streams, one of 49°, another of 60°, and two of 80° each, several streams on the mountain flowed down banks of scoriæ twenty-five and thirty feet high. The fusion was complete — the streams cooled in a perfect state.

"I saw thin strata, say one inch thick or less, which had flowed down the face of perpendicular rocks, adhering to the rocks like paste, and thus cooling. Will you say that I spoil my demonstration *by proving too much*, when I assert that I saw more than one place where the lava flowed at an angle of 95° — like the Indian's tree which grew so bolt upright

1 "Les coulées, qui se présentent sous un angle de 4° ne sont plus que des agglomerations de fragments incoherents." *Terrains volcaniques des environs de Naples*, iv. 342.

2 *Philosophical Transactions of the Royal Society*, part ii. vol. cxlviii. for 1858.

that it 'leaned the other way,' — thus flowing down a bank until it came to where the rock *retreated*, it would follow the inward curve in a thin layer like molasses, adhering to the rock and thus cooling."[1]

I have myself seen precisely such cases as Mr. Coan describes, and the consolidated lava often looks like mud slowly oozing through the cracks and down the surface of a perpendicular wall. I have seen a bed of lava several feet thick and quite compact, which had solidified at an angle of 35°. Cases have been cited where the lava has flowed over a bank in a thin stream which has formed layer after layer until the angle has been reduced to 3°.

Cooling of Lava.

It has been shown that the lava cools very rapidly on the surface, so that a stream may be walked upon a few hours after it has been incandescent. The lava on the surface of the Halemáumau crusts over almost instantly after the action ceases, and the fragments of lava thrown into the air cool almost before their rapid motion can change their form. Instances have been cited where the lava, dashed upon a tree by a passing flow, has consolidated in rings around the branches without burning into the bark. The casts of the trees, occurring quite through a bed twenty feet thick, show that where the caloric can escape through any good conductor the lava becomes solid. The crust is however a most excellent non-conductor, and under its protection the lava may run for months, or remain heated for years. The flow of 1840 was steaming for more than ten years after it ceased to run, and while the other recent flows have cooled in a much shorter time, it is owing to their being quite thin and cracked.

The more rapidly lava cools the more vitreous will be its texture, as is shown in the Pélé's hair, in the drops of lava thrown from the lake into the air, which are as vitreous as obsidian, and in the surface of lava-streams. I obtained many specimens of crust from the wrinkled streams, and while the inside was quite porous, the outer surface, to the depth often of half an inch, was quite compact and vitreous, as will be seen from the impression of a section of crust. The lava poured out of the pools in Kilauéa, and some of that in the summit eruptions, cools very rapidly, and the whole surface much resembles the thin glass flakes produced in the process of stamping bottles at a glass-house. Where melted lava is thrown into water, it is broken and granulated into a glossy coarse sand or gravel.

Fig. 47. Impression of lava crust.

The temperature of the Hawaiian lavas has never been determined, although from their extreme liquidity it is probably very high.

Formation of Pit Craters.

Kilauéa, and the similar craters on Maunas Lòa, Hualalaì, and other mountains of the group, are simply orifices left by the overflowing lava, and by no means the remains of

[1] Silliman's *Journal of Science*, [N. S.] vol. xxi. p. 142.

collapsed bubbles, as Mr. Scrope and others seem to think. They have not been formed by a falling in of the top of the mountain, but the process is this: When the lava subsides in the tube after a surface overflow, it leaves a well or depression, which will have perpendicular walls. A violent commotion in the lava at the bottom of this pit at a recurrence of volcanic activity will crack and dislodge portions of the wall, which will be swallowed up in the melted mass. The lava may again rise and overflow the rim, and its heat will both melt and crack the walls, and thus the crater of an active volcano of the Hawaiian type constantly increases in diameter. When the lavas no longer overflow, they may yet reach the base of the encircling wall and remove the debris, which falls, maintaining the perpendicularity of the cliffs. This has been the case at Kilauéa, and the fragments broken from the upper walls now form a low ridge some distance from where they fell, having been transported by the fiery currents. The natives declared to Mr. Ellis, on his first visit to the crater, that it had grown much since ancient times.

Neither in these craters nor anywhere on the mountains can I see any signs of "a single, sudden swelling up of previously formed horizontal beds of lava and scoriæ into a hollow bladder."

Influence of constant Winds.

The north-east trades blow during nine months of the year with considerable force, and their influence is seen in the tufa cones which always are higher and broader on the south-west, as the comparatively light tufa is easily blown by the winds. But in the ridges themselves there is a curious feature which probably owes its origin to the cooling influence of these winds. The general direction of all the spurs is from the north-east. The windward sides of the islands usually present perpendicular precipices, or short steep ridges where the islands are broken, as in Oáhu and Molokaì, while Hawaii presents to the force of the waves, unbroken by any protecting coral reef, a precipice several hundred feet above, and at least as many below the sea level.

Makapùu Ridges.

A direct result of a constant direction of the wind is the more rapid decomposition of the walls of the smoking crater by the action of the sulphurous vapors, causing a crumbling of the walls when the action is long continued.

Earthquakes not a necessary concomitant of Eruptions.

It has been remarked that the eruptions of Mauna Lòa are wholly unaccompanied by any great commotion of the earth. While earthquakes do occur on the Hawaiian Islands, they are never severe, and seldom are noticed during an eruption. They seem to confirm Mallet's theory of vibrations, as they almost always radiate from the solid axis of the centre of an island. A slight shock was felt on Oáhu in the winter of 1865, when the vibrations were distinctly felt from the mountain to the sea on all sides of the island.

[The remarkable difference in level between lavas in the same mountain will be considered in the Topography of Kilauéa.]

Sea Waves.

It is not unusual, during littoral or submarine eruptions, for the sea to be agitated by great and unusual tides. Such sea waves have not attended the recorded eruptions of the

Hawaiian volcanoes, but have been observed on these shores at times when the volcanic vents were not unusually active.

The first recorded took place in May, 1819, when the tide rose and fell thirteen times in the space of a few hours. The elevation was not very great, nor was there any earthquake shock on the land. On the 7th of November, 1837, a more remarkable commotion took place. At six o'clock the sea retired to a depth of eight feet, leaving the reef surrounding the harbor of Honolulu quite dry. The water then slowly returned, and in twenty-eight minutes had risen to the height of an ordinary high tide. Without a pause it again fell six feet, and this ebb and flow was repeated at intervals of twenty-eight minutes. At the third flow it rose four inches above ordinary high-water mark, and fell again six feet four inches. After the fourth flow the motion became irregular and gradually diminished, but did not return to the ordinary course of the tides until the next day. The meteorological observations do not show any extraordinary disturbance in the atmosphere.[1]

11 P. M.	Thermometer	74°.	Fahr.	Barometer	30.04.
11.30 P. M.	"	73.5°.	"	"	30.03.

At Kahulùi on the windward shore of the Isthmus of Máui, the sea retired suddenly twenty fathoms. The natives followed with delight picking up the stranded fish, when suddenly the water rose like a wall before them and overwhelmed them in a wave which swept up on the shore destroying the village. Happily only two lives were lost here, as the people were quite at home in the water. At Hìlo the first fall of the water took place at half-past six, half an hour later than at Honolulu, and the returning wave rose twenty feet above high-water mark.

May 17th, 1841, a similar although less violent commotion of the sea took place. In the harbor of Honolulu at twenty minutes past five P. M., the water was observed to be "discolored and breaking like a tide rip." It then fell rapidly, leaving the reef and portions of the harbor bare. Twice during forty minutes this ebb was observed, and the sea then assumed its ordinary appearance. At Lahaìna, nearly a hundred miles distant, the first ebb was almost simultaneous, but the rise and fall was quite rapid, at intervals of four minutes. It is said that a similar sea-wave occurred on the coast of Kamtschatka.[2]

The effects of such waves in undermining the cliffs along the shore must be very great, and it was perhaps during one of these extraordinary tides that the loose craters on the shores of Ka-ù were partially demolished; certainly the cliffs were broken away in that district by this means, and I am inclined to attribute to the same powerful agent erosions on the lee shore of the other islands of the group.

MAGNETIC EFFECTS OF MELTED LAVA.

It would be most interesting to try the effect of a lava-stream in motion on the magnetic needle. In the vicinity of the Halemáumau in Kilauéa the needle of the theodolite compass was strongly affected, and the variation at the different stations on the upper bank was considerable but inconstant, doubtless owing to the presence of moving lava currents, as the disturbance was most marked in the vicinity of the pools. In several cases the variation has been noted on the map of Kilauéa. (Pl. XV).

[1] *Hawaiian Spectator*, vol. i., p. 104. Observed by Dr. T. C. B. Rooke.

[2] Jarves's *History of the Hawaiian Islands*, p. 22.

Erosion.

The effects of erosion have been considered evidences of the age of the Hawaiian mountains, and it would be well perhaps to examine the extent to which rains, rills, and rivers rushing rapidly, rend rocky regions, remove rock remains, leaving lofty ledges, perpendicular palis or precipices, and in a word work wonderful changes in the smooth, swelling summits of these volcanic islands.

The original form of the mountains was probably quite similar to that of Mauna Lòa — smooth rounded domes; but the present aspect is, as we have seen, quite different. Wherever the trade winds have driven the rain clouds against the mountains, streams have formed, and while at first they have been absorbed by the porous lava and carried by subterranean paths to the sea level, the decomposition of the lava produced by constant moisture has at last formed a soil capable of retaining surface streams. The nature of the rock has much to do with the rapidity of this process, and the shape of the central compact core is not without its influence. The continued rains, finally retained on the surface until they have acquired sufficient volume to form brooks, commence the erosive process.

Mauna Lòa is smooth; no rivers run over its slopes, and its only ravines are the work of streams of lava or the earthquake. The same is true of Hualalaì, and both these mountains are on the leeward side of the island of Hawaii. A glance at the map (Pl. XIV.) will show their position, and also that of Mauna Kéa and Mauna Kohála, whose peaks almost entirely intercept the vaporous clouds which the constant winds bring from the ocean. The windward slopes of these latter mountains are deeply channelled by the permanent streams and frequent freshets, while on the south and west they are as smooth as the sides of Mauna Lòa. The gorges on Mauna Kéa from Hìlo to Laupahòehoe, are both numerous and deep, and indicate as long continued erosion as those on Kauaì. Many extend more than half way up the mountain through the dense forests on the north-east, and while some, as that at Laupahòehoe, have been worn down to the sea level so as to form valleys of considerable extent, the majority meet the ocean in a fall of several hundred feet on the very shore. In all these cases the rock is essentially of the same nature and arrangement; and where the streams are of equal size, the height of the fall is about the same, indicating curiously enough the synchronous origin of all these streams. At Laupahòehoe, the stream is not very large, but there are indications of earthquake rents which assisted the eroding waters. I was unable to examine this valley as I could have wished.

On Máui (Pl. XIII.) the windward portions of Háleakala, comprised in the district of Hána, are grooved in the same way as we have described them on Kéa, but like the mountains of Hawaii the destroying valleys have not yet reached two thirds of the height of the summit. The leeward slopes are not eroded. Eéka is lower, and the torrents have completed their work on the north-east, and have even invaded the other sides, until, like the Tahitian mountains, only a skeleton is left. This result is owing to the depth of the craters and their shattered walls, as well as to the streams of water. These cavities were so deep that they penetrated the solid core of the mountain to a considerable depth, and thus retained water to supply streams.

On Lanai and Kahooláwe (Pl. XIII.), the ravines are not the work of surface streams.

This I infer from their presence mostly on the leeward side of the islands which are themselves on the lee of Máui, and also from the entire absence of running water even in small quantities; the severest rains even hardly form a brook. Molokaì has been eroded by both sea and rivers. The eastern end at Halàwa is undoubtedly worn by waves when at a lower elevation than at present, and the same agent has removed the windward slopes. On the south side the valleys are not deep, but exceedingly irregular, and often bear marks of the severe freshets that sometimes occur during certain winds. In many cases the streams which have formed the ravines seem ridiculously inadequate to the immense task of excavating the great valleys through which they quietly flow, but these occasional torrents explain the true agency. The craters on the summit of the ridge are the usual sources of the permanent streams which run, almost without cascades, to the sea. This general absence of cascades of any considerable height, — there are several at the eastern end which may compare with some on Hawaii, — characterizes this island.

Oáhu presents many of the features of Molokaì (Pl. XII.), and is eroded by the sea on the windward side, while on the south-west of the Konahuanùi range the valleys cut into the heart of the mountain. In speaking of the origin of Oáhu, attention has been called to the linear craters and their broken walls. Nuuánu has been cited as an example of a crater completely broken through on both sides. Manóa was also in all probability opened towards the south by the final eruption, and the waters have only had to enlarge the rent thus formed for their passage.[1] The Kaàla range is only eroded on the windward side and does not present deep valleys.

Kauaì (Pl. XI.) is deeply channelled on both windward and leeward sides, and the ravines reach deep into the core of the mountain; indeed, the Hanapépé and Waiméa valleys are deeper and have more precipitous sides than Hanaleì, Wainìha, and Lumahaì on the north. From the flat and crater-crowded summit the overflow of the marshes which abound there winds down on all sides; the Hanaleì and Hanapépé rivers rising from the same swamp and flowing in exactly opposite directions.

On all the islands the effect of destroying the timber has been very marked. On Oáhu especially the rainfall has been much diminished on the mountains, and the little stream in Nuuánu valley which supplies Honolulu with water is greatly wasted. The introduction of goats and cattle which run loose on the mountains destroying the young and tender shoots of the ohia and koa, the principal trees, and the wasteful and improvident way in which the natives destroy wood, has converted portions of the once moist and wooded mountains into dry pastures where the indigo alone of shrubs flourishes. Should the government take no measures to stop the wanton destruction of the forests, Oáhu may become like Niihau or even like Lanai. It would be instructive to present the annual rainfall since the introduction of goats, but no accurate observations have been kept regularly, although the zeal of amateur meteorologists has been awakened from time to time, especially at the Punahoù school. In 1837 and 1838, Dr. T. C. B. Rooke kept a careful register of atmospheric changes, from which it will be seen that at Honolulu, the thermometer and barometer were tolerably constant through both years while the winds varied considerably and the rainfall was more than doubled in the last year. During the rainy season of 1864–65, the following measurements were taken: —

[1] For an admirable explanation of the formation of valleys see Dana's *Manual of Geology*, p. 635; also *Exploring Expedition, Geological Report*, p. 290, and Silliman's *Journal* [N. S.], vol. ix., pp. 48 and 289.

Punahoù.[1]				Nuuánu Valley.[2]			
Dec. 1 . . .	.013	Dec. 8 . . .	.207	Dec. 4 . . .	2.80	Dec. 13 . . .	1.50
" 3 . . .	.024	" 13 . . .	2.950	" 5 . . .	.35	" 14 . . .	4.50
" 4 . . .	1.052	" 14 . . .	3.921	" 6 . . .	6.00	" 15 . . .	8.25
" 5 . . .	1.215	" 15 . . .	4.499	" 7 . . .	2.10	" 16 . . .	12.00
" 6 . . .	.833			" 8 . . .	.45		
" 7 . . .	.486		15.200	" 11 . . .	.08		38.03

At Punahoù, from the twelfth to the nineteenth of February, the rainfall was as follows:—

In the morning,	13th	14th	15th	16th	17th	18th	19th	
inches,	.496	.480	.099	.698	.080	.408	.050	— Total, 2.311 inches.

These were my own measurements. Dr. Rooke's table is as follows:[3] —

Time.	Barometer.			Fahr. Thermom.			Winds.			Weather.			
	Average height at 7 A. M.	Average height at 2 P. M.	Average height at 10 P. M.	Average at 7 A.M.	Average at 2 P.M.	Average at 10 P. M.	Trades — Days.	Kóna — Days.	Variable—Days.	Fine — Days.	Rainy — Days.	Variable—Days.	Rainfall, inches.
1837.													
January . .	29.970	30.006	30.043	69.9	76.6	71.3	10	14	7	24	3	4	2.0
February .	30.076	30.030	30.060	71.1	77.7	72.7	22	4	2	19	3	6	1.7
March . .	30.098	30.057	30.087	69.6	76.6	72.4	19	6	6	22	2	7	2.5
April . .	30.128	30.092	30.117	72.1	78.4	73.7	30	0	0	25	4	1	1.2
May . . .	30.109	30.085	30.097	73.4	80.2	75.0	30	1	0	29	1	1	0.9
June . .	30.093	30.081	30.085	76.1	81.9	77.5	29	0	1	21	3	6	1.4
July . . .	30.115	30.095	30.107	76.4	81.5	77.3	28	1	2	21	7	3	2.8
August . .	30.077	30.086	30.087	76.9	82.8	78.1	30	0	1	22	3	6	2.0
September .	30.095	30.060	30.097	76.5	83.0	77.0	29	1	0	29	1	0	0.7
October . .	30.116	30.076	30.120	74.8	80.6	76.0	26	4	1	28	1	2	0.4
November .	30.070	30.029	30.071	72.7	77.9	73.8	19	7	4	18	8	4	4.5
December .	30.124	30.072	30.115	69.9	76.5	71.1	23	6	2	27	1	3	1.0
Average . .	30.128	30.060	30.090	73.1	79.5	74.8	295	44	26	285	37	43	21.1
1838.													
January . . .	30.060	30.028	30.054	69.3	75.6	71.5	21	5	5	25	3	3	0.8
February .	30.016	29.970	30.005	71.2	75.3	72.1	20	3	5	18	6	4	8.5
March . .	30.105	30.064	30.095	72.0	75.1	72.5	22	3	6	21	4	6	2.1
April . .	30.127	30.095	30.140	71.5	76.7	72.8	29	1	0	27	1	2	1.0
May . .	30.149	30.139	30.162	73.2	80.3	75.5	25	5	1	28	1	2	0.5
June . .	30.085	30.040	30.090	75.5	81.7	77.1	20	7	3	17	3	10	2.5
July . . .	30.091	30.068	30.092	76.4	82.5	77.9	26	3	2	24	3	4	1.5
August .	30.078	30.052	30.078	77.2	83.2	78.4	30	1	0	28	1	2	1.2
September .	30.073	30.035	30.068	76.7	82.6	78.4	27	2	1	25	3	2	2.5
October . .	30.040	30.021	30.142	75.0	80.1	76.9	16	7	8	20	5	6	12.0
November .	30.041	30.008	30.144	72.3	76.6	73.7	18	9	3	19	5	6	6.7
December .	29.978	29.876	29.993	71.5	76.3	73.3	4	25	2	23	6	2	7.5
Average . .	30.087	30.033	30.072	73.5	78.8	75.1	258	71	36	275	41	49	46.8

1 The measurements are taken at 7.30 A. M. Average temperature 72° Fahr. Winds violent from the north, followed by a calm, and variable south and south-east winds.

2 Taken each day at 8 A. M., by Dr. G. P. Judd.

3 Jarves' *Hawaiian Islands*, p 15. The temperature at Lahaìna on Máui during ten years ranged between 86° and

In addition to the severe rains of the tropics, water-spouts have from time to time broken in the mountain valleys, and flooded the plains near the shore. Native traditions are full of such catastrophes, and a number have, within the last half century, visited Máui, Molokaì, Oáhu, and Kauaì.

Melting snows do not often produce a debacle, owing to the porous nature of the mountain summits. Snow is common on Maunas Lòa and Kéa, not uncommon on Háleakala and Waíaleale, but does not extend down the sides below an altitude of eight or nine thousand feet.

The Place of the Hawaiian Volcanoes in Volcanic Systems.

In endeavoring to ascertain the connection between the volcanoes of the Hawaiian group and other Pacific ranges, most geologists have noticed the parallel linear arrangement of the Pacific insular volcanoes which trend generally north-west and south-east, and have inferred the existence of as many primary fissures in the earth's crust as there are parallel groups of volcanic islands.

The question arose in my mind whether volcanoes presented in themselves any indication of mutual relation other than mere position on the same line. I did not endeavor to connect the periods of activity or eruption, because I have seen so much independent and apparently irregular action in the same vent, as in the lava pools of Kilauéa, or in neighboring vents, as Kilauéa and Mauna Lòa. It was in the shape and position of the craters themselves that I thought the desired clew might be found.

Craters of eruption are almost invariably oval or elliptical in outline, and the usual explanation of this shape is that the ejections which build up the crater reach the surface through a rent in the earth's crust, and not through a circular aperture, or through one formed by a stellate fissure, as would be the case were the superficial strata of the earth's crust raised around an axis to form the so-called craters of elevation. While the fact of the existence of many elliptical craters has long been known, no importance has been attached to the direction of the major axis. As the elongated form is caused by a rent of greater length than breadth it would perhaps be supposed that the major axis would coincide in direction with the volcanic train, or in other words with the primary fissure in the earth's crust over which the craters occur.

The trend of the Hawaiian Group is N. 64° W., but there is no crater on the islands whose major axis is parallel to this line. On the contrary a very interesting parallelism is observed among all the cratérs, and invariably the longest diameter is north and south, or at an angle of twenty-six degrees with the supposed primary fissure. Kilauéa, Mauna Lòa, Hualalaì, Háleakala, Leáhi, Puawaìna, Aliapaakaì, the ancient crater of Kauaì, all have the same direction, and so with all the craters on the other mountain ridges. Such a deviation from the line on which these craters were supposed to have been formed must have some explanation. Are there in any other volcanic regions like examples? To answer this question we must know the shape and direction of the craters, and this has been almost always neglected in accounts of volcanoes. I give below, however, a list of such as I have been able to determine the position of, from which it will be seen that *the major axes are always at right angles to the mountain chains* in which they are situated. Another fact will be shown, that the Mexican volcanic train of the nineteenth degree north latitude, commencing with

51° with no greater daily variation than 19°. At Waiméa, Hawaii, at an elevation of four or five thousand feet, the average is 64°, the lowest 48°. At Kolòa, Kauaì, 88° to 50°. At Waiòli, Kauaì, 90° to 55°.

Tuxtla on the Gulf of Campeachy, and extending to the Revillagegido Islands some two hundred miles west of the Pacific coast, exhibits this transverse direction most remarkably. Now if this line be extended westward forty degrees it passes through the Hawaiian Islands where the craters also range north and south.

Commencing with the Andean volcanic line, and placing the larger end of each oval crater first, as indicating the larger part of the subjacent fissure, we have the following result: —

VOLCANOES.	VOLCANIC LINE.	MAJOR AXIS OF THE CRATER.
Deception Island	Andean line S.—N.	E.—W.
† Antuco	" " "	E.—W.
† Aconcagua	" " "	E.—W.
† Sangay	" " "	E.—W.
† Sinchulagua	" " "	E.—W.
Antisana	" " "	E.—W.
Pichincha	" " "	E.—W.
Cayambi	" " "	E.—W.
† Mombacho	Central American line N. 55° W.	N. E.—S. W.
† Masaya	" " " "	N. E.—S. W.
† Coseguina	" " " "	N. E.—S. W.
† Isalco	" " " "	N. E.—S. W.
Agua	" " " "	N. E.—S. W.
† Fuego	" " " "	N. E.—S. W.
Tuxtla	Mexican line E.—W.	S.—N.
† Citlaltepetl or Orizaba	" " "	S.—N.
† Popocatepetl	" " "	S.—N.
Istaccihuatl	" " "	S.—N.
Toluca	" " "	S.—N.
Jorullo	" " "	S.—N.
† Colima	" " "	S.—N.
† Kilauéa	Hawaiian line E.—W.	S.—N.
† Mokuawéowéo	" " "	S.—N.
Hualalaì (several craters)	" " "	S.—N.
Háleakala	" " "	S.—N.
Eéka (several craters)	" " "	S.—N.
Leáhi	" " "	S.—N.
Puawaìna	" " "	S.—N.
Aliapaakaì	" " "	S.—N.
Kauaì (ancient crater)	" " "	S.—N.
† Shasta	North American line S.—N.	E.—W.
San Francisco	" " " "	E.—W.
† Mt. Hood	" " " "	E.—W.
† Klutschewskaja Sopka	Kamtschatkan line N. 25° E.	N. 60° W.
† Tolbatsch	" " "	N. 60° W.
† Awatschka	" " "	N. 60° W.
† Wiliutschinskaja Sopka	" " "	N. 55° W.
† Opalinskaja Sopka	" " "	N. 55° W.

† Active volcanoes.

Volcanoes.	Volcanic Line.	Major axis of the Crater.
† Ushiuruyama	Japanese line N.—S.	E.—W.
† Komanartaki	" " "	E.—W.
† Fusiyama	" " "	E.—W.
Usugatalee	" " "	E.—W.
† Wunsen	" " "	E.—W.
Guguan	Bonin line N.—S.	E.—W.
Farallone de Tores	" " "	E.—W. (?)
† Taal	Philippine line N.—S.	E.—W.
† Mayon	" " "	E.—W.
Egmont	Maori line N.—S.	E.—W.
† Tongariro	" " "	E.—W.
Tuhua	" " "	E.—W.
† Putanaki (Edgcumbe)	" " "	E.—W.
Pihanga	" " "	E.—W.
† Ruapehu	" " "	E.—W.
† Rangitoto	" " "	E.—W.
Mangere	" " "	E.—W.
Puketutu	" " "	E.—W.[1]
† Gelungung	Javan line E.—W.	S.—N.
† Papandayang	" " "	S.—N.
† Gunungtenger	" " "	S.—N.
Guevo Upas	" " "	S.—N.
Ararat	Western Asiatic line N.—S.	W.—E.[2]
Aden	" " " "	W.—E.
† Djebbl Tur	" " " "	W.—E.
† Santorini	Hellenic line N. 60° W.	N. 35° E.—S. 35° W.
† Argentiera	" " "	N. 33° E.—S. 33° W.
† Ætna	Latin line S.—N.	
† Volcano	" " "	E. 5° S. — W. 5° N.
† Volcanello	" " "	E. 5° S. — W. 5° N.
† Stromboli	" " "	E. 10° S. — W. 10° N.
† Vesuvius	" " "	E. 8° S. — W. 8° N.
† Solfatara	" " "	E. — W.
Astroni	" " "	E. — W.
Mont Dore	Gallic line N.—S.	E. — W.
Cantal	" " "	E. — W.
Mezen	" " "	E. — W.
† Heckla	Icelandic line N. W. — S. E.	S. W. — N. E.
† Eyafialla Yokul	" " " "	S. W. — N. E.
Myrdals Yokul	" " " "	S. W. — N. E.
† Kotlugia	" " " "	S. W. — N. E.

1 F. von Hochstetter, *Geologie von Neu-Seeland.*

2 Abich, *Bull. Soc. de Géographie* Sér. 4, tom. 1.

VOLCANOES.	VOLCANIC LINE.	MAJOR AXIS OF THE CRATER.
Teneriffe	Atlantic line N.—W.	N. 60° E.[1]
† Chahorra	" " "	N. 60° E.
† Teyde	" " "	N. 60° E.
Cone of 1798	" " "	N. 60° E.
Fuente agria	" " "	N. 60° E.
Palma	" " "	N. 55° E.
Lanzarote (Montana de Fuego)	" " "	N. 55° E.
St. Vincent	Caribbean line N. — S.	E. — W.
† Montagne Pélée	" " "	E. — W.
† Guadaloupe (La Soufrière)	" " "	E. — W.
Mauritius	South-east African line N. W. — S. E.	N. E. — S. W.
† Isle of Bourbon	" " " " "	N. E. — S. W.

The superficial cracks are very much as represented on the Map of the Group (Pl. XII). The circles or ovals enclose the centre vents while the radiating lines indicate the supposed fissures which have given rise to the minor lateral vents and tufa cones. It will be seen that all the smaller cones are referred to some centre, and the interesting parallelism of the connecting lines will be evident. I connect Kaúla with the centre of Púuokapélé, while Lehùa is undoubtedly an offshoot of Niihau. On Oáhu, Laelóa and the Waianaè craters belong to Kaàla; Aliapaakaì, Puawaìna, Leáhi, and Kóko, to Konahuanùi. On Máui, Molokìni is secondary to Háleakala, and the craters near Haliimaìla and Malìko all fall on two lines, one to the north-east and the other to the north. Hawaii presents a very regular system of subordinate cones, all that have been observed ranging approximately on north and south and north-east and south-west lines. The cones behind Hìlo belong to Mauna Lòa, and the Kapóho series in Púna, to Kilauéa.

THEORIES OF VOLCANIC ACTION.

I cannot feel satisfied with the various theories which have been proposed to account for volcanic and telluric phenomena. I am not ready to admit that either electric currents or the waters of the ocean are the source of the heat which presents us with melted rock on the surface of the globe. For in the first case we should have more electricity sensible at the outlets of melted matter, while the lightnings which often accompany eruptions are no doubt due to the expansion and condensation of vapor in the atmosphere; the magnetic variations are such as may easily be accounted for by the motion of imperfectly fluid basalt which contains much iron; and both are totally inadequate to the production of such vast results as we witness constantly in various volcanic foci. On the theory that water gaining access to the interior through fissures, causes the liquefaction of rocks through the oxidation of metallic bases, little need be said, as the originator of this theory (Davy) himself abandoned it as untenable. Water may, if it once obtains access to a mass of melted matter, cause explosions and sudden eruptions; but such action must be exceptional, for the instant water approaches an intensely heated mass it assumes the spheroidal state, and no contact takes place. If it be argued, however, that the water would be under great pressure, that under

[1] Von Buch, *Isles Canaries.*

great pressure it can be heated red hot without assuming the condition of vapor, and that sudden motion or changes of pressure, such as we know are constantly taking place in the earth's crust, might bring about a contact, in such a way as to cause an expansion of the water into steam, and cause an elevation of the combined water and melted mass to the surface, we must point to the quiet welling out of the Hawaiian lavas, and ask for an explanation of that.

What we see with these lavas is quite contrary to the supposition that water causes their activity. Often they pass into the ocean and cool rapidly beneath the water; at other times when the motion is violent, the water obtains access to the interior of the mass and cools it still more rapidly, breaking it into sand. Where the fresh water gains access to the incandescent lava the effect is to cool it more or less rapidly in proportion to the quantity of water. Everywhere on the surface the tendency of water is to cool the melted mass by its evaporation, and whatever its action may be at great depths, under great pressure, on being set free on the surface it should cool the mass from which it escapes. There is not enough water set free from any volcano known, to account for the elevation of such vast weights of lava to such great heights. To do the work steam must pass from a high tension to a lower one, and must finally escape into the air. In its high tension it may be condensed to water by extreme pressure, but on reaching the atmosphere it must lose all this tension and become ordinary steam at the pressure of sixteen pounds to the square inch, or unite chemically with the lava. Analyses show us that the last is not the case, and no more steam is evolved from the Hawaiian volcano than must result from the rainfall on the heated surface of the exposed lava. Prof. Dana intimates that the rainfall may be the fuel of the volcano; if so, why should not constant eruption attend a season of rain? I have been on the banks of the lake of liquid fire during a severe rain, and the water that fell on the surface, instead of stimulating to increased action, darkened the crust. and nearly closed the vent.

We know so little of the laws of combined heat and pressure, that at present theory runs wild on the condition of the interior of our globe. One supposes a solid core surrounded by a melted coat, which in turn is covered by the solid crust of the earth; another supposes pockets or reservoirs of heated matter left in the solid crust of the cooling globe. All, however, are obliged to admit some source for the great streams of lava which are poured out upon the earth's surface. To explain all the phenomena of volcanoes it matters little what the interior of the earth may be, so long as we have a crust and a bed of melted rock below it. In the earliest ages of the globe, when the crust was thin, it was frequently broken as the earth cooled and contracted, owing to its being a poor conductor of heat, and contracting on its surface faster than it transmitted heat from beneath, and the escaping caloric found vent in numerous volcanoes over these fissures, precisely as on a smaller scale the surface of the lava in Kilauéa hardens and cracks, and allows the lava to boil up through the cracks. As the crust became thicker, the rate of cooling diminished, and the escaping heat needed fewer orifices, so that volcanoes became extinct. But the cooling process does not go on perfectly regularly; the crust is a better conductor in some places than in others, and this conductive power may vary from time to time. A high mountain with its rough surface abstracts more caloric from the earth by radiation than a smooth lake; continents more than the ocean. The balance is destroyed, and caloric must be transmitted through the earth to restore it. In what way the temperature of the earth's crust, at moderate depths, is kept so uniform we do not know; but we do know that the relative level of the land and sea is constantly changing, generally, as on the coast of Norway and the eastern coast of the United States, raising the land gradually at the rate of a few feet in a century, or in a similar way depressing the bed of the Pacific, the Baltic, and a part of the Indian Ocean. Or the change may be sudden, as during an earthquake.[1]

The bed of the ocean seems to be sinking and the land rising; but our knowledge of the earth's surface is yet too limited to inform us how extensively this is the case. The Hawaiian Islands are rising, and the atolls in the same ocean are sinking; and if we admit that the shallow bed of the Pacific, extending from the Hawaiian Islands to the China Sea, was once a continent, we have a case the reverse of those previously cited.

Wherever this change of level occurs over a tract of greater or less extent, there will be cracks of greater or less size along the boundary of this area; and here will the contracting crust force the lavas beneath, through to the surface. This fact was long since recognized by Humboldt, who says: "I am inclined to believe that islands and coasts are only richer in volcanoes, because the upheaval effected by internal elastic forces is accompanied by depression of the bed of the adjacent sea; so that an area of elevation borders on an area of subsidence, and at the limit between these areas great and profound clefts and fissures are occasioned."[2]

If the continents were not rising it would be difficult to see how they could maintain any height above the general surface of the globe, for meteoric influences constantly degrade and lower their peaks and slopes, and the material taken from them is constantly poured into the bed of the ocean, tending to fill that up, and reduce all to a common level.

The theory of a contracting crust, although not based on a sufficient knowledge of cosmic forces, yet seems to satisfy the known condition of volcanoes better than any other; and it also explains earthquakes which have been repeatedly shown to be unnecessary to eruptive action.

This theory, briefly expressed, is this. The earth's crust contracts unequally owing to its various composition, structure, and form, causing certain portions to fall below the general level, opening rents at the boundaries, and forcing up molten matter to the surface. The vibration of this gradual change of level, and consequent disruption of beds of rock, giving rise to earthquakes.

Mineral Products of the Hawaiian Volcanoes.

In the classification of the Hawaiian minerals I have followed the arrangement of Prof. Dana. The rocks, however, present some difficulties, since the metamorphic influences are both continual and considerable. The usual division of lavas into *basaltic* and *trachytic* is most unsatisfactory, since the lavas under consideration are mostly intermediate, of the *clinkstone* variety. If we attempt to draw a line between the recent and ancient, there are lavas yet hot which can hardly be distinguished from some that have been exposed to meteoric influences for centuries. Nor is the chemical composition sufficiently constant to serve as a basis of classification.

1 The island of Tongatabu in the Friendly Group, during a recent earthquake, was depressed on the north-east side, so that the sea advanced on the land two miles, while the western coast rose several feet.

2 Kosmos, iv. 415, Sabine's trans.

I have therefore placed first, the fresh lavas which reach the atmosphere in a liquid condition, a class varying in each crater, and even in consecutive eruptions of the same crater; next, the lavas acted upon by gases while still heated; lavas more or less decomposed by aqueous and acid vapors; lavas acted upon by the atmospheric agents simply; and finally lavas which reach the air through water, by which they are more or less comminuted and decomposed, forming tufas.

As the Hawaiian lavas are extremely liquid, the component parts have every opportunity for free motion, and from this perhaps results the homogeneity of most of the ejected matter. With the exception of chrysolite and augite no minerals have been found in the lavas which have not been formed, in all probability, since the matrix has cooled.

Native Sulphur.

This mineral is found principally on the outer walls of Kilauéa, and over the fumaroles in Púna which are in close connection with this crater. As the sulphur is first deposited in the crust of the decomposed lava, near the surface, it is usually in fine almost acicular crystals of great beauty. The heat varies from time to time, and the crystalline deposits are often melted by the high temperature (220° Fahr. observed), and form on cooling thin and irregular layers or veins which show an almost prismatic structure, breaking readily in planes at right angles to the surface of the layers. The color is usually pale lemon yellow, but occasionally the presence of selenium is indicated by a deep orange color. The crystals are seldom perfect, being usually formed of concentric coatings with cavernous faces. A remarkable specimen is represented in the figure of the actual size. It was found in Púna and drawn on the spot; it was so exceedingly brittle that it broke in fragments on removing it from the slab of lava under which it formed. The opposite ends of the vertical axis are not symmetrical, and while the successive layers commence at the upper pole and terminate abruptly at equal intervals as they approach the diagonal axes, the layers on the lower half of the crystal commence on the plane of the diagonal axes, and terminate as on the upper half, but in reversed order. This was by no means an unique specimen, many similar ones were observed.

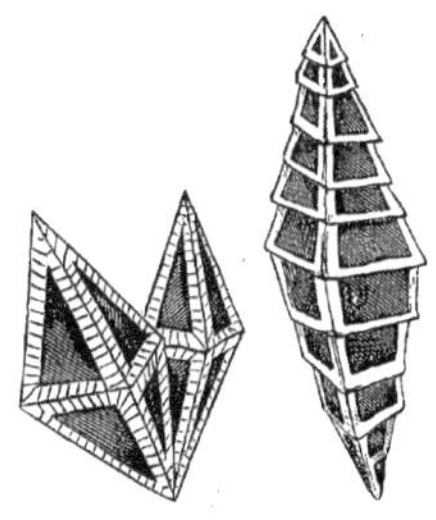

Sulphur Crystals.

The whole amount of sulphur on the Hawaiian Islands is small, and it will perhaps never become an article of commerce, but the deposits are generally quite pure and easily reached. The absence of this mineral, so commonly considered a necessary concomitant of volcanoes, on the other islands, with the exception of the few traces on Háleakala, arises perhaps from the fact that sea-water does not intercept or commingle with the sulphurous fumes. The Sicilian deposits were probably due to the presence of the sea above the lower parts of Trinacria where the sulphur is mostly found. So in Spain, and at Husavik and Krisuvik in Iceland, and at the sulphur-beds of Japan.

Pyrites.

This is not found in any recent lava, but apparently arising from decomposition of the silicates containing a large proportion of ferruginous oxides, by aqueous action; as the globular or reniform nodules, the most common form, are usually found in wet places where the ancient lava has long been exposed to the water. So comparatively rare is this mineral, that natives have often brought me a carefully treasured fragment believing it gold, and eager to find more.

Common Salt.

This mineral is not common in the crater of Kilauéa, and there are no traces of it in the tufa cones, with the exception of Aliapaakaì where it is deposited in crusts and concretions every dry season, to be redissolved at every freshet. In former times this salt lake furnished a large supply of good salt, but for some years it has been wholly neglected. This is found on the upper walls as well as in the basin.

Sal ammoniac.

Generally this salt is much contaminated with iron in Kilauéa, where it is found in the caves, and just beneath the crust of the floor of the crater. B. Silliman analyzed a specimen obtained by the United States Exploring Expedition with the following result:—

NH^4Cl	$FeCl$	Fe_2O_3	$AlCl$	Insoluble and loss.	
65.53	12.14	8.10	13.00	1.23	= 100.

Specimens nearly pure were obtained in a crevice of a burning cone.

Hydrochloric Acid.

Taking Vesuvius as a model, it has been supposed that hydrochloric acid is a usual product of active volcanoes; it is, however, quite rare in Kilauéa, and I cannot find that it has been observed in the eruptions of Mauna Lòa. Very little is found even in combination.

Hæmatite.

Although the basaltic lava contains a large proportion of iron, enough to color the resulting soil bright red, no available deposits of iron ore have been found. A few fragments of hæmatite were found loose in the beds of streams on Kauaì, and near Nuuánu pali on Oáhu. They were much worn, and did not exhibit any external crystalline form. Perhaps an altered Limonite. A fine red powder was found on Oáhu which makes an excellent pigment.

Limonite.

On the edge of the lava flow of 1855 from Mauna Lòa, where it passed through a wooded land, rounded masses of this mineral were found from three to twelve inches in diameter and of the consistency of fresh putty, so that they could easily be cut with a knife, or moulded with the finger. On drying, these lumps crumbled and exhibited a fibrous structure. At Kaliiwàa on Oáhu, an ochre occurs of a finer texture. Both of these ochres form pigments of considerable body, little grit, and the color of burnt sienna. The impure varieties found near the sulphur banks, have been used in former times as paints, but are now wholly superseded by the better, imported ochres. It is highly probable that a more careful exploration, on the windward side of Oáhu, on Kauaì, and possibly in the northern districts of Hawaii, may result in the discovery of small beds of this important ore.

Sulphurous Acid.

The cloud of vapor which overhangs the active portion of Kilauéa, is mostly sulphurous acid. Boussingault found, in the volcano of Cumbal, hydrosulphuric acid only in the higher and cooler parts, where the temperature of the fissures did not exceed 185° Fahr., while in the hotter fissures sulphurous acid was abundant.[1] Humboldt saw, from the summit of Pichincha, that at a considerable depth in the crater blue flames moved about, and he distinctly recognized the smell of sulphurous acid.[2] The sulphur banks of Kilauéa have a temperature of 210° Fahr. just beneath the outer crust, while at a depth of several inches, near the steam cracks, the temperature rises as high as 220° Fahr.

This gas combining with hydrosulphuric acid, which is found in the cooler portions of the crater, especially when largely diluted with aqueous vapor, is decomposed, and furnishes the deposits of sulphur in the sulphur banks. Over the more intensely heated Halemáumau the hydrosulphuric acid is consumed on reaching the atmosphere, and this seems to be the source of most of the aqueous vapor in the cloud which overhangs the crater. The steam is in very small quantities, for the smoke is remarkably dry and consists almost wholly of sulphurous acid.

Sulphuric Acid.

In crevices in the sulphur banks small quantities of dilute sulphuric acid were observed, probably the result of the decomposition of hydrosulphuric acid. Many years ago Breislak observed that unless this gas was considerably heated when coming in contact with the atmosphere, no sulphur was deposited, but sulphuric acid was formed.[3]

Carbonic Acid.

Nowhere in the crater is carbonic acid evolved; and I have not seen proofs of its existence in a free state anywhere about the Hawaiian volcanoes. It is by no means a usual concomitant of volcanoes, and seems limited to those which, like Vesuvius, penetrate limestone strata of a former age.

Sassolin — Boracic Acid.

This was observed in minute quantities in only one fumarole, although looked for with care. It encrusted the decomposing lava, and was much mixed mechanically with sulphate of lime and with silica.

Quartz.

Fine crystals have been found in *cavities* of ancient blue basalt at Onomèa, Hawaii, which were from half an inch to an inch in length, quite symmetrical and without modifications, usually attached by the basal pyramid to the basaltic matrix. The cavities in which they were found were generally smooth within. Milky quartz is quite common on Molokaì and other islands, and occurs in irregular rounded masses, from one to eight inches in diameter; it is often colored superficially by oxide of iron. Chalcedony is found in botryoidal masses, and mamillary concretions, often of considerable beauty, on Kauaì, and has been formed by the solution of the silica in the lava by the soda, set free, perhaps, by atmospheric agency; and this soluble silicate of soda is again decomposed, depositing the silica in thin layers. The silica, separated from the basalt in the sulphur banks, forms a cement for the aluminous earths with which it seems mechanically united, and so far as I have observed, is not separated in these places in distinct masses. The quartz crystals found at Onomèa were undoubtedly formed after the lava cooled, as they were found within spherical cavities attached to one side, with perfectly sharp angles. The stratum of blue basalt was about twenty feet thick,

[1] *Annales de Chim. et de Phys*, t. lii. p. 5.

[2] *Ibid.*, t. xxvii. p. 129.

[3] Bischof, *Chem. Geol.*, vol. i. p. 330.

covered with four feet of earth and about a foot of good soil, the crystals being near the bottom of the bed which was cut away to form a roadway.[1] The most common form is milky quartz stained with oxides of iron, found on Molokaì and Kauaì. I have never seen this form from the other islands, although it doubtless occurs.

Augite.

Augite is the common constituent of all the recent Hawaiian lavas, but it is only in the tufa cones that crystals of any size occur. The variety termed Palagonite by Von Waltershausen is common at Leáhi, Kóko, and Aliapaakaì, where the rather rough crystals are imbedded in the tufa, and seem to be broken and worn. The Hawaiian specimens have not been analyzed, but the composition of this variety is so remarkably uniform that I quote the analyses of Von Waltershausen.

	$Si\,O_3$	$Al_2\,O_3$	$Fe_2\,O_3$	Ca O	Mg O	Na O	K O	H O		
Krisuvik	40.68	14.59	14.24	6.95	7.65	1.84	0.45	13.60	=	100
Heckla	40.75	8.42	17.99	8.64	4.54	0.62	0.44	18.60	=	100
Gallapagos	38.07	13.03	9.99	7.54	6.58	0.70	0.94	23.15	=	100
Val di Noto	40.86	10.07	20.54	4.46	3.28	3.99	1.10	15.70	=	100

Chrysolite.

This mineral is very common in most of the lavas that have issued low down the flanks of the mountains. On the summit no traces are found in the massive clinkstone which forms the crater walls. In the flow of 1840 from Kilauéa the a-a is full of it, and where the stream entered the sea the matrix was so pulverized that the chrysolite was set free and is now washed up in the clefts of the rocky shore as a green sand or gravel. The larger grains are amorphous, half an inch in diameter, while the smaller sand is used in mortar for fire-bricks. At Aliapaakaì fine spheroidal masses, sometimes four to six inches in diameter, are found, and in these the grains seem to be flattened against each other. I found chrysolite in some scoriæ on the top of Hualalaì, and in a lava of ancient date in Kilauéa. It is not uncommonly altered by the oxidation of the iron into a red and softer mineral. It is found changed to a red color in cellular basalt on Oáhu containing Thompsonite.

Garnet.

Only two specimens of garnet were seen, both at the summit of the cliff at Aliapaakaì. The crystals were dark red, a quarter of an inch in diameter, dodecahedrons, with the edges truncated by the planes of a tetragonal triakis-octahedron.

Biotite.

A few small tabular hexagonal crystals, nearly black, with a submetallic lustre, were found imbedded in the tufa at Aliapaakaì.

Labradorite.

It is not uncommon in the crater of Háleakala, also on Mauna Lòa, where it occurs in

[1] Quartz crystals, with perfect pyramidal faces at both ends of the crystal, were found in trachyte in the Andes of Bolivia, by Forbes. *Quart. Journ. Geol. Soc.*, xvii., pp. 26 and 29.

glossy colorless crystals. It is doubtless a component of many of the basalts. An analysis of a specimen from Máui by Schlieper gives —

$Si\,O_3$	$Al_2\,O_3$	$Fe_2\,O_3$	Ca O	Na O	K O	Mg O
53.98	27.56	1.14	8.65	6.06	0.47	1.35 = 99.21.

Orthoclase — Feldspar.

Feldspar has not been found in separate crystals, but enters into the composition of the phonolites of the higher mountain regions, and the solid mountain core. The decomposition of feldspathic rocks by sulphurous vapors sets free the silica, and results in the recombination of the elements into various species. Clays are found on all the islands, especially on Oáhu and Máui, and in the district of Hána. On the latter island, much coarse pottery was manufactured some years ago. Bricks also have lately been made.

Prehnite.

It is found in the cavities of ancient basaltic rock on Oáhu, in pale green compact granular masses. Seldom found near the surface of the rock, so only seen when the rock is quarried for building purposes. Not common.

Thompsonite.

This mineral is found in lavas containing much olivine on Oáhu and Hawaii; it usually completely fills the cavities, forming an amygdaloid.

Natrolite.

Natrolite is found in the same rock as the last, and is usually of a gray color, vitreous lustre and radiating structure. I have never seen it *in situ*, but in fragmentary rocks the centre of radiation seems to be always on the same side of each cavity in the same specimen.

Scolecite.

A radiated crystalline mass, much resembling natrolite, gave the well-known blowpipe indication of scolecite, but was not further analyzed. Other zeolitic minerals will doubtless be found in the older lavas whenever the rocks are excavated to any extent. In many places I have been struck with the resemblance between some Hawaiian lava beds, and those in the Ghâts of Western India, where such rich deposits of apophyllite and other zeolites have been found, especially in the deep excavations at the Bore ghât. The so-called amygdaloid in this place is no older, apparently, than some of the cellular lavas on Oáhu, and is of the same nature.

Gypsum.

This is found beautifully crystallized in Kilauéa, both beneath the crust around the fumaroles and on the tube stalactites in the caves. Sometimes the long slender tubes pendant from the roof are completely covered with opaque white rhombic crystals thickly agglomerated, and at other times with long transparent acicular crystals often stellate. Both varieties are found in the same cave and even on the same tube, but always where both forms are so closely associated, the transparent crystals are at the end of the tube, and as this grows by successive deposits of silica and other soluble parts of the superincumbent rock, the opaque crystals form over and conceal the former. The temperature of the caves where the gypsum is deposited is not high, as will be seen in the description of the stalactitic formations farther on.

No beds of gypsum have been found in the upraised coral reef, and there does not seem to have been any submarine emission of sulphur vapors to produce this deposit.

Specimens of the gypsum-coated tubes of both varieties have been deposited in the Museum of the Society.

Cyanosite.

An impure sulphate of copper is sometimes, though rarely, found in the sulphur beds of Kilauéa. An analysis, given in the Geological Report of the United States Exploring Expedition, is as follows: —

$HO\,SO_3$	$Na\,O$	$Cu\,O$	Al+Fe	Mn	K Cl	$Si\,O_3$ (insol.)	Si and loss.	
37.97	16.80	10.80	5.0	4.0	trace	21.00	4.43	= 100.00

Soda Alum — Solfatarite.

A strongly ferruginous soda alum is found in the smoking cones (fumaroles) in Kilauéa.

Halotrichite.

As the fibrous silky mass of the alum often contains little soda, it seems to run into halotrichite. The free sulphuric acid in this mineral is often quite perceptible, and wholly destroys the paper in which it is placed for a few days.

Copperas.

It is found in the sulphur bank on the southern edge of Kilauéa; it is quite impure, and from its solubility is usually dissolved as soon as formed, and is absorbed into the porous earth resulting from the decomposition of the lava rock.

Glauber Salt.

At Kailùa, on the western shores of Hawaii, this mineral was abundant twenty years since, forming in a cavern on the shore by the action of hot sulphurous gases on sea-water. These gases have ceased to flow, and the springs are no longer hot. I did not visit the place, but was told that no sulphate of soda was now found there. In Kilauéa it is not uncommon as a deposit on the under-surface of lava crusts, and contains a little sulphate of lime and sulphate of iron.

Nitre.

Found in small quantities in Kilauéa on a ledge in a cave, in delicate acicular crystals. The rock on which it was found was too porous to hold water, and the crystals must have formed from a vaporous solution, or grown from the saturated rock.

Calcite.

The chief deposits of carbonate of lime on the Hawaiian Islands are the extensive coral beds. These are often very compact and solid, often baked by lava-streams to a compact limestone, and ringing when struck. Where the lava has broken through the raised coral reef, as in the shore craters of Oáhu, the particles of coral are carried up with the tufa, and may be found imbedded in an almost unaltered condition. It is usually, however, acted upon by heat and sulphurous gases forming gypsum and aragonite. As a white incrustation it is exceedingly common on all the tufa cones on the ancient reef, and sometimes is of quality and quantity to be used as chalk, especially the deposits at Leáhi and Laelóa. In the caves at Haéna, on Kauaì, the roof is in many places covered with a thick incrustation of agaric mineral, and specimens were obtained several inches thick. I am inclined to refer to calcite the insoluble scum which was mentioned as occurring on the water in the second cave. It was here that the incrustation formed extensively, and the unevaporated water which had percolated from above dropped constantly from the roof. The incrustations are mamillary and botryoidal, and of a reddish-yellow tinge, often cellular in structure.

The coral rock is burned for quicklime, which is not, however, considered of so good quality as that made from other limestone. The calcareous matter, however, cements together fine volcanic sand, forming the coral-shaped masses of sandstone at Kolòa on Kauaì, the beach sandstone of Hanaleì and elsewhere, and the curious sand tubes of the Isthmus of Máui. It also cements together the black gravel near Honolulu, forming cylindrical and rounded masses, often resembling fossil bones.

Arragonite.

Sometimes found mixed largely with calcite incrusting caves. The crystals are small and inconspicuous, and the corolloidal form is more common.

Hawaiian Rocks.

Fresh Lava.

The lava spattered out of the pools cools rapidly in the air, and presents when cold a glossy black exterior usually quite smooth, somewhat resembling coal tar, while the interior of the drops is sometimes hollow, and oftener filled with a cellular mass perfectly vitreous. The lava drops are indeed miniature volcanic bombs. Although as they are seldom projected to any considerable height the contained gas has no opportunity to burst the solidified shell in a rarer atmosphere; and as the lava is still red-hot when it strikes the ground, provided the pieces are more than half an inch in diameter, the drops flatten and lose completely the spheroidal shape they assumed during projection. The drops are exceedingly brittle, and split readily with the least jar, presenting a conchoidal fracture. The lava of which they are composed is so poor a conductor of heat that a fragment, a quarter of an inch thick, may be held in the hand within an inch of the red-hot extremity.

Pélé's Hair.

The filamentous lava formed by the adhesion of the drops to each other, or to the surface of the pool, varies in color and fineness. During the eruptions on the slopes of Mauna Lòa, when the lava fountains often play to a great height, the wind spins out Pélé's hair in clear green or yellow threads, sometimes three feet in length and rather coarse. In Kilauéa, the threads are finer,[1] and although clear and transparent when first formed, are soon corroded on the surface by the sulphurous vapors so abundant there. This decomposition is rapid, and on the leeward banks a strong cement is formed with the dissolved silica.

Various analyses have been made of this curious product, and as the drops are of essen-

[1] I have seen a bird's nest wholly made of this Pélé's hair, beautifully interwoven. When found in the crater, it contained two eggs. It is now in the possession of Mr. D. R. Hitchcock of Hilo.

tially the same material, the results of examinations of both these forms may be placed side by side.

	SiO_3	Al_2O_3	FeO	Fe_2O_3	MnO_2	CaO	MgO	NaO	KO	HO			
I.	49.0	13.0	15.0	——	7.8	8.9	0.4	4.5	2.3	——	=	100.9	C. T. Jackson.[1]
II.	49.2	7.8	——	13.7	13.0	8.4	5.1	1.8	trace	0.5	=	99.5	J. C. Jackson.
III.	51.19	——	30.26	——	——	——	18.16	——	——	——	=	99.61	B. Silliman, Jr.
IV.	39.74	10.55	22.29	——	——	2.74	2.40	21.62	——	.33	=	99.67	" "
V.	50.00	6.16	28.72	——	——	7.40	——	2.00	6.00	——	=	100.28	J. Peabody.
VI.	50.67	——	33.62	——	——	3.66	1.13	10.52	——	——	=	99.60	B. Silliman, Jr.
VII.	51.93	14.07	16.91	——	——	6.20	1.73	6.31	——	——	=	97.15	" "

I. Lava drops. Color dark bottle-green; very frangible, like unannealed glass. Sp. gr. 2.7; from Halemáumau. II. Pélé's hair from Kilauéa in 1864; both protoxide and peroxide of iron were present, but owing to the presence of oxide of manganese the proportions could not be determined. III. Pélé's hair from Kilauéa in 1840 (United States Exploring Expedition). IV. Pélé's hair, ditto. V. Pélé's hair light colored, ditto. VI. Vitreous lava from Kilauéa; Sp. gr. 2.91. VII. Scoria from Kilauéa 1840; Sp. gr. 2.505. Of the last five the solubilities in hydrochloric acid were as follows: —

	Soluble in hydrochloric acid.	Insoluble.
III.	49.51	50.49
IV.	48.80	51.20
V.	——	——
VI.	42.50	57.50
VII.	45.84	54.16

Crust. The fresh crust from the surface overflow of the pools often looks quite firm on the surface, while within it presents a series of small cells surrounding larger, all with the walls of a brilliant metallic lustre. Its composition closely approaches that of Pélé's hair. The lava that breaks out of the cones in Kilauéa is less porous than this scum, but is still quite cellular. It is viscid, and where it runs over light scoriæ does not sink into the porous mass, but flows above, bending slightly, where unsupported, between the fragments. Often a fractured surface is brilliantly iridescent. The bubbles or air-cells are generally, but not always, elongated in the direction of the flow. Usually the fresh lava exhibits chrysolite in exceedingly small particles, and so red as to mislead at first in regard to its true nature. Where a large quantity of lava escapes at once, the cooled crust is quite distinct from the cellular portion under it, and is quite compact, vitreous, and easily separable from the rest of the mass. As the small streams cool almost equally above and below, the melted matter solidifies in a cylindrical form which twists if one side cools faster than the other, and produces the rope-like masses so common on the outskirts of lava flows. If the supply is very abundant, the cooling goes on principally at the upper surface, and broad sheets of a sort of pahoehoe are formed. What is most curious, while the general mass of a lava flow — I am now speaking of the comparatively insignificant flows from the pools in the crater — is of a tolerably compact stony nature, a thin layer of very cellular lava separates it from the compact vitreous crust. It is so often declared that the surface of lava is porous and spongy from the escaping gases, that I have been surprised to find that this is not the case. The surface, although covered with glassy scales, perfectly flat and by no means bubbles, is more impervious to gases than is the lower stony mass. The lava as it flows out is not in an effervescent state; it is simply melted, not boiling rock, and evidently

[1] This, and other analyses, were kindly made for me by Dr. C. T. Jackson and his son Mr. J. C. Jackson.

is not brought to the surface by the rise and expansion of inflating vapors. That vapors accompany it is perfectly true, but the molten mass is often drawn from a cone some yards below the surface of the liquid which emits gases, and the product is smooth and glassy; not a bubble disturbs its rapidly hardening surface, and often no vapor accompanies its egress.

That the lava is not much above the melting point on the surface of the Halemáumau and other pools in Kilauéa, is evident from the great rapidity with which it becomes granular. Where the substance is drawn out by gravity the granules are very distinct, even when the lava was liquid enough to form pendants a foot long. Several stalactites formed from melted lava exhibit this structure admirably. The lava is melted as the Rowley rag is melted in the furnaces of the Messrs. Chance, and is not a simple solution in some vehicle. Dolomieu, in speaking of volcanic fire, says: "Il produit la fluidité par une espèce de dissolution, par une simple dilatation qui permet aux parties de glisser les unes sur les autres, et peut-être encore par le concours d'une autre matière *qui sert de véhicule à la fluidité*."[1] Elsewhere he supposes this vehicle to be sulphur, a supposition not more improbable, judging from Kilauéa alone, than the theory of Mr. Scrope, that water is the interstitial fluid which imparts mobility.[2] The fusion is perfect as seen in the Pélé's hair, and when the lavas granulate they do so without any disengagement of vapor. I have seen the streams or rills of lava moving with such entire freedom from any thing like smoke, that had I not been watching, they might have passed near me unnoticed. Wherever the melted rock passes over combustible matter, or through swamps, the vapor generated is sufficient to convert the surface and mass also into a porous rock. It must not be inferred that gases never inflate the lava in the crater. Much of the surface overflow is, as has been said, a spongy scum, but it is only the surface overflow that is so porous, and if water is necessary — if vapors are necessary to the elevation of the matter — these gases must be in a state of greater tension lower down in the column, and ought to froth out when an outlet is provided; and we should have, with the pressure of a column of lava three thousand feet in height, a result similar to that produced by the sudden expansion of liquid carbonic acid, and a black or green snow would surround the vent. Something like this seems to occur, but in quantities wholly inadequate to the agency supposed. Around the orifice of 1859 on Mauna Lòa are several cartloads of a very light porous substance, called by the natives *límu* or moss. It is dark green and smooth on the surface of the irregularly rounded nodules, while the interior is light green. The same límu forms large beds on the leeward bank of Kilauéa, and there its origin is explained; it is simply the scum from the Halemáumau blown away by the wind, not by liberated gases, and its formation is going on with that of Pélé's hair.

Pumice.

The structure of the fresh lava is not easy to understand, some parts of the same stream having a clear ring when struck, others being dead and flat. The mode of granulation certainly has much to do with the phonetic qualities of lava, as the a-a or simple granules sound quite differently in different places, although of the same composition and appearance. The a-a of Kilauéa contains but little olivine, and that in small grains; this is true also of that formed on the slopes of Mauna Lòa from the summit discharges; but the flow of 1840 from Kilauéa at a considerable depth, produced an a-a full of large grains of this mineral. The specific gravity of a specimen from Kilauéa is 2.47. The formation of this rough and curious product has already been discussed.

A-a.

1 *Les Isles Ponces*, 1788, avant propos, p. 8.

2 Scrope *on Volcanos*, p. 116.

Rapilli. When the melted lava is thrown into water, the black gravel called lapillo or rapilli results, and the iron which it contains as peroxide becomes magnetic. From the loose form of this gravel it is readily transported by water, and is generally spread out in horizontal layers near the shore, often covered, as near Honolulu, with other alluvial deposits.

In one blow-hole, Mr. Rexford Hitchcock found some very curious forms of lava which, for want of a better name, may be called as in the margin, for I conceive them to have been formed by the action of electric currents on a plastic mass containing much iron. The masses are of considerable specific gravity (2.857), and the surface is arranged precisely as the iron filings place themselves around the poles of a magnet. Similar specimens were found in Vesuvius, and are in the Museum of the Society; but in Kilauéa only this one locality has been discovered.

Electric Lava.

Only in the eruption of 1789 has volcanic sand or ash been ejected, and this is simply irregular, angular, and rounded grains of the ordinary lava of the pools, comminuted perhaps by the explosive violence of the eruption. It is not so fine as the ash of Vesuvius, and although it is apparently but little acted upon by meteoric influences, rounded particles of calcareous matter are found in it in considerable quantities.

Sand.

Heated Lava acted upon by Gases.

The immediate result of gases, usually sulphurous vapors, is to change the external color of the lava, so that as it cools it assumes various shades of brown, red, blue, yellow, and often a metallic hue, so as to resemble brass. The color imparted in this way is quite superficial, and the action of the gas is but momentary, but the results are often very beautiful. The heat of gas-jets seems to remelt the angles of the consolidated lava. Much more important, however, is the

Decomposition by Aqueous or Acid Vapors.

A formation which always excites the curiosity of visitors to Kilauéa, is found in many of the caves in the floor of the crater which have been undisturbed for several years. At the first glance the tubes which hang from the roof, and the curiously formed droppings beneath these, seem to be of igneous origin, or droppings of melted lava from the roof. An examination *in situ* shows that this was not the case. The roof of these caves is about two feet thick and generally unbroken; the stalactites do not occur under cracks, and indeed there is often no fresh lava over the surface. The formative process may be clearly seen, as the tubes grow from day to day; and I have caught the steel gray deposit in the drops on the end of the tubes upon my finger and watched its solidification. Usually the tubes are straight cylinders, from one to three eighths of an inch in diameter, and sometimes more than two feet long. The bore is almost never continuous, and while externally they are smooth, within, a mass of stony cells of considerable size is presented. As long as these tubes grow downward in the quiet upper region of the cave they hang perpendicularly, but when they reach farther down the currents of air and steam blow the deposits to one side and the tube becomes distorted; it may even return on itself. The drip on the bottom forms much thicker and more irregular stalagmites[1]

Tubes.

[1] A very beautiful stalagmite of shining black obsidian from Iceland, formed with surprising regularity, is in the cabinet of Harvard College.

as will be seen from the figure, which represents three actual forms, not occurring, however, in the same cave. Specimens have been found which exceed eight inches in diameter, and these are usually low and flat-topped. The more slender ones sometimes rise to a height of two feet; and so rapidly is the silica deposited, that they seldom increase in diameter, but are true acrogens, none of the suspended silica running down the sides. In one cave the growth of the stalactites was at about the rate of an inch a week, but owing to the varying amount of water or steam the production is quite irregular. They are often coated with beautiful white crystals of gypsum, sometimes tipped with needle-like transparent crystals of the same mineral, where the cave is high. The natives collect them with the upper open joint of a long bambu.

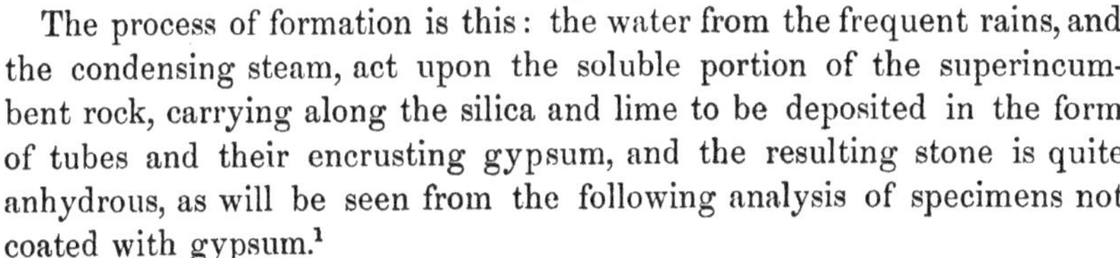

The process of formation is this: the water from the frequent rains, and the condensing steam, act upon the soluble portion of the superincumbent rock, carrying along the silica and lime to be deposited in the form of tubes and their encrusting gypsum, and the resulting stone is quite anhydrous, as will be seen from the following analysis of specimens not coated with gypsum.[1]

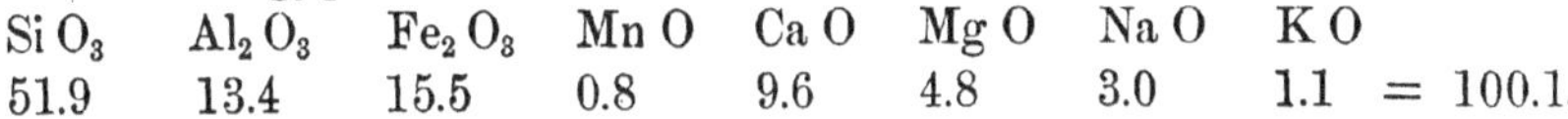

SiO_3	Al_2O_3	Fe_2O_3	MnO	CaO	MgO	NaO	KO	
51.9	13.4	15.5	0.8	9.6	4.8	3.0	1.1	= 100.1.

Fig. 48.

Specific gravity, 2.9. The temperature of the caves is usually from 80°–95° Fahr.

Other specimens, examined by Prof. Dana, had a hardness of 5–5.25, and a specific gravity of 1.656.[2]

The imitative forms arising from the evaporation of the siliceous solutions in the caves, are often quite curious, some resembling bunches of dried raisins, from a partial collapse of the encrusting bubble. The structure of all is stony and very cellular.

Acid vapors exercise a more extensive influence, but only in combination with steam. The surface of the black lava is first colored white or yellow, and the decomposition extends throughout the mass, rendering it after a while friable, and if the aqueous vapor is in excess, reducing it to an earth which is often again consolidated by the dissolved silica. A portion of spattered lava exposed to this action may be colored quite differently from the rest of the mass. Thus yellow or orange drops appear on a red ground, brown on a purple, and so on in great variety.

In the sulphur banks changes are going on quite rapidly, and the soil which results from the decomposition of the ancient lava of the outer walls of Kilauéa does not differ in appearance from that formed in the crater from the fresh black vitreous lava. The stony lava is always first decomposed, and the vitreous crust resists longest. In Púna I have raised large slabs of the crust which were nearly entire, while the stony stream underneath was reduced to a red earth for more than eighteen inches deep. Wherever cracks permit the passage of gases through the crust the interior is attacked. Most of the salts are deposited in these cracks and beneath the crust.

Clays are formed both by acid vapors and by simple meteoric influence. Those near

1 Analyzed by Mr. John C. Jackson in the laboratory of Dr. C. T. Jackson.

2 *Geology of the United States Exploring Expedition*, p. 201.

Kilauéa result from the former agency, and are usually bright red, tenacious, and gritty. The undecomposed lava contains more silica than is required to form clay with the alumina, and consequently clays are not always produced. At the sulphur banks a curious alternation of earths containing more or less silica has been observed, the more clayey containing twigs or other vegetable matter from the cliffs above, in a more or less fossil state, while the siliceous layers are thin and comparatively free from foreign substance.

Clays.

Decomposition by Meteoric influences.

Under this head we may range all the ancient lavas, and thus almost the entire mass of the Hawaiian Islands. I have already pointed out that the lava rock in the centre of the volcanic mountains is by no means the oldest; like granitic veins penetrating sedimentary strata its actual formation may have been long subsequent to the surface overflows which have formed the innumerable coatings of the dome. Wherever this central mass is visible, as in the deep valleys, it exhibits an amorphous, compact structure, gray or dark blue in color, and of considerable specific gravity. The composition is slightly different on the different islands, Háleakala containing a rock of lighter color and less specific gravity than Konahuanùi. I have never seen in either any cells which would permit the formation of zeolites.

Clinkstone.

The clinkstone beds on the summit of Maunas Lòa and Kéa are of two kinds, differing chiefly in color, one being gray, the other pale red or light brown. A partial analysis by Mr. J. C. Jackson gave: —

$Si\,O_3$	$Fe\,O + Fe_2\,O_3$	$Al_2\,O_3$	$Ca\,O + Mg\,O + Na\,O$	
52.0	25.2	20.6	2.2	= 100.0 Sp. gr. 2.91.

This is a very tough compact rock, chips with a conchoidal fracture, and is used for adzes. In ancient times, the only implements for cutting wood and shaping canoes were made from the rock of Hawaii, which was considered better for the purpose than any other. The composition of most of the summit lavas is trachytic. They take a good polish, and have the characteristic ring of phonolites. Olivine is quite rare, and I have never seen a single specimen from these compact rocks. The phonolites, like the other lavas, are in beds and much fissured. Both Kéa and Lòa are capped with this rock, mingled with the ordinary trachydolerite of Abich, which is the only stone on the other mountains.

Graystone.

The ordinary rock of the walls of the craters, both on Hawaii and on the other islands, is a compact heavy graystone, not cellular to any extent, and containing much olivine, usually of a pale yellow color. A mass in Kilauéa, evidently from the outer walls, has a specific gravity of 2.2. The summit of Háleakala, and consequently the walls of the crater, are of a vesicular trachydolerite, light brown on the surface where acted upon by the weather, but brownish black within. Fracture conchoidal and splintery. Specific gravity, 2.7. Much of this rock has in spots a structure similar to that of highly fermented dough — coalescing bubbles with intervening bundles of fibres. A specimen of stony lava procured by the Exploring Expedition gave —

$Si\,O_3$	$Fe\,O$	$Mg\,O$	$Na\,O$	
59.80	31.33	1.71	4.83	= 97.67 B. Silliman, Jr.

Specific gravity, 2.93. Soluble in Hydrochloric acid, 24.55; insoluble, 75.45.

Although the trachytes are often columnar, it is in the basaltic varieties that this structure is most beautifully shown. In many of the deep flows of lava from Kéa and Lòa, especially in the valley of the Wailùku, the columns are very perfect. So on Kauaì near Hulèia and in the Hanapépé valley. The dykes so common all over the group are usually of basalt, and the structure is generally prismatic, the prisms often separated by a thin calcareous film. Basalt.

Lavas which have been ejected through Water.

On all the islands there are found shore craters, and those on Oáhu have attained considerable size. The tufa of which they are principally composed is simply comminuted lava, cemented together by ferruginous or calcareous cement. The stone thus formed is tolerably firm and compact. It is in layers varying in thickness from half an inch to a foot. Where the eruption has taken place through the coral reef, the limestone thus mingled with the ash or mud is gradually decomposed, and fills the cracks with calcareous deposits. Sometimes this is so abundant as to whiten the whole surface of the rock. In a climate where frosts prevail, the loose porous tufa could not long hold together; and even in the tropics the rains fast reduce the hardest to soil. Sometimes the grain is coarse and much mottled with lime, while at the same place other layers may be fine and homogeneous throughout. In the tufa of Kóko small crystals of augite are seen, and also what closely resembles these, particles of obsidian. At Aliapaakaì, these and garnets, mica and chrysolite, have been found, the latter abundantly in the tufa. Tufa.

Soils.

All the soil about Honolulu and Waikìki is simply tufa debris, and it does not differ essentially from that resulting from the decomposition of other lava. It is often bright red, like the original tufa. We have spoken of the clay soils, but they are not common; the usual earth is light, requiring constant irrigation to render it fertile. In the valleys and on the windward slopes of the mountains the rains are abundant; but where these fail all is dry and sterile; yet the soil is equally good, covering itself with verdure during the rainy season, although dry and brown all the rest of the year, and yielding good crops of cane, bananas, and cotton whenever artificially irrigated. The vegetable acids produce a rich black soil in the forest.

It will be seen that the lavas contain but little potassa, no titanium, so far as analyzed, and a large amount of iron oxides. The different varieties run into each other, and a complete chain may readily be formed from the clinkstone of Mokuawéowéo to the basaltic dykes of Hanapépé.

EXPLANATION OF THE PLATES.

Plate XI. Kauaì, Niihau, Kaúla, and Lehŭa.

This Map has been constructed from several manuscript maps kindly furnished by residents. As no general survey has ever been made, either of Kauaì or any other island in the group, it is not as accurate as could be desired, but is believed to be an improvement upon any yet published. The island of Niihau has been surveyed by Mr. G. N. Wilcox of Kauaì.

Plate XII. Oáhu and the Hawaiian Group.

The Map of Oàhu is drawn mainly from that given by Prof. Dana in the "Geology of the Exploring Expedition." The exact position of many of the valleys is as yet undetermined, and it has been necessary to merely indicate their general form and relation to each other. For the same reason the dotted line which represents the fringing reef denotes the position and general extent rather than the exact topography of the coral formation.

The Map of the whole group shows both the relative position of the various islands and action of the volcanic vents. Where these have clustered around a single point, as on Hawaii and Máui, a circle represents the position; where the line of eruption is elongated, as on Oáhu, an elliptical figure is used for the same purpose. The radiating lines serve to connect with these centres the various lateral cones which stud the great domes in determinate lines to the very shores, or even extend into the sea, as in the crater of Molokìni. So far as is known, all the lateral cones will fall into the lines represented, and it will be seen at once that they are remarkably parallel to four directing lines. The centre on the western part of Kauaì has been divided, to show the relation of Niihau as previously suggested. The same has been done with Lanai and Kahooláwe, although this is perhaps unwarranted.

Plate XIII. The Máui Group.

West Máui has been drawn chiefly from a manuscript Map by Mr. Horace Mann, and represents fairly the relative positions of the valleys.

Plate XIV. Hawaii.

One of the original features of this Map is the lava flows. Those along the coast have been represented from actual observation, and are only those whose aspect is still perfectly fresh and distinct; farther up the slope they are lost in the dense forest, and although they proceed from near the summit in almost every case, their upper course has never been traced. Mauna Koháла has been represented nearly in its true position, and Kilauéa has been recognized as an independent mountain. The region in the district of Hìlo south of Laupahòehoe is not represented in its true character, as it would be difficult to even indicate on so small a scale the extraordinary nature of the intersecting ravines. The streams show the position of the largest, but as there are more than fifty large streams in a distance of thirty miles less than half are shown.

Plate XV. The Crater of Kilauéa.

This plan has been constructed from a careful survey by the author. Starting from the house at the north-east bank the circumference was chained, making the distance between the twenty stations on the wall of the crater 8.6865 miles. From each station bearings were taken with a large theodolite made expressly for the purpose. The summit of the Cathedral in the crater was made a central point to determine the relative height of the banks. The side crater, Poli-o-Keàwe, was not measured. Many of the cracks in the walls of the principal crater are not figured, and other details are omitted. A section across the southern end from A to B will give a fair idea of the elevation of the bottom towards the centre.

At each station the magnetic meridian was compared with the true meridian, obtained by careful observations oı the pole star at its east and west elongation and the remarkable variation observed in the neighborhood of the

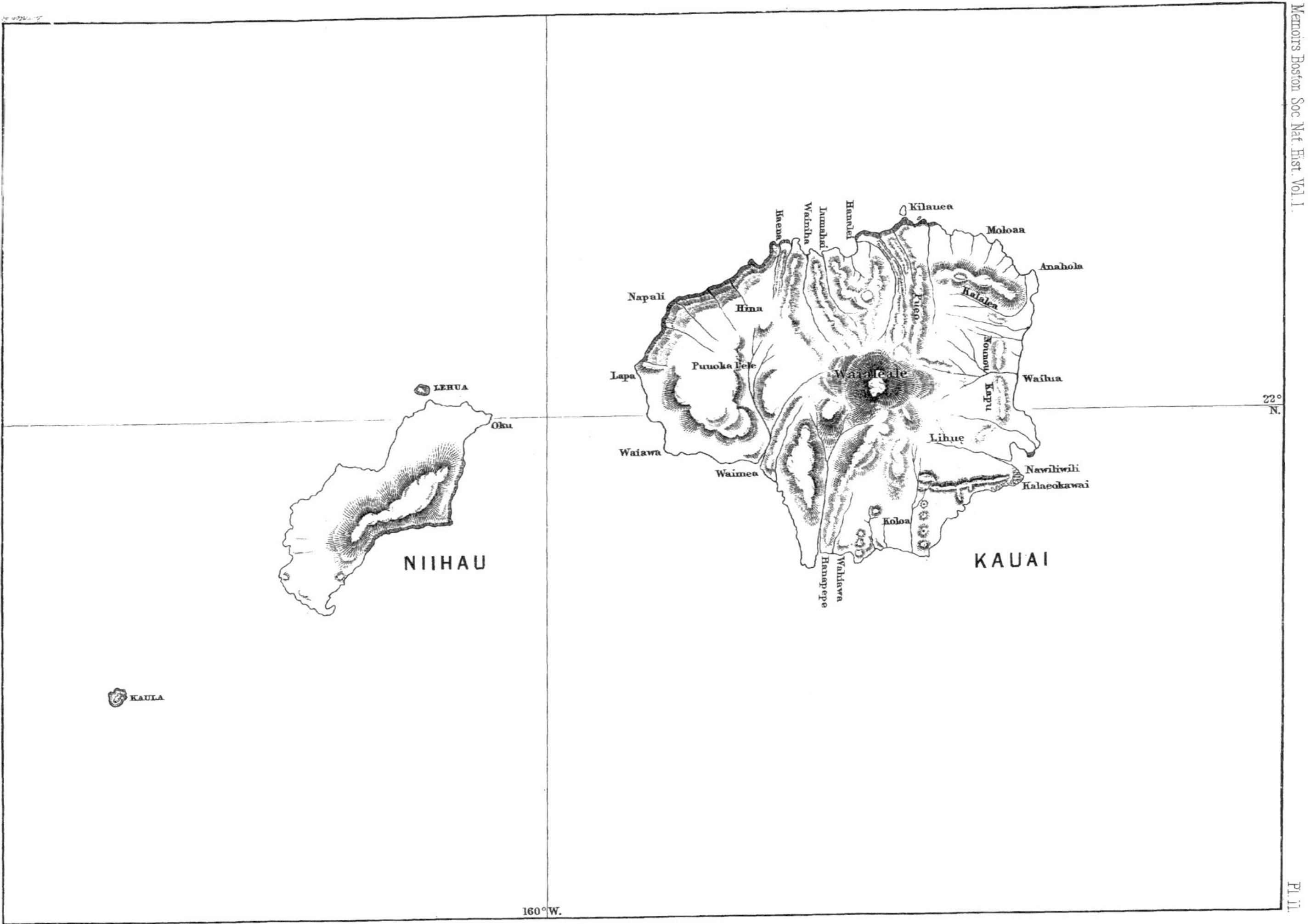
KAUAI
Kilauea
Moloaa
Anahola
Kalalea
Haena
Wainiha
Lumahai
Hanalei
Napali
Hina
Pueo
Nounou
Wailua
Kapu
Puuoka Pele
Waialeale
Lapa
22° N.
Lihue
Waiawa
Waimea
Nawiliwili
Kalaeokawai
Koloa
Hanapepe
Wahiawa
NIIHAU
LEHUA
Oku
KAULA
160° W.

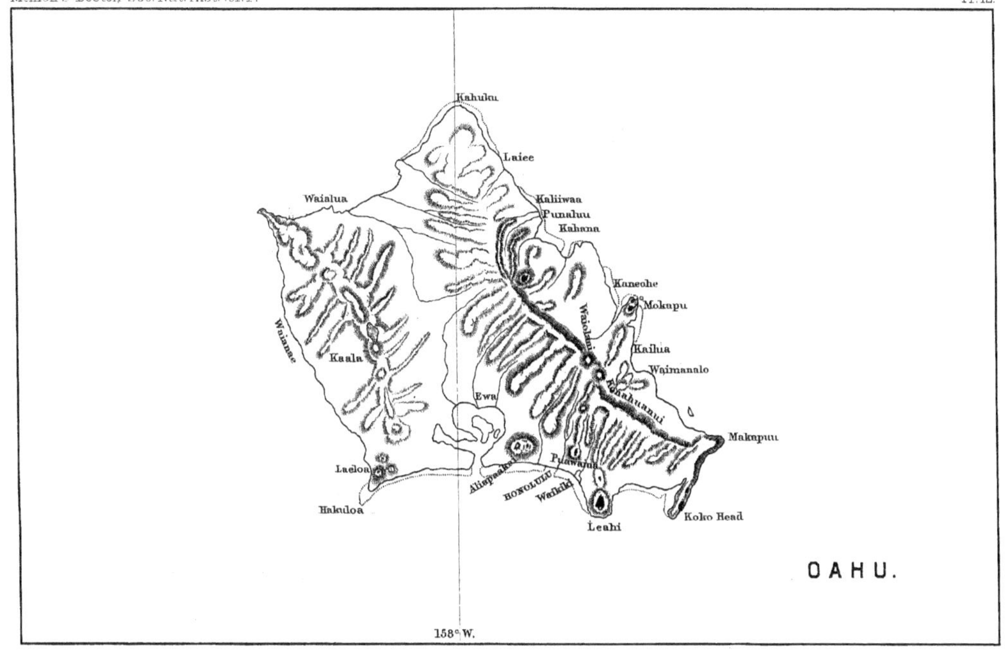

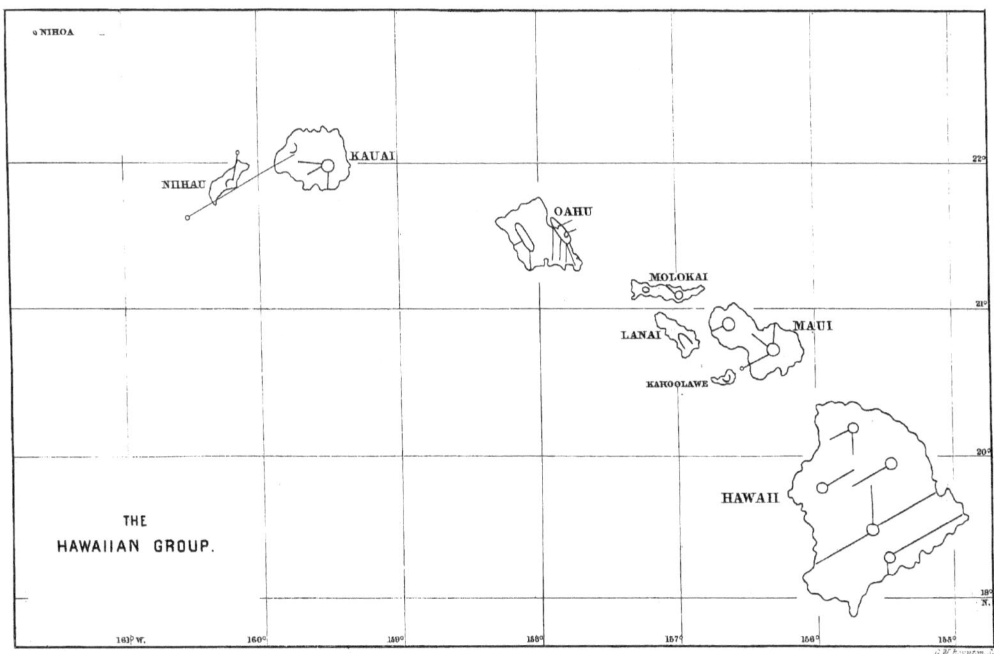

Wm. T. Brigham on Hawaiian Volcanoes.

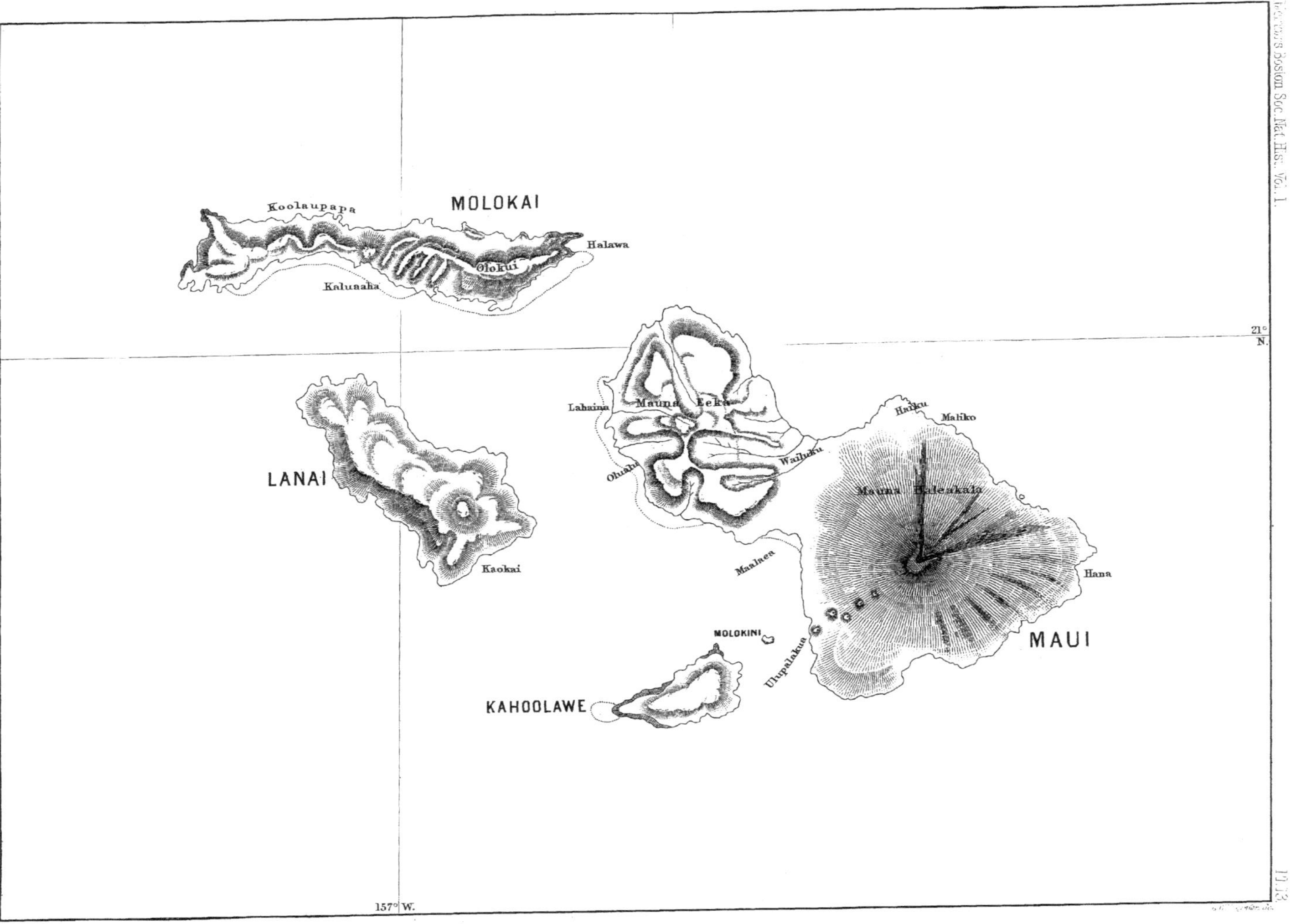

Wm. T. Brigham on Hawaiian Volcanoes.

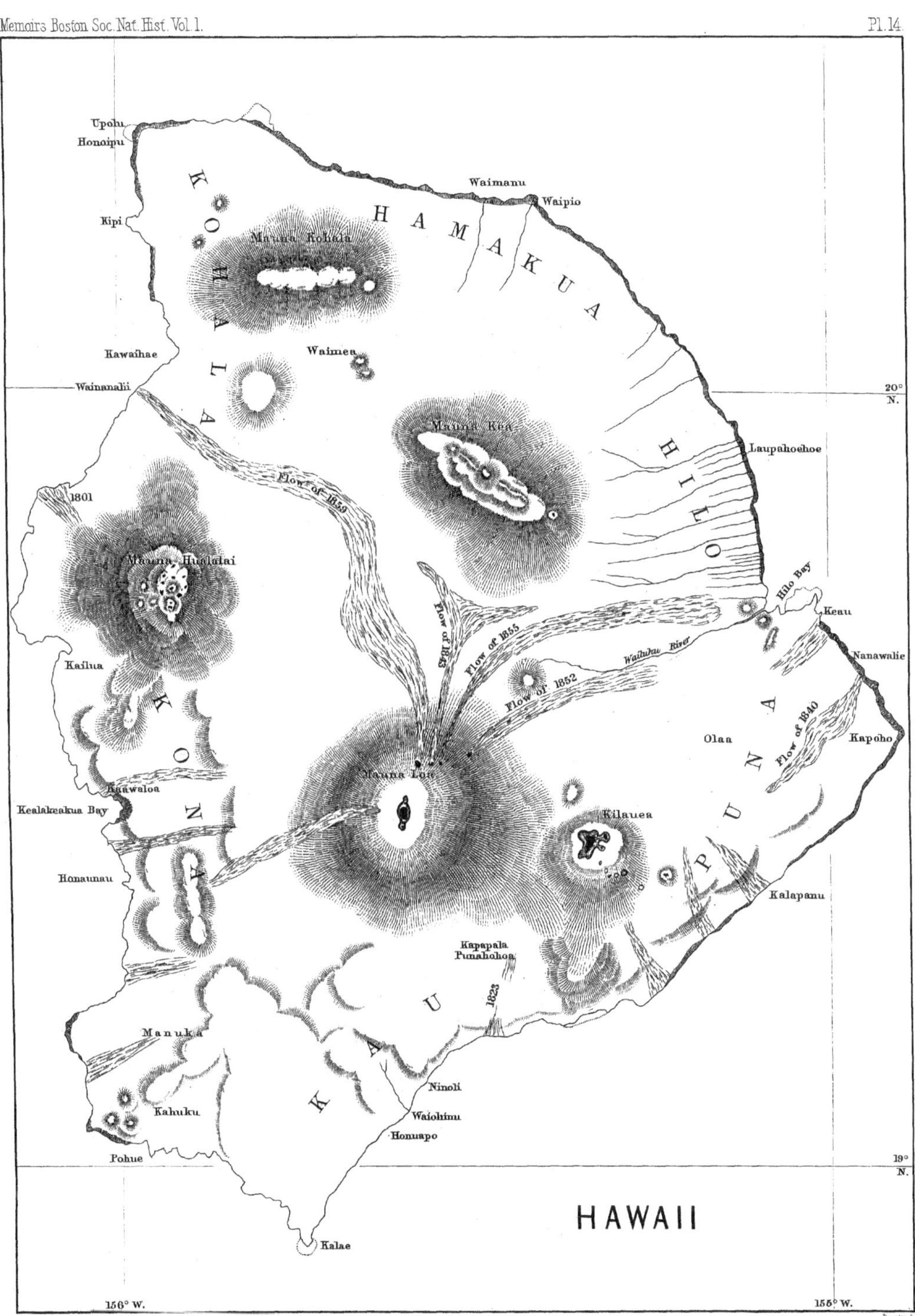

Wm T. Brigham on Hawaiian Volcanoes.

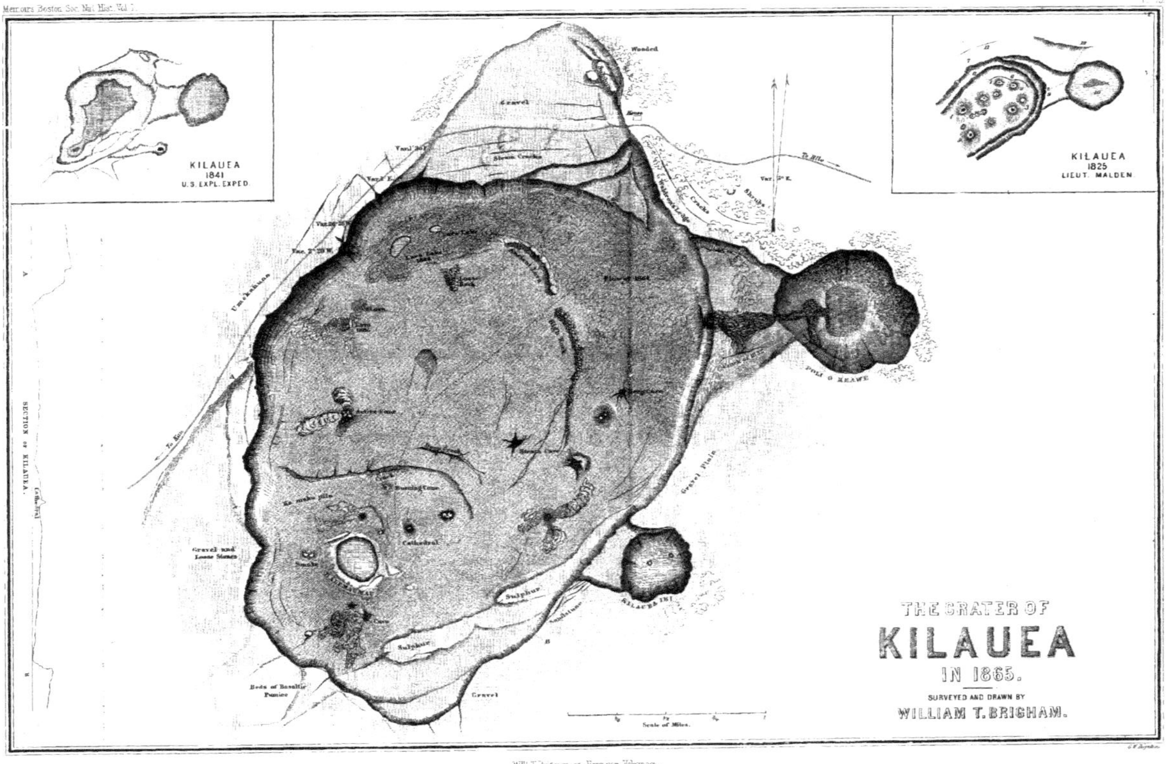
KILAUEA
1841
U.S. EXPL. EXPED.
KILAUEA
1825
LIEUT. MALDEN
SECTION of KILAUEA.
Wooded
Gravel
To Hilo
Umekahuna
Poli o Keawe
Gravel Plain
Cathedral
Gravel and Loose Stones
Sulphur
Kilauea Iki
Beds of Basaltic Pumice
Gravel
Scale of Miles.
THE CRATER OF
KILAUEA
IN 1865.
SURVEYED AND DRAWN BY
WILLIAM T. BRIGHAM.

northern pools has been noted on the plan. As the author was unassisted, save by a few kanakas who knew nothing whatever of surveying, he was unable to make the numerous measurements necessary to the construction of a relief model, but so far as the plan goes it is believed to be accurate.

The sketch of the Exploring Expedition Survey shows the Black Ledge, and with the plan by Lieutenant Malden, who accompanied Lord Byron in 1825, will indicate the constant changes taking place in the topography of Kilauéa. Neither of these plans, however, were measured with sufficient detail to serve as standards of comparison except in a general way.

The explanation of the numerals on Lieutenant Malden's plan, is as follows:—

1. Crater in action visited by Lord Byron.
2. Sulphur crater.
3. Crater that broke out on the 29th of June.
4. A cone very active all the night of the 29th.
5. Largest crater, always emitting fire and smoke.
6. Deep fissure in the lava.
7. From this point it was 932 feet to the Black Ledge.
8. Black Ledge 400 feet from the bottom of the crater.
9. Lord Byron's encampment.
10. A deep wooded crater.
11. Steam cracks.
12. A descent of twenty feet.

On the northern bank there was a constant smoke from the sulphur banks, and the western end of the crater was quite hidden by the thick vapors. Poli-o-Keàwe was "thickly covered with green underwood;" the descent on to the neck between this and Kilauéa was one hundred and fifty feet.

In 1846 a sketch map was made of Kilauéa, and on this the Black Ledge was estimated at 650 feet below the highest bank. The whole interior was elevated from one hundred to one hundred and fifty feet above the Black Ledge; rough and broken, sloping towards the north. Halemáumau was some twenty feet above this plain. The lava cataract of 1832 was estimated at three hundred feet in height. The walls of Poli-o-Keàwe were four to five hundred feet in height, and at the bottom was once a lake of lava thirty to fifty feet deep. Now the crust has fallen in and is marked with tree holes; it was from the outbreak of 1832. The variation near the house was 8° W. Steam issued from the south-west bank near the spot marked on the large plan "Beds of Basaltic Pumice."

Levelling revealed the curious fact that the surface of the various pools of melted lava was of different heights. Halemáumau presented a surface sixty feet above the Lakes of 1864, and fifty feet above those of 1865. Even the two pools of 1864 were not at the same level, but two or three feet different. With the great pressure lava must exert, and the apparently free communication between the several vents, it is difficult to understand this, unless the viscidity of the lava is greater at a considerable depth than on the surface. All the pools are above the base of the outer walls.

EXPLANATION OF THE WOODCUTS.

[From Drawings and Photographs by the Author, unless otherwise specified. Engraved on wood by R. B. Dyer, except numbers 37 and 38.]

INDEX AND VOCABULARY.

[EVERY Hawaiian word is divided into as many syllables as it has vowel sounds: *ae, ou, au,* and *ai,* are sometimes pronounced as diphthongs, although not correctly: *a* as in arch, *e* as *a* in late, hate, &c.; *i* as in pique, *o* as in note, *u* as *oo* in coo. The consonants are pronounced as in American. Hawaiians do not strongly accent many of their words, usually only to distinguish words of the same sound but different signification; but for convenience, Hawaiian words have here been accented on the prominent vowel sound, ˋ grave where that is long, ˊ acute where short.]

Published February, 1868.

www.ingramcontent.com/pod-product-compliance
Lightning Source LLC
LaVergne TN
LVHW021412110826
845150LV00007B/1885

* 9 7 8 1 4 2 5 5 1 0 6 8 8 *